Promoting Law Student and Lawyer Well-Being in Australia and Beyond

University can be a psychologically distressing place for students. Empirical studies in Australia and the USA highlight that a large number of law students suffer from psychological distress, when compared to students from other disciplines and members of the general population.

This book explores the significant role that legal education can play in the promotion of mental health and well-being in law students, and consequently in the profession. The volume considers the ways in which the problems of psychological distress amongst law students are connected to the way law and legal culture are taught, and articulates curricula and extra-curricula strategies for promoting wellbeing for law students.

With contributions from legal academics, legal practitioners and psychologists, the authors discuss the possible causes of psychological distress in the legal community, and potential interventions that may increase psychological well-being. This important book will be of interest to legal academics, law students, members of the legal profession, post-graduate researchers as well as non-law researchers interested in this area.

Rachael Field is an Associate Professor in the Faculty of Law at Queensland University of Technology, Australia. She holds an ALTC Fellowship (2010) for Stimulating Strategic Change in Legal Education to Address High Levels of Psychological Distress in Law Students, focussing on the potential of non-adversarial legal practice to better engage, motivate and support student learning and wellbeing in law.

James Duffy is a lecturer in the Faculty of Law, Queensland University of Technology, Australia. He researches in the areas of Alternative Dispute Resolution, Non-Adversarial Justice and the Law/Psychology nexus. His teaching excellence has been recognised at the institutional and national level.

Dr Colin James is a solicitor and a senior lecturer with the Australian National University. His areas of practice include family law and domestic violence. He teaches in clinical legal education and professional legal training programs and serves on the management committees of law societies and community legal centres. His research areas include emotional intelligence, coaching psychology, professional development, academic integrity, legal history and domestic violence.

Emerging Legal Education

Series Editors

Meera E. Deo, *Thomas Jefferson School of Law, USA* and
Paul Maharg, *Australian National University, Canberra, Australia,*
Elizabeth Mertz, *University of Wisconsin-Madison/American Bar Foundation, USA*

Emerging Legal Education is a forum for analysing the discourse of legal education and creating innovative ways of learning the law. The series focuses on research, theory and practice within legal education, drawing attention to historical, interdisciplinary and international characteristics, and is based upon imaginative and sophisticated educational thinking. The series takes a broad view of theory and practice. Series books are written for an international audience and are sensitive to the diversity of contexts in which law is taught, learned and practised.

Other titles in this series:

Legal Education in the Global Context
Opportunities and Challenges
Edited by Christopher Gane and Robin Hui Huang

Legal Education
Simulation in Theory and Practice
Edited by Caroline Strevens, Richard Grimes and Edward Phillips

The Calling of Law
The Pivotal Role of Vocational Legal Education
Edited by Fiona Westwood and Karen Barton

Law and Leadership
Integrating Leadership Studies into the Law School Curriculum
Edited by Paula Monopoli and Susan McCarty

The Moral Imagination and the Legal Life
Beyond Text in Legal Education
Edited by Zenon Bankowski and Maksymilian Del Mar

Promoting Law Student and Lawyer Well-Being in Australia and Beyond

Edited by
Rachael Field, James Duffy and Colin James

Routledge
Taylor & Francis Group
LONDON AND NEW YORK

First published 2016 by Routledge

2 Park Square, Milton Park, Abingdon, Oxfordshire OX14 4RN
52 Vanderbilt Avenue, New York, NY 10017

Routledge is an imprint of the Taylor & Francis Group, an informa business

First issued in paperback 2020

British Library Cataloguing in Publication Data
A catalogue record for this book is available from the British Library

Library of Congress Cataloging-in-Publication Data
Promoting law student and lawyer well-being-in-Australia and beyond / by
Rachael Field, James Duffy and Colin James.
pages cm. — (Emerging legal education)
Includes bibliographical references and index.
ISBN 978-1-4724-4529-2 (hardback : alk. paper) —
ISBN 978-1-4724-4530-8 (ebook) — ISBN 978-1-4724-4531-5 (epub)
1. Law students—Australia—Psychology. 2. Law—Study and teaching—Australia—Psychological aspects. I. Field, Rachael, editor. II. Duffy, James (Law teacher) editor. III. James, Colin, editor.
KU52.4.P76 2016
340.071'194—dc23
2015029341

ISBN: 978-1-4724-4529-2 (hbk)
ISBN: 978-0-367-59674-3 (pbk)

Typeset in Times New Roman
by Apex CoVantage, LLC

Contents

Figures

Tables

Contributors

Paula Baron: Dr Paula Baron is Chair of the Common Law at La Trobe University and recently completed a three-year term as Head of the Law School. Prior to this, Paula was Dean of Law at Griffith University and, earlier, was the first woman professor appointed in law at Victoria University Wellington. She has published nationally and internationally in the areas of contract law, intellectual property, legal professional ethics, legal education, company law and gender and the law. She is the General Editor of *Law in Context*. In 2013, as Chair of the Council of Australian Law Deans' Standing Committee for Legal Education, Paula was the lead author of *Promoting Law Student Well-Being Good Practice Guidelines for Law Schools*.

Judy Bourke: Judy Bourke is a Senior Lecturer in Practical Legal Training at The College of Law. She is a solicitor with over 30 years' experience in a legal environment, including with city and suburban firms, in sole practice and in practical legal education.

James Duffy: James Duffy is a lecturer in the Queensland University of Technology (QUT) Faculty of Law. He teaches primarily in the first year of the law degree in Introduction to Law and Dispute Resolution. James researches into alternative dispute resolution, non-adversarial justice and the law/psychology nexus. His teaching has been recognized at university and national level.

Maxine Evers: Maxine Evers is a Senior Lecturer in the Faculty of Law at the University of Technology, Sydney (UTS). She has taught in the Practical Legal Training (PLT) programme and core degree since 2004. Maxine has an interest in the legal profession, legal education and the student experience as seen in her roles as Programme Head of PLT, University Student Ombud and Director of Students in the Law Faculty. As an executive member of the Australasian Professional Legal Education Council (APLEC), she contributed to the 2015 revised Competency Standards. She was also involved in the design of a new professional programme, including the addition of a resilience component, for students undertaking PLT at UTS. Maxine has published on the role of PLT in preparing students for the profession; lawyers' certification as to reasonable prospects of success; the duties of in-house counsel; legal costs; the ethics of collaborative practice; and the role of the student ombud. In 2011, Maxine co-authored the *Good Practice Guide for the TLO (Threshold Learning Outcome) 2* on ethics and professional responsibility.

Rachael Field: Dr Rachael Field has been an Associate Professor in the QUT Law School since 2012. Her key teaching interests are in the first year experience and dispute resolution. Rachael has received a number of institutional and national learning and teaching awards, and in 2010 was made an ALTC Teaching Fellow to work on strategic reform of law curricula to promote law student wellbeing. Through the Fellowship she initiated the Wellness Network for Law. She received an Australian Awards for University Teaching (AAUT) Teaching Excellence award in 2014. In 2010 Rachael worked with Professors Sally Kift and Mark Israel on the development of the nationally influential Threshold Learning Outcomes for Law. Rachael has also co-authored two first year law texts: *The New Lawyer* and *Lawyering and Positive Professional Identities*. Both texts seek to make a contribution to curricular resources that support law student wellbeing through good learning and teaching practice. In 2013 Rachael was named Queensland Woman Lawyer of the Year.

Tony Foley: Dr Tony Foley is an Associate Professor at the Australian National University (ANU) College of Law. He teaches in clinical and practical legal education programmes. Tony is a practising lawyer and appears regularly in court on behalf of Legal Aid. He also sits as a senior member of the ACT Civil and Administrative Tribunal. Tony's most significant contribution (together with colleagues Vivien Holmes, Margie Rowe and his co-author Stephen Tang) to the research field of lawyer wellbeing is empirical research investigating professional identity formation in new lawyers. His own research focuses on the development of conceptual frameworks to better understand the practice of law, particularly alternative responses to criminal wrongdoing, restorative justice, juvenile justice and court interpreters.

Anna Huggins: Anna Huggins is a Senior Lecturer in the Queensland University of Technology School of Law. Anna's primary research and teaching interests lie in the fields of administrative law and regulation in both domestic and global contexts. Her recent research explores the implications of administrative proceduralization in diverse settings, including global environmental regulatory bodies and Australian higher education regulation. Anna is also passionate about legal education research and practical strategies to promote law students' wellbeing. Her Master of Laws (Research) thesis examined the changing higher education regulatory context in Australia, and proposed theoretically informed strategies for implementing the law TLO on self-management. Anna publishes widely, and presents at national and international conferences, in relation to her areas of research interest. She was previously the Assessment and Curriculum Development Fellow at UNSW Law, and prior to entering academia worked in environmental law at the NSW Department of Environment and Climate Change.

Colin James: Dr Colin James is a solicitor and a senior lecturer with the ANU. His areas of practice include family law and domestic violence. He teaches in clinical legal education programmes and serves on the management committees of law societies and community legal centres. His research areas include emotional intelligence, coaching psychology, professional development, academic integrity, legal history and domestic violence.

Nick James: Professor Nick James is the Associate Dean (Learning and Teaching) and the Acting Executive Dean of the Faculty of Law at Bond University, Queensland. He is a former commercial lawyer, and has been an academic since 1996. His areas of teaching expertise include business and commercial law, 'law in society' and legal theory, company law, the law of succession and property law. He has won numerous awards for his teaching, including a National Citation for Outstanding Contribution to Student Learning, and he is the author of three textbooks: *Business Law*, *Critical Legal Thinking* and *The New Lawyer* (with Rachael Field). He has written numerous journal articles and conference papers in the areas of legal education, critical thinking and critical legal theory. Professor James is presently the Editor-in-Chief of the *Legal Education Review*.

Wendy Larcombe: Dr Wendy Larcombe is an Associate Professor at Melbourne Law School (MLS), where she teaches legal theory, legal research and legal method and reasoning in the JD programme. She is currently undertaking research into sexual offences and also legal education. For five years, Wendy has been either Director of Learning Support or Director of Teaching at MLS. She is currently chairing the MLS Student Wellbeing Working Group, which is implementing a range of wellbeing measures in response to student data collected in 2011–2013. Wendy has received 14 awards and grants related to development of student learning and educational policy, including a Universitas 21 Fellowship in 2008; a 2011 Australian Learning and Teaching Council Citation for her Outstanding Contribution to Student Learning; and a 2014 Australian Office for Learning and Teaching (OLT) grant for a project to stimulate curriculum innovation to support student mental wellbeing.

Judith Marychurch: Judith Marychurch is the Assistant Dean – Teaching and Learning at Melbourne Law School. Prior to this appointment, Judith was a senior lecturer and the Associate Dean – Teaching and Learning in the Law School at the University of Wollongong (UOW). Judith's interests include legal education, particularly student wellbeing and innovation in assessment; also evidence and corporate law, with a specialization in the legal issues surrounding forensic accounting. She is a co-author of *Uniform Evidence in Australia* (2015). Judith received a national Carrick Citation for Outstanding Contribution to Student Learning in 2006 as well as the UOW Vice Chancellor's award for Outstanding Contribution to Teaching and Learning (OCTAL).

Patricia Morgan: Dr Patricia Morgan is currently a postdoctoral fellow at Canberra University researching the impacts of connectivity through ICT. Before taking up this position her research was sited at the intersection of contemplative practice and learning. She has lectured on contemplation and legal practice and study with Professor Prue Vines at UNSW's School of Law, and developed contemplative education courses for the Office of Student Life and Learning, UNSW. Dr Morgan has recently completed a fellowship with the Mind and Life Institute, Massachusetts, USA, where she investigated current methods being used to examine first-person consciousness. She writes in the area of contemplative studies and pedagogy, and has most recently published an article on the contemporary history of contemplative education.

Molly Townes O'Brien: Molly is an Associate Professor at the ANU College of Law, where she teaches evidence, litigation and dispute management and human rights in the Australian context. Molly has served on the law faculties of Emory University, the University of Akron and the University of Wollongong. Prior to entering the academy, she worked as a judicial clerk and as a public defender. She has an AB from Brown University (1982), a JD from Northeastern University (1986) and an LLM from Temple University (1997). She is currently Director of Teaching Development at the ANU College of Law and a Senior Fellow in the Higher Education Academy. On student wellbeing, her recent articles include: 'The Power of Naming: The Multifaceted Value Of Learning Students' Names' (2014, co-authored with Tania Leiman and James Duffy); 'Bring Your Whole Self to Law School' (2013); and (co-authored with Tony Connolly) 'The Challenge of the How: Developing a Process for Legal Education Program Renewal' in *The First-Year Law Experience: A New Beginning* (ed. Leon Wolff and Maria Nicolae, 2014).

Helen Stallman: Dr Helen Stallman is a clinical psychologist and senior lecturer in the School of Psychology, Social Work and Social Policy at the University of South Australia. She lectures in clinical psychology, developmental psychology and mediation and conflict resolution. Helen is a leading international researcher of the mental health of university students. Her work has involved understanding the prevalence and correlates of mental health problems as well as prevention, promotion and early interventions to support student wellbeing and success. Helen has led the development of population-based interventions for students, including Staying on Track, *thedesk* and The Learning Thermometer. Helen and her colleagues have received multiple awards for their work, including: the International Education Association of Australia (IEAA) Award for Best Practice/Innovation; the University of Queensland Faculty of Health Sciences Award for Programs that Enhance Learning; ANZ Mental Health Services Achievement Award; Uniquest Trailblazers Award; and Queensland Mental Health Week Achievement Award.

Alex Steel: Alex Steel is a Professor in the Faculty of Law, University of New South Wales. His roles have included both Associate Dean (Education) and Associate Dean (Academic) of UNSW Law; co-convenor of the Legal Education Associate Deans Network (LEAD); consultant to the Australian Law

Schools Standards Committee; and membership of the UNSW Academic Board. His publications in legal education focus on assessment and student attitudes. He is the author of two commissioned Australian Good Practice Guides to teaching law: *Law in Broader Contexts* (2013) and *Statutory Interpretation* (2015). Alex is also widely published in the areas of theft, fraud and dishonesty law. Alex's professional roles have included consultant to the NSW Attorney General's Department Criminal Law Review Division; membership of the Criminal Law Committee of the NSW Bar Association; and expert advisor to the NSW Law Reform Commission. He is a recipient of an Innovative Teaching and Educational Technology Fellowship (2003); a UNSW Learning and Teaching Award (2005/6); a Vice Chancellor's Award for Teaching Excellence (2008); and the LexisNexis-ALTA Award for Excellence and Innovation in the Teaching of Law Highly Commended (2013).

Stephen Tang: Stephen Tang is a lecturer and psychologist at the Australian National University (ANU) Legal Workshop. His research interests are at the intersection of law, clinical psychology and decision science. Stephen has been involved in research about psychological wellbeing and distress in law students and lawyers since 2008. He takes an empirically led approach to understanding the experience of students and practitioners in context, which extends into cognate areas such as professional identity, behavioural ethics, values, uncertainty and perceptions of conflict. Stephen has been involved in running quantitative and qualitative projects with first year LLB/JD students, Practical Legal Training (PLT) students and new lawyers in their transition to practice. He has also been active in the research-informed pedagogical approach of ANU Legal Workshop, and also provides psychological support to students in the programme. Stephen was previously a lawyer in commercial and government practice, and has clinical experience as a psychologist in community and acute mental health settings. He is also currently a consultant to the World Health Organization on international mental health law, policy and human rights.

Prue Vines: Prue Vines is a Professor in the Faculty of Law at UNSW. She has been the Director of First Year Studies there since 1996 and has set up many programmes for first year students which have been widely copied. She is the author of *Law and Justice in Australia: Foundations of the Legal System* (3rd edn, 2013) and co-editor with Carolyn Sappideen of *Fleming's The Law of Torts* (10th edn, 2012) as well as many other articles, texts and monographs on torts and succession law and legal education.

Penelope Watson: Penelope Watson is a senior lecturer and Director, Learning and Teaching, at Macquarie Law School, Sydney. Penelope joined Macquarie Law in 1999, having previously worked at UOW and UNSW. She is course co-ordinator of remedies, torts and advanced torts, and has also taught contracts for a number of years. Penelope is convenor of the Australasian Law Teachers' Association (ALTA) Torts and Contracts Interest Group. She served for three years on the editorial committee of legal professional journal *Precedent* and is currently on the editorial committee of the *Legal Education Review*. Penelope has received a number of prestigious teaching awards, including a National Carrick Citation for Outstanding Contribution to Student Learning and a Macquarie Learning and Teaching Fellowship. Her research interests include legal education generally – especially assessment, graduate capabilities including teamwork and leadership, peer-assisted learning and distance education; torts generally, with specific interests in emerging torts and novel adaptations of old torts; privacy; educational malpractice and school law; school and workplace bullying; medical/health law, including wrongful life and birth; tobacco and alcohol litigation; toxic torts and class actions; civil actions and remedies for sexual injury; negligence; causation; and remedies generally, especially personal injury damages and remedies for non-economic loss. Recent publications include C Sappideen, P Vines, H Grant and P Watson, *Torts Commentary and Materials* (10th edn, 2009. Penelope is currently working on her PhD in the area of novel torts and judicial decision-making. In 2010 Penelope was awarded the LexisNexis-ALTA Award for Excellence and Innovation in the Teaching of Law.

Acknowledgements

This book is dedicated to those who have experienced the stressors of legal education and/or practice and have encountered psychological distress as a result. It is also dedicated to those who maintain their well-being by making psychological health a priority in their studying and working lives.

Legal education and practice will always involve a degree of stress. The challenge for the legal professional community is to scrutinize practices and activities that negatively impact on mental health, and to promote well-being broadly. There are many examples of those who not only endure an imperfect legal profession, but also take active steps to make it better. The Jepson family; Shane, who contributed to the introduction in this book; the Australian Wellness Network for Law . . . the list goes on. We know there is value in asking the right questions about law student and lawyer well-being. While we don't have all the answers, we hope this book is received as a step in the right direction.

Any and all royalties from the sale of this book will be donated to the Tristan Jepson Memorial Foundation (http://www.tjmf.org.au/).

Rachael Field
James Duffy
Colin James

Introduction

Rachael Field, James Duffy and Colin James

University can be a psychologically distressing place for students. Empirical evidence in both the USA and Australia suggests that the stresses of law school do impact upon the psychological well-being of some law students. It has been found that symptoms of psychological distress rise significantly for some students in their first year of law (compared to levels in the general population) and persist throughout the degree to post-graduation. Research also tells us that members of the legal profession have higher incidences of depression and psychological disorders than other professions and the general community. One reason that explains the poor mental health experienced by some law students and lawyers is the way in which law is taught and practised, at least in parts of the profession. In Australia, law schools and the profession have joined together to consider the issue of mental health.

This book is a collection of works on this important issue by members of the Australian Wellness Network for Law. It explores the role legal education can play in promoting mental health and well-being in law students, and consequently in the profession. The book examines the links between psychological distress amongst law students and the way law and legal culture are taught, and offers strategies for promoting well-being for law students. The work's perspective is based on current Australian experiences, but the research is relevant to law schools in other common law jurisdictions. Our hope is that this work has international application and appeal.

The chapters of this work reflect a growing body of scholarship on a new focus in legal education. The intention of this work is to assist law schools wanting to enable students to develop in compassionate, mindful and emotionally intelligent ways, while learning the law at their cognitive best. The authors are experienced legal educators sharing their knowledge and research on what works in helping students thrive during their law school experience.

The thinking evident in this work also reflects an important shift in the Australian legal academy towards taking responsibility for the promotion of law student mental health. The chapters reflect an acceptance amongst the authors that there is now a strong imperative to *do something* in response to what we know (as a result of robust and defensible empirical evidence) about law student mental well-being. Each of the chapters offers a different perspective on the problem of mental ill-heath at law school, as well as different solutions. However, there are a number of common themes that emerge, including: the need to adopt justifiable and evidence-based interventions; and the need to adopt integrated whole of school curricular and extra-curricular based approaches across all levels of legal education, including practical legal training.

The work begins with Stephen Tang's piece, 'Valuing Persons and Communities in Doing Wellness for Law Well', which introduces several of the challenges faced by legal academics working to promote law student well-being. Tang brings our shared visions for wellness in the study and practice of law together, and offers strategies to help us avoid some of the hazards which might hinder progress or inadvertently make things worse. Tang argues that the two objectives of promoting well-being and addressing distress require distinct strategies and interventions, and that maintaining this distinction will ensure that our practice and interventions develop appropriately. Further, he reminds us of the importance of creating and adapting theories of well-being and distress to guide the development of our evidence-based models and approaches.

In Chapter 2, Wendy Larcombe recognizes the school-level implications of the movement to promote law students' mental well-being and argues for the development of integrated, whole-school approaches. Larcombe offers a way of sustainably conceptualizing and embedding such approaches, using the guiding principles of the World Health Organization's Charter for Health Promotion ('the Ottawa Charter') and the Australian national mental health initiative for primary and secondary schools. Her insightful chapter provides a comprehensive, coordinated, evidence-based and sustainable framework for mental health promotion in law schools.

In Chapter 3 Paula Baron considers the persistent nature of law student distress, recognizing that the reasons as to why law students experience such high levels of distress remain largely speculative and that, notwithstanding law school responses to the issue, the problem continues to persist. The chapter provides some insights from Lacanian psychoanalytic theory as to the potential causes of the distress of law students and lawyers, and the remarkably robust and persistent character of this distress.

Chapter 4, by Alex Steel and Anna Huggins, considers the issue of lifestyle pressures for law students and their relevance to student well-being. Using the results from a 2012 survey of law students at the University of New South Wales (UNSW), the chapter examines how students spend their time outside the classroom, including: the amount of time spent reading and preparing for class and assessments; the amount of paid and volunteer work done; the extent to which students have family caring responsibilities; and the time students devote to leisure activities. The chapter highlights the desirability of better understanding student lifestyle patterns and pressures if we are to be able to appropriately support student well-being during their time at law school.

Chapter 5, also by Huggins and Steel, explores the relationship between class participation and law students' learning, engagement and stress. Drawing also from the data from the Law School Student Assessment Survey (LSSAS), conducted at UNSW Law School in 2012, the chapter provides preliminary insights into whether assessable class participation at law school is alienating and stressful for students.

In Chapter 6 Judith Marychurch explains the *Vitality for Life and Law* programme. This programme, an example of an innovative, preventative approach, was developed at the University of Wollongong to foster student resilience, empowerment and well-being. The chapter explores the programme's design strategies to support the development of student understanding of stress, and considers the range of techniques taught through the programme to facilitate and support sustained optimal performance for students in both their personal and professional lives. The chapter also considers the implications of the programme's elements for the support of law student transition to law school and to the legal profession, and for the design of the law curriculum, including the implementation of the *Bachelor of Laws Threshold Learning Outcome (TLO) 6: Self-Management.*

Judy Bourke and Maxine Evers offer the practical legal training (PLT) perspective on resilience and well-being programmes in Chapter 7. Acknowledging the important role of PLT in the student experience of transition from law school to the profession, the chapter discusses the role of PLT in legal education, with reference to well-being programmes developed by two PLT providers.

In Chapter 8 Colin James explores the notion of resilient lawyers and strategies that can maximize student and lawyer well-being. Using the concept of resilience not as a trait or a practice, but as a personal quality that emerges from a dynamic relationship between the individual and his or her environment, James argues that the more we model, enable and motivate in ourselves, our students and colleagues the development of self-awareness, the more we can support the development of a capacity to manage challenges with purpose and a sense of acceptance that the stressors of law do not need to be a barrier to a good and happy life. James argues that concepts of peak performance and flow can be attained by legal professionals working in challenging circumstances who have integrated well with their environmental domains, including their own physical, cognitive, affective and ethical potential. Importantly, James highlights the responsibility that institutions such as law schools, law firms and law societies share to act on the knowledge we now have about law student mental well-being.

Penelope Watson's Chapter 9 considers the use of peer-assisted learning to develop resilient and resourceful learners of law. Focusing on the learner and the development of characteristics that enhance well-being, the chapter discusses how a student-run peer-assisted learning programme, designed in accordance with principles from positive psychology and self-determination theory, can help students to help themselves to become more resilient and resourceful learners and individuals by actively fostering autonomy, resourcefulness, competence and relatedness. The chapter discusses the LAWPAL model of peer-assisted learning operating at Macquarie University Law School, which encourages and enables learners to acquire and embed transferable and sustainable attitudes, skills and values.

In Chapter 10, Tony Foley and Stephen Tang consider the connections between uncertainty, ignorance and well-being. Foley and Tang acknowledge the stressful, challenging and deeply complex nature of the process of becoming a lawyer. The chapter argues that the way law schools teach students to 'think like a lawyer' tends to inflate the importance of certainty, knowledge and an answer-driven worldview at the expense of understanding and managing the many unknowns of the law and legal practice. They suggest that this is unhelpful, and that a more constructive approach is to help students to recognize the importance of uncertainty, lack of knowledge and a questioning perspective. They argue that neglecting this perspective sets up blind spots and false expectations about the nature of legal practice.

James Duffy considers in Chapter 11 lessons for law student well-being that can be learned from positive psychology, particularly in terms of the importance of balance. Duffy calls for the legal academy to go beyond fixing what is wrong, to include a strengthening of what is going right, suggesting that adversarialism should be balanced with alternative dispute resolution, pessimism with optimism and the cognitive with the affective. He argues that striving towards these balances may help address the imbalance of psychological distress experienced by law students.

Chapter 12 by Molly Townes O'Brien re-examines law school student well-being from a remedial standpoint, considering student discomfort, suggesting some possible remedial options, and making some recommendations about how a positive law student culture can be promoted in order to graduate a group of engaged, connected and confident lawyers.

The chapter asks, and attempts to answer, two difficult questions: What changes in the law school curriculum would promote a 'more connected' and more engaged experience? And, more importantly, how can the lawyer's role as problem solver be thoroughly incorporated into the legal curriculum?

In Chapter 13, Prue Vines and Patricia Morgan offer contemplative practice as a method for breaking barriers to learning and resilience. They argue that the increasing use of contemplative practices in law schools is significant because it can support resilience and diminish stress and depression by enhancing focus, the ability to prioritize, the optimization of objectivity and higher-order thinking. They also contend that the management of ethical issues of professional practice, which are known triggers for depression, may also be improved by contemplative practices, because such practices enhance students' and lawyers' ability to articulate their personal and professional ethics.

In Chapter 14, Rachael Field discusses the importance of intentionally designing the law curriculum to promote law student well-being, and argues that this work is particularly important in the context of the first-year experience of legal education. Field argues that given the empirical information which exists about law student well-being, legal academics have an ethical obligation to create positive learning experiences for our students, and to 'do no harm' through legal education. The chapter suggests that what is taught, how it is taught and how it is assessed are all decisions that legal academics make, which have well-being implications for law students.

In Chapter 15, Helen Stallman and James Duffy go beyond the curriculum to consider the well-being of law students within their broader environment, seeing the entirety of the university environment as an influence on health and well-being. Stallman and Duffy argue that proximal social and physical environments, including the learning environment, affect the ongoing development of the student as a person. They highlight the important role a university plays in the ongoing development of students through community reputation, student recruitment strategies, physical and virtual environments, and teaching. They contend that in order to promote law student well-being, these systemic influences need to align with factors that are known to support psychological health.

The final chapter of the work, by Nick James, addresses the issue of dealing with resistance to change by legal academics. James notes that the responses of individual legal academics to wellness initiatives in law schools are varied, ranging from enthusiastic to ambivalent to resistant and oppositional. The chapter examines the nature of academic resistance to wellness initiatives, identifying the various forms it takes, describing the various reasons and justifications for it, and offering some possible strategies for addressing the resistance.

The significance of the ideas discussed in these chapters is evident in the voice of those we serve. So we conclude the introduction to this work with the words of a law student who has experienced the issues we address.

An Open Letter to the Participants of the 2015 National Wellness for Law Forum

To those whose support has made all the difference.

I began writing this as a personal diary while I went through this journey. It never once crossed my mind that this could be a help in any way to others, but I hope my story is useful to you as you work to develop student wellness in the legal community.

I am a final year law student at the Australian National University. I come from a stable, loving family, am in a great relationship, and work part time as a paralegal at a law firm which has become my second family over the past two years. Whilst I've scraped through law school, without grades I could be really proud of, in most regards I have been, and am, very lucky.

Nevertheless, I was diagnosed with moderate depression just before the final exams. The biggest obstacle was coming to terms with depression, which has not been an easy journey. It is one thing to understand what depression is, and another to internalize this understanding. More often than not, it is a concept which doesn't make full sense until depression has consumed you or someone you know. Life goes on, regardless of whether you can get out of bed, and you end up living with the consequences.

One of the hardest things in coming to terms with my diagnosis was dealing with the demands of work and university. Anxiety and depression make a really poor couple. I wavered between caring too much about doing well and giving up completely. Days where I couldn't even get out of bed grew in number, and I went from being a capable worker under high pressure to staring blankly at walls because there was no point trying. The more I worried, the more I couldn't do it; and I hated myself for not caring and not being able to do anything at all. This simply fuelled my worries and I fell into a self-fulfilling cycle. The internal conflict was terrible – the idea of letting my parents down, of being the 'worst' in my social circle, simply ate away at me. I could not hurt myself because I had no ability to even get myself out of bed. I am so grateful that my partner recognized the signs then and pushed me to see a doctor. Even though I had been like this for half a year, it was still better late than never.

When I received my diagnosis, it was already a couple of weeks before exams. Though I knew I might fail, I could hardly bring myself to study. The times I tried, I found myself struggling to understand and absorb things that weren't even conceptually difficult. This too, fuelled my feelings of worthlessness. The doctor gave me a letter for special consideration, but I couldn't face the lecturers when I couldn't even tell my family. I am especially thankful that the only lecturer I did speak to made this process easier – her understanding and words really did help, although I couldn't tell her at the time. That in itself was so draining I didn't end up talking to the rest of my course conveners. At that time, I would rather have them think I was merely faking an illness to get out of doing work than tell them the truth, because frankly, the truth meant I was not good enough, and that was harder to face.

Having come from a background where mental illness is pretty much equivalent to madness, I fully appreciate and am so thankful that the ANU has a system in place to help those who inevitably fall hard along the way.

Would anything else have helped me then? This is a tricky question for me. If anyone had spotted the signs earlier, that would have helped greatly; but this is, of course, idealistic and a lot to ask of tutors/lecturers who encounter hundreds of students every day. The fact that the ANU College of Law considers and provides an avenue for students who do struggle with mental illness is a huge step forward in itself.

If I could change anything about law school at this point, it is probably to increase the awareness of depression and the avenues a struggling student could take. One of the hardest things I had to do was ask for help. It is not something that comes naturally to everyone, and, when crippled by anxiety and depression, is not something you particularly want to do. The fear of being judged and regarded as pathetic, whether true, is always on your mind, ready to remind you of your failure as a 'law student'. Perhaps, if issues of psychological distress and depression were more widely talked about in lectures or classrooms as a reality, and it was acknowledged more widely that this actually happens to law students, it would have made it easier for me to figure out how to survive and deal with my university life when the rest of my life felt like it had already crumbled.

I would also like to see a wider acceptance for what success in law school means. The support of friends is essential to recovery, and if most of a law student's friendships are formed in law school, the culture amongst law students – one based on pride, achievement and, to some extent, pretension – is of concern. There exists a need to keep up an image of being the conscientious, hardworking student who also undertakes internships/volunteer work, while perhaps working a part-time job (or two) to make yourself employable. While we should always do our best where we can, it is also necessary to recognize that not everyone goes down that same path. Law students need to be reminded that even if you don't manage to become the stereotypical success, it is ultimately okay.

I would like to end by saying that in this process of coming to terms with depression and me not being able to maintain the image of the typical 'law student', I've realized how important it is for law schools to understand – to show students that understanding, and encourage a culture of acceptance. It was only when I finally picked up the courage to face my course convener and would-be Honours supervisor that I began to realize not everyone places that kind of pressure on law students, despite my general impression. It is this wider understanding and acceptance which will go a long way in helping students deal with depression and mental illness, especially in such a high-pressure environment such as law school.

It doesn't take a big or grand gesture to make a difference. A simple step like talking about depression is in itself a good start. This for some could mean the difference between suffering and recovery.

Thank you for taking the time to read this. I hope that this has been useful, and I am thankful for having been given the opportunity to contribute to the development of the legal community in regard to the mental well-being of students.

Yours sincerely,
Shayne

PS. I cannot translate the feeling of struggling to find the right words to explain your depression, and having your course convener (who probably doesn't even know who you are) look at you without judgement, and offer you kind words and advice laced with understanding. Nor can I possibly explain how much it means to have your potential Honours supervisor reply to your apology for not qualifying (not being able to make it) and yet consistently offer support, encouragement and alternative avenues to explore. That kindness after having beaten yourself up internally about your inability to do anything makes educators more real, and the legal profession more human. That weight that lifts off your shoulders when the people who make up the very environment that places the pressure on you make you feel like it is all going to be okay is a feeling that is impossible to describe. It has made all the difference to me.

1 Valuing Persons and Communities in Doing Wellness for Law Well

*Stephen Tang**

Introduction

During the brief history of Australian research and practice about wellness in legal education and the profession, we have been actively pursuing three goals: (i) understanding the onset and causes of psychological distress; (ii) developing ways to prevent and ameliorate distress; and (iii) fostering and promoting wellbeing within law schools and the legal profession.[1] This chapter addresses the latter two objectives, and considers how we can be most effective when developing strategies and programmes which address psychological distress or promote psychological wellbeing. Rather than discuss the merits of specific wellbeing programmes or initiatives, this chapter will step through several challenges in working together with our law students and legal professionals towards these objectives. Acknowledging these issues critically helps us to reach our shared visions for wellness in the study and practice of law, while avoiding some of the hazards which hinder progress or inadvertently make things worse.

From here, the chapter briefly surveys the normative landscape in which wellness is now situated and the ambiguities that have arisen during this time of transition. It then provides a psychological basis for reconciling the tension between understanding the unique personal experience of wellbeing and distress and our strategies and programmes which generally operate at a community level. Next, the chapter considers the two objectives of promoting wellbeing and addressing distress as two different strategies. Maintaining this distinction ensures that we develop appropriate programmes which address each set of needs and priorities. Finally, the study discusses the importance of creating and adapting theories of wellbeing and distress which guide our programmes. This requires us to develop our own evidence-based models and practices, which is predicated on the shared task of understanding the personal and collective experiences of our students and lawyers.

I write this as a psychologist embedded within a law school. Not only does this set me apart from other helping professionals, but it also means that my views do not adequately consider the sociological, philosophical or ethical considerations of wellbeing. I acknowledge my disciplinary bias, but I suggest that any boundaries are permeable and should not have a limiting or deterring effect on our work. These are therefore my reflections, rather than prescriptions, on our journey so far and what might lie ahead. I am aware of the cognitive bias known as the false consensus effect whereby I may be overestimating how much others may view this work through the same psychological lenses as I do.[2] Much of this, accordingly, is a self-directed reminder about being mindful and respectful of the assumptions, explanations and blind-spots about wellness that we all have. During the past few years where we have discovered many new ideas and occasionally changed our minds,[3] this chapter is also a search for some uniting principles which may help us to be flexible in pursuing our objectives while staying well ourselves.

Wellbeing: It's a Thing Now?

Promoting wellbeing and addressing distress in law students and lawyers is not a new idea. It has always been an integral part of legal education and the profession as part of good pedagogy, pastoral care, and personal and professional development. However, there has been a change over the past few years from a stance of raising awareness of mental health and wellbeing in legal education and practice[4] to taking direct and practical action on wellness as part of establishing positive norms or in compliance with new regulatory requirements.

In legal education, for example, the Council of Australian Law Deans' 2013 *Guidelines on Promoting Law Student Well-Being* specify that it is 'good practice' to 'actively educate and disseminate information around the issues of mental illness and student distress';[5] to 'integrate strategies for the promotion of law student well-being into teaching and learning practices';[6] and to 'evaluate the efficacy of interventions' about wellbeing.[7]

Similarly, the Law Admissions Consultative Committee's recently revised *PLT Competency Standards* place a positive duty on practical legal training providers to 'make applicants aware of the benefits of developing and maintaining personal wellbeing in their professional and personal lives'.[8] Although this requirement is phrased in terms of information and awareness, the outcomes envisaged could only be achieved through experiential programmes rather than learning the 'rules' of wellbeing.

The Tristan Jepson Memorial Foundation's *Best Practice Guidelines* on psychological wellbeing also envisage a more active role for legal organizations in directly addressing wellness as part of a psychologically safe workplace.[9] The guidelines encourage psychological health and resilience programmes to be available for all employees, and anticipate the use of specific psychological and social support interventions.

This is not the place to consider the appropriateness of this turn towards recognizing, and possibly inadvertently reifying, wellness. Wellness in law is now a normative project. The evidence about levels of distress and ill-health in lawyers and law students that has brought us to this point speaks for itself.[10] What remains is the challenge of translating 'wellness' or 'wellbeing', which are usually undefined at this level, into strategies and programmes which are effective and meaningfully integrated into legal education and practice. Without a suitable framework for how to do this, our objectives risk being dismissed as a regulatory overhead. The concept of wellness may even be co-opted into other incompatible agendas. To establish a base for proper action, therefore, we return to the person and the community.

The Psychological: Persons and Communities

A psychological approach has often been adopted in the Australian and international research on wellness in law students and lawyers. Psychological and psychometric methods are commonly used in the measurement of distress and wellbeing. Psychological or psychosocial theories are used to explain wellbeing or its absence. Wellbeing programmes are often informed by evidence-based psychological interventions and other psychotherapeutic techniques.

However, we must be clear what we mean by 'psychological' before we can effectively develop effective strategies and programmes. There are two ways in which this term can be misconstrued. First is the view that the word 'psychological' limits the scope of 'wellness'. Such a misreading holds that psychological wellbeing is a *psychologized* definition of wellness, which is necessarily individualistic, decontextualized and technical.[11] This is behind the charge that psychological strategies and programmes for wellness address the wrong problem, only making the situation worse at the sociocultural level.[12]

Alternatively, the word 'psychological' may invoke an attitude of deference towards those who apparently have the expertise in wellbeing, especially 'psy' professionals such as psychologists, psychotherapists or psychiatrists.[13] This is based on the false assumption that the knowledge and skill to achieve our wellness objectives is situated outside of our legal communities. Moreover, it reinforces the underlying attitude that wellness is purely a personal problem separate from what the legal profession or law schools should be concerned about. If we do propose psychological strategies and programmes in this climate, we may already run into barriers between those who have the perceived authority to intervene and those who are the objects or 'targets' of such action.

Some of this potential confusion may be because we are straddling two different levels of analysis. Part of our work is informing ourselves about students' and lawyers' personal experiences of law school or legal practice and how they may be related to wellbeing or distress. Yet we also tend to work at a collective level, identifying trends and differences across groups. Sometimes we aggregate these findings into descriptions of the average or typical student or lawyer. Our actions are typically to consider our entire community, or at least large segments within it, rather than establishing one-on-one therapeutic or pastoral responses. Rather than individualising the problem, here we may instead run the risk of homogenising our students and lawyers.

Understanding and Empathy

There is no need to treat these two perspectives as inherently incompatible, and thereby force a choice between them. We can embrace both the individual and community levels concurrently as a dialectic, with each informing the other. As a starting position towards reconciling the two approaches, I am inclined towards a theory of the person in the humanistic psychological tradition.[14] Following in the footsteps of Gordon Allport, Abraham Maslow, Carl Rogers and others, we can view a person as being irreducible to parts and always in search of meaning, connection and creativity.[15] Sass describes the humanistic psychological tradition as recognising a person's freedom and choice, the uniqueness of each person's character, values and goals, and recognising the subjectivity and 'innerness' of experience.[16]

Wellbeing and distress, therefore, are also embedded within the unique subjective experience of a person as a whole, rather than just being attributes of a person. There is a danger of skipping too quickly from the person to a description of a person, even though there is a legitimate place for theory and abstraction. Our understanding of people begins instead with empathy as a 'way of being', to borrow Rogers' phrase.[17] Such empathy is more than a technique. It is an ongoing sensitivity and attunement to the world of the person, which is also useful as a guide for our work alongside law students and lawyers:

> I am not trying to 'reflect feelings'. I am trying to determine whether my understanding of the Client's inner world is correct – whether I am seeing it as he/she is experiencing it at this moment. Each response of mine contains the unspoken question, 'Is this the way it is in you? Am I catching just the color and texture and flavor of the personal meaning you are experiencing right now? If not, I wish to bring my perception in line with yours.'[18]

Empathy also means understanding the person in her or his continuity and change, rather than as a frozen snapshot. Personality psychologist Dan McAdams says that to understand a person in this full sense requires more than a set of static traits or types, but requires an appreciation of the stories which tell of the unity and purpose of a person's life.[19] This psychological approach places a primary emphasis on upholding the integrity and relatability of the entire person. As psychoanalyst and philosopher Donna Orange writes:

> We believe that our involvement in humankind means all human experience is in principle understandable through empathic dialogue, including its nonverbal or embodied forms. This means that although you or I may not be able to understand every patient, no patient, no psychosis, no cultural difference, no form of otherness lies outside the possibility of understanding by someone.[20]

However, as Paul Bloom has argued, this kind of immersive empathy does not scale well from the individual level to the community or policy level.[21] The reasons are mainly prosaic: limits on our time and psychological resources. We could not possibly develop a deep empathic relationship (as between a therapist and client) with everyone in our law school or profession. But this misses the point. A humanistic psychological approach to wellness means that we maintain our focus on the person as the beginning and end of all that we do, while acknowledging that much can happen in between due to the complexity of their lives, of which we only see a small fraction.[22]

We can validate that a person's experience *can be* understood, even if practically this is not possible for us to do personally. Indeed, we need to avoid elevating ourselves as authority-figures who dispense empathy to students or lawyers. We are not the protagonist in each person's story of wellness. Rather, we hope to see each person develop as an empathic agent, as well as a recipient of empathy supported by their community.

A psychological approach to wellness therefore also means keeping our focus on the person, rather than on methods and techniques. This is particularly important when working at the aggregate level. Being person-centred is not inconsistent with the use of psychological methods and tools, such as the quantitative surveys that we have been using. It is, however, a reminder – not only to the researcher but also to those interpreting the results – that these data come directly from the personal experience of each participant. We know, both theoretically and empirically, that these tools are imperfect, but we can still allow the data to speak to the person. For instance, when we invite students and lawyers to complete the DASS-21, we are asking whether their current experience resonates with a set of specific experiences associated with psychological distress (for instance, 'I felt I wasn't worth much as a person', or 'I was worried about situations in which I might panic and make a fool of myself').[23]

Even when statistically aggregated, these data are used to inform us about the kinds of experiences people are having – and the variability of such experience – at an individual and collective level. While we need to be cautious of staying too long at the aggregate level, these methods can inform us about the person and the community in ways which may not be immediately accessible or directly apprehended. They may be rough measurements from afar, but always yield openings for further inquiry and closer understanding.

As anthropologist Clifford Geertz recognized, we are always moving between two different stances in our inquiry: the *experience-near* and the *experience-distant*.[24] The former involves the immediate experience through relational understanding and empathy; the latter is the systematic symbolic representation of the near through categories, data and theory, as is common in the social sciences as a way to understand complex phenomena. Just as we move between individual and community, we also mindfully weave between experience-near and experience-distant modes so that the person as a whole, and the observed and measured aspects of a person, can be understood in relation to one another.[25]

People in Context

Despite this complexity of the person, one aspect is particularly visible to us: their identity as a law student or lawyer. Unlike a counsellor in private practice, we have a privileged proximity with the people we see. We relate to them not just in the universal humanity of a person meeting another person, but within our shared social contexts. We seek to promote wellbeing and prevent distress not just in *a* community, but in *our* communities.[26]

This raises a broader set of psychological questions. Here our goal is to understand wellbeing and distress by looking beyond the individual and into the environments and structures in which lawyers or students find themselves, which overlap with the spaces we also inhabit. A psychological approach at this level entails recognising the uniqueness of each community and its collective experiences, in parallel to recognising the uniqueness of persons. Appreciating this context then helps the community to work together towards empowerment and change, especially directed at structural, institutional and socioeconomic arrangements which contribute to problems at an individual or collective level.

It may seem that this community level is an appropriate place for what Paul Ricoeur termed the 'hermeneutics of suspicion'.[27] This is a sceptical way of interpreting a person's experience, looking for hidden motivations and meanings. It presumes that we are not only deceptive to others and ourselves, but also that this non-transparency is caused by dynamics of power, oppression and interests involving underlying social, economic and political forces. We should identify and address these concerns as they relate to wellbeing.[28] However, doing this does not require primarily deconstructing and challenging others' motivations and view of reality, as this introduces even more distance from those with whom we are seeking to work together for collective positive change. Instead, a 'hermeneutics of trust' is favourable, even at a community level. Our presumption is that people in communities are the experts of their collective experiences. The dialogic and empathic presence of others within the community allows each person to express and refine their understanding of their common world.[29] Whatever we then choose to do is planned and done together as a community, while learning from and supporting other communities.[30]

Although there is room for improvement in terms of cooperative participation, we have already begun to do this kind of community psychological work. Our wellness work has always been situated within the context of legal education and practice in our particular local settings. Our focus has never just been on the narrow issue of the incidence of mental health problems or of individual 'happiness'.[31] While requiring a deep understanding of the expression and experience of wellbeing and distress, the Australian wellness project has been inextricable from broader innovations and reforms about teaching and learning, ethics, conflict and dispute resolution, social justice and the future of the legal profession.[32]

By furthering this work, we actively reject the view that people are principally blinded by invisible social forces by creating an environment where not only inclusion and hospitality are felt but also critique and change is possible. We seek to understand the collective psychological experience and the effect of broader systemic influences within a community which models wellness through its willingness to listen and relate. Our challenge then is to move intentionally and smoothly between the individual and the community levels, just as we move between the near and distant in organising what we know and what to do. There is nothing gained by having a bifurcated wellness movement which addresses two artificially separate issues from supposedly irreconcilable perspectives.

What Are We Hoping For?

What we are trying to achieve when we talk about promoting wellbeing and addressing distress? Taking the time to consider our motivations and objectives is particularly important given the tempting ease to jump directly to action. For instance, a quick scan of the literature will show a wide range of neatly packaged programmes which have been successfully run for law students, lawyers or a related population. Commercial wellness 'solutions' are also – unfortunately – too easily accessible and attractive. Delivering such a programme will probably yield some positive results, and not only because of the placebo effect.[33] However, to act without considering and communicating the reasons for acting is short-sighted and may lead to unintended adverse consequences, including the distortion of what the community understands 'wellness' to mean. The chief reason is that the programme would not have been a result of understanding the problems and needs of the local community and generating responses from within.

We may be wise to separate our *strategies* from our *programmes*, borrowing a distinction often made in relation to (mental) health policy at a national level.[34] The broad objectives of promoting wellbeing and preventing or ameliorating distress operate at the *strategy* level. These are long-term general objectives identifying broad areas for action. On the other hand, the specific actions or interventions are situated at the *programme* level, which address specific strategy-level priorities over a short period and usually working with a smaller segment of the population. This is to say that we should not mistake a wellbeing programme – even an apparently successful one – for a well-developed strategy.

Being clear about our strategy and strategic priorities is made more critical because the two objectives of promoting wellbeing and preventing/ameliorating distress are very different. The absence of distress is not the same as wellbeing, and wellbeing does not mean the absence of distress. Promoting wellbeing entails persons moving towards improvement, development and values-oriented growth. Consistent with the picture of the person described earlier,[35] this strategy is underpinned by a hopeful striving towards flourishing in each person which goes beyond momentary happiness but involves living well according to one's virtue and potential.[36] Promotion-based wellbeing programmes, which often find their roots in positive psychology, encourage growth of character, exploration and connection. Collectively, programmes may involve building social engagement and relationships; fostering positive collective or organizational identity; developing positive approaches to leadership or learning; or changing the environment to create opportunities for connection, resilience and empowerment.[37]

On the other hand, a focus on psychological distress is primarily about stopping and reversing declines in psychological health where distress or impairment are already present, although it is increasingly also about preventing the incidence of poor mental and psychosocial health in the first place. At this point, it bears repeating that we are interested only in addressing *pathological* distress or that which is associated with a mental or psychosocial disability, not just any stress which forms part of the normal spectrum of human emotion and experience.[38]

Prevention and amelioration programmes involve addressing dysfunctional and distress-causing aspects of the person's experience, behaviour or environment. This may involve structured psychological therapy, especially for more serious problems and impairments, but can often be informal and less intense in applied contexts, taking the form of providing information, social support and opportunities to learn and practise new life skills. We are primarily interested in these latter options, while keeping appropriate channels open for supportive (rather than dismissive) referral where the level of care required is beyond our competence. At the community level, prevention programmes typically involve the management of psychological risks,[39] as well as addressing systemic issues known to be harmful, such as poor teaching methods or management practices.

While both promotion and prevention/amelioration strategies are equally important, they are not interchangeable. Programmes promoting wellbeing may also help prevent or alleviate distress, and vice versa; but each strategy has very different theoretical roots leading to different kinds of actions. Programmes designed for one strategy cannot be assumed to achieve the other. Implying that these strategies are the same dilutes their potential and sets up misleading expectations.

What Do We Do?

Theory, Evidence and Their Limits

The substance and process of any wellness programme depends on its underlying theory of why people experience psychological distress and get better, or how they develop or maintain positive wellbeing. There is no shortage of such explanations, and there is therefore an abundance of possible programmes.[40] Doing wellness well requires being aware of these explanatory models and adapting and applying the most appropriate ones to our local context.

Many of the wellness programmes in the Australian and international legal context have been influenced by evidence-based clinical (treating and preventing distress) or positive (developing or maintaining wellbeing) psychological theory and evidence. It would, however, be a mistake to characterize this process as choosing the most appealing theory from a menu of options. Just because a programme is described as evidence-based does not necessarily mean that it will be efficacious towards our strategies in our contexts.

Every underlying theory also is incomplete, and technically speaking, false.[41] No theory can adequately explain a person's individual experience of wellbeing or distress, or the infinitely varied and interrelated causes and influences which led to this point. Theories are typically universal models, built on all-encompassing explanations and pathways which can be applied to everyone.[42] However, many current wellness theories also tend to presuppose responses and interventions at the personal level. As such, the programmes which follow may not be appropriate or sufficient, by themselves, to support our communities of students and lawyers.

Reclaiming the Middle

I suggest that there is a middle level of theory between the idiographic of each person's experience and the nomothetic of explaining all human experience.[43] There is a valuable intermediate space in which we can develop, test and share theories of wellbeing and distress within our particular law-related environments. We can intentionally use this space to examine the common issues which are faced by law students and lawyers and their relationship to wellbeing and distress. These include topics which we have already started to explore, such as the role of the curriculum[44] or lifestyle pressures;[45] or for lawyers, careers pressures and expectations,[46] heavy workloads[47] and inadequate preparation for the complexities of legal practice.[48]

Our task, however, is not just to identify possible correlates of wellbeing or distress, but both to integrate and dismantle these contextual influences in order to account for as much individual and collective experience as possible using the simplest explanations. Locally appropriate theories of wellbeing help us plan and prioritize what to do and know when to do it. Having our own theory and evidence minimizes the risk of 'Band-Aid' solutions which may mask or even legitimize underlying problems. While this requires the language of systematized experience-distant tools and language to formulate our explanations, we are always informed by the experience-near at both the individual and community level, and iteratively check what we think we know.

None of this local enquiry should be separated from what we already know in terms of general psychological theories. Well-established theories, such as self-determination theory (SDT),[49] can be extended and adapted to our explanatory model. In the case of SDT, for example, the legal workplace or law school environment can be examined more closely to see what contributes or subtracts from the satisfaction of the three basic psychological needs of autonomy, competence and relatedness. We could, for example, investigate if there are sub-categories of each need which are specific to the legal environment at various points in time, thus making a universal theory more relevant to our legal contexts.

The objective is to reshape existing psychological theories, rather than start afresh or, worse, filter what we see in our communities through the lens of a universal theory. The maxim from statutory interpretation, *generalia specialibus non derogant*, applies here: the general does not detract from the specific. We should have the courage to tinker with theories of wellbeing and distress, assured this is never the end point of our inquiry. Our focus is always on the people in our communities from whom the theory is generated, and for whom the theories serve.

But What Do We Do?

So far, this may feel like a pure research project, rather than implementing a wellness programme. My response is that the process of collective discovery and understanding will already be the basis of a very sound and meaningful programme. Theory, inquiry, action and reflection are part of a continuous loop. How might this look, as good practice?

Listening

The first step involves mapping out the distinctive or important features of the community, especially relating to wellbeing or distress, while also bringing to light that which may be so ordinary or familiar it is not noticed.[50] This should be done as an exploratory joint project within your communities (i.e., together with law students or lawyers). Immersive qualitative methods such as participatory action research may be particularly useful to build relationships and share goals. Surveys may be an important part of a mixed-methods approach to provide further information about specific topics. Understanding and creating meaning together in this step is often a powerful wellness-promoting activity in itself, and should not be seen merely as a time-consuming prefatory step.[51]

Systematising

The next step is to see if the themes identified resonate with models proposed in legal education/practice or in wider psychological theories. Depending on what psychological processes are identified – e.g., did issues arise about how people think or feel; relationships, what people are doing or not doing; issues of identity? – the theories on these topics may be useful. The clinical and positive psychological literature may help explain why these things go wrong and what good outcomes may be possible, and provide examples of the kinds of programmes that others have developed in their contexts.

This stage of theory development should also look at what other disciplines (e.g. in the sociological, feminist or critical scholarship) have said in terms of experience-distant theory, as well as what wellness-related programmes and strategies others (especially in professional disciplines such as medicine) have tried as experience-near understanding and responses. Integrating these observations and explanations is at the heart of forming a locally appropriate working theory of wellness.

Experimenting and Evaluating

By this stage, recurring suggestions for possible actions will usually have surfaced in the process of collaborative discovery. These ideas should be checked against your wellness-related strategic priorities. If compatible, they can be formulated into plans for specific small-scale and time-limited programmes. Developing these plans informed by what others have done within their legal education/practice communities is beneficial; but this requires asking why others did what they did, rather than just imitating techniques and interventions in search of immediate outcomes.

Questions of access, inclusion and continuity also arise here: who are the intended participants? Who is not eligible to, could not or is unlikely to participate? Programmes are intentionally time-limited but the underlying strategy should be ongoing. What happens when the programme finishes? What other programmes and resources are available? How do they all integrate towards the strategy?

Evaluating the programme is essential. Even if a formal mixed-methods evaluation is not possible, there should at least be a qualitative inquiry about participants' experience, including an honest appraisal of unexpected or undesired effects. Evaluation begins even before a programme commences in assessing *a priori* attitudes and expectations. Pilot testing with a small sample of the intended audience can provide such valuable feedback and opportunities for adjustments, especially in terms of communicating expectations. The results of the evaluation should be considered part of the programme results, which must be shared with the participants. Follow-through and ongoing dialogue is important in valuing participants as part of the community rather than as experimental subjects.

Reflecting, Learning and Sharing

The final step is to reflect on how the programme and the evaluation results informed your theory. How well did the theory explain participants' experiences and expectations before, during and after the programme? Were there important phenomena left unexplained by the theory? What is the limit of what you can say was achieved? Now is the time to update the model based on your evidence before cycling back to the first step.

The working theory at this point is likely to explain wellbeing or distress at one point in time, or over a wide timespan (e.g., across a whole law school). The next step is to expand this into a developmental theory, one which accounts for changes over time. This may include identifying, explaining and responding to particular points of growth, instability or homeostasis which are relevant to wellbeing and distress.

Sharing these reflections about the status of your theory is just as important as communicating the results from the programme itself. It provides the underlying rationale and context of what you did, what you learned from it and what remains unknown or unresolved. These lessons are valuable for our broader community of research and practice.

We therefore have the opportunity to create a theory and evidence base for wellness in legal education and practice. We can learn from both the similarities and differences in others' experience compared with the characteristics of our local communities. Having our own expertise and models ensures that our programmes are truly evidence-based, rather than transplanting techniques and programmes which may be evidence-based in another context but may be inappropriate or even counterproductive in our own communities.

The steps outlined above may still seem too abstract to form the basis of a concrete programme aimed at promoting wellbeing or addressing distress. De-emphasising prescriptive techniques may be unsettling. It may appear too easy, or naïve, that the contents of a programme could emerge through the indeterminacy of dialogue.[52] It is therefore worth considering the consistent (but often ignored) findings from large systematic reviews showing that there is very little difference in outcomes between the major 'brands' of evidence-based psychological interventions.[53] Despite having very different and sometimes incompatible techniques and rationales, they all seem effective. This is not to say that we can do anything as a wellness programme and be guaranteed success. It does, however, suggest that we should be wary of overt technique and method as the determining factors.

What, then, explains why people seem to get better across these therapies? Despite their differences, there are also substantial similarities between them. These are known as *common factors*.[54] One of the most important common factors is the therapeutic relationship between therapist and client, the quality of which accounts for the client's progress more than the distinctive features of each kind of therapy. The therapeutic relationship has a number of dimensions, including the presence of a helping professional; the intentional time and space in which the client can speak and be heard; and the hope and expectation that comes from the routines and rituals of therapy. To be effective, we should also pay sufficient attention to these qualities in our wellness programmes.

Taking this further, Arthur Bohart persuasively suggests that it is therefore ultimately the client themselves who is the most important common factor.[55] He disputes the implicit idea that the therapist is the 'hero' who makes the recovery or growth happen. In fact, it is the client (in our case, the student or the lawyer) who, through dialogue and as an intelligent active agent, will take the programme and use it as appropriate in her or his own life and context.[56] Bohart therefore suggests that therapy is mostly a learning space. As we know, learning involves not only content and skills, but also having the environment and scaffolding in which to learn experientially and effectively. It is the client themselves, with support, who is learning how to self-heal. Therefore, our aim should be towards:

> develop[ing] collaborative, relationship-based models that emphasize mobilizing hope and optimism, active client involvement, . . . and helping clients mobilize their own intrinsic intelligence for solution-finding rather than models that rely on cookbook lists of manualized interventions for specific disorders.[57]

The same could apply to what we seek to do together with our students and lawyers as part of our wellness strategies. It applies both individually and collectively. At the community level, there is the extra dimension of empowerment and critique against systemic or institutional sources of impaired wellbeing. This comes from recognising collective experiences and drawing on the shared resources needed to respond, while encouraging each person to be ever more aware of the depth of their life stories, relationships and values.

Of course, the specific activities we undertake will have procedural and technical qualities which could be described like a recipe. Such systematized knowledge is important, but must then be translated through the active process of mutual understanding. Creating such a participatory learning space does more than nurture integrative and creative action. It also affirms the capacities of the community and each person, including (but never limited to) their experience and identity as a law student or a lawyer.[58]

Conclusion: Wellbeing, Being Well

Doing wellness well should not be an impossible pursuit. Nor should it come at the expense of our own wellbeing. The approach outlined in this chapter relies on the most basic of human needs and abilities: understanding and being understood. This should therefore be easy, but only to the extent that relationships are easy. A relational foundation to wellness, however, means that we do not do this alone. Any perceived personal responsibility (and stress) for the success of a wellness strategy or programme is therefore not primarily personal, but shared with members of the community across programmes and strategies. The success of establishing dialogue, trust and empathy within the community is already a significant step towards the conditions for wellness.

This connection also extends to the Wellness Network for Law, whose increasing diversity provides new opportunities not only to observe and learn about theory or data, but also to engage in our own experience-near dialogues. We may sometimes do things differently, but we can respect that (and communicate how) these differences are based on distinctive priorities and experiences at the local level. We can integrate others' experiences into our own models and practices, while always being informed by good psychological theory as well as a hopeful and holistic view of the person.

Our wellness work together with lawyers and law students also creates or rediscovers communities which act as containers for our own experiences, doubts, joys and frustrations. These common spaces are vital in keeping ourselves well, as we navigate the strategies of promoting wellbeing and preventing or ameliorating distress. We can appreciate experience and move towards understanding the experience of people and our communities, just as we ourselves and our hopes for legal education and practice are understood.

Notes

* Stephen Tang is a lecturer and psychologist at the Australian National University (ANU) Legal Workshop. E: stephen.tang@anu.edu.au.

1 Wellness Network for Law, *About Us* <http://wellnessforlaw.com/about/>.

2 Lee Ross, David Greene and Pamela House, 'The "False Consensus Effect": An Egocentric Bias in Social Perception and Attribution Processes' (1977) 13 *Journal of Experimental Social Psychology* 279.

3 An earlier version of this chapter was presented at the 2014 National Wellness for Law Forum. With the benefit of reflection, and the wisdom and patience of the editors, the present chapter is now less polemic and more positive in tone. I am also deeply grateful to Mabel Tsui, who translates for me the principles of genuineness, unconditional positive regard and empathy which Carl Rogers identified into an experience-near reality (see below) and for her valuable editorial support.

4 Kath Hall, 'Do We Really Want to Know? Recognising the Importance of Wellbeing in Australian Law Schools' (2009) 9 *QUT Law and Justice Journal* 1.

5 Council of Australian Law Deans, *Promoting Law Student Well-Being: Good Practice Guidelines for Law Schools* (2013), guideline 2.

6 Ibid., guideline 4.

7 Ibid., guideline 10.

8 Law Admissions Consultative Committee, *PLT Competency Standards for Entry-Level Lawyers* (2015) [4.6].

9 Tristan Jepson Memorial Foundation, *TJMF Psychological Wellbeing: Best Practice Guidelines for the Legal Profession* (2014) ('TJMF Guidelines').

10 Wendy Larcombe, Stephen Tang and Rachael Field, 'Reflecting on the Evidence, Ethics and Politics of Student Mental Health and Legal Education' (forthcoming).

11 Katie Wright, 'From Target Interventions to Universal Approaches: Historicizing Wellbeing' in Katie Wright and Julie McLeod (eds), *Rethinking Youth Wellbeing: Critical Perspectives* (Springer, 2015); Jim Orford, *Community Psychology: Challenges, Controversies and Emerging Consensus* (Wiley, 2008) 8; Christine Parker, 'The "Moral Panic" Over Psychological Wellbeing in the Legal Profession: A Personal or Political Ethical Response?' (2014) 37 *UNSW Law Journal* 1103, 1127–30.

12 But see Katie Wright, 'Theorizing Therapeutic Culture: Past Influences, Future Directions' (2008) 44 *Journal of Sociology* 321; Mike M Martin, 'From Morality to Mental Health: Virtue and Vice in a Therapeutic Culture' (Oxford University Press, 2006) ch 5.

13 A critique and reaction to this is found in the concept of empowerment in the mental health and community psychology literature: Suarla Fitzsimons and Ray Fuller, 'Empowerment and its Implications for Clinical Practice in Mental Health: A Review' (2002) 11 *Journal of Mental Health* 481, 483.

14 For what 'humanistic' does not mean, see Donna M Orange, *Thinking for Clinicians: Philosophical Resources for Contemporary Psychoanalysis and the Humanistic Psychotherapies* (Routledge, 2010) 6–9.

15 Stella Resnick, Arthur Warmoth and Ilene A Serlin, 'The Humanistic Psychology and Positive Psychology Connection: Implications for Psychotherapy' (2001) 41 *Journal of Humanistic Psychology* 73, 75.

16 Louis A Sass, 'Humanism, Hermeneutics, and Humanistic Psychoanalysis: Differing Conceptions of Subjectivity' (1989) 12 *Psychoanalysis and Contemporary Thought* 433, 435. Sass includes a fourth element, self-transparency (the 'certitude and clarity of subjective experience'): ibid. 441–2.

17 Carl R Rogers, 'Empathic: An Unappreciated Way of Being' (1975) 5 *Counselling Psychologist* 2; Orange, above n14, 8.

18 Carl R Rogers, 'Reflection of Feelings' (1986) 1 *Person-Centred Review* 375.

19 Dan P McAdams, 'What Do We Know When We Know a Person?' (1995) 63 *Journal of Personality* 365.

20 Donna M Orange, 'Kohut Memorial Lecture: Attitudes, Values and Intersubjective Vulnerability' (2009) 4 *International Journal of Psychoanalytic Self Psychology* 235, 238.

21 Paul Bloom, 'The Baby in the Well: The Case against Empathy', *New Yorker* 20 May 2013 <http://www.newyorker.com/magazine/2013/05/20/the-baby-in-the-well>.

22 Isaac Prilleltensky, 'Values, Assumptions, and Practices: Assessing the Moral Implications of Psychological Discourse and Action' (1997) 52 *American Psychologist* 517.

23 The DASS-21 is the 21-item version of the Depression Anxiety Stress Scale, a standardized self-report measure for three aspects of psychological ill-health: Steven H Lovibond and Peter F Lovibond, *Manual for the Depression Anxiety Stress Scales* (Psychology Foundation, 2nd ed, 1995). Wendy Larcombe et al, 'Does an Improved Experience of Law School Protect Students against Depression, Anxiety and Stress? An Empirical Study of Wellbeing and the Law School Experience of LLB and JD Students' (2013) 35 *Sydney Law Review* 407; Molly Townes O'Brien, Stephen Tang and Kath Hall, 'Changing Our Thinking: Empirical Research on Law Student Wellbeing, Thinking Styles and the Law Curriculum' (2011) 21 *Legal Education Review* 149; Stephen Tang and Anneka Ferguson, 'The Possibility of Wellbeing: Preliminary Results from Surveys of Australian Professional Legal Education Students' (2014) 14 *QUT Law Review* 27.

24 These terms were first used by humanistic psychotherapist Heinz Kohut: *The Analysis of the Self* (International Universities Press, 1971). They were later adopted by Clifford Geertz: 'From the Native's Point of View: On the Nature of Anthropological Understanding' (1974) 28 *Bulletin of the American Academy of Arts and Sciences* 26.

25 Lynn Froggett and Stephen Briggs, 'Practice-Near and Practice-Distant Methods in Human Services Research' (2012) 8 *Journal of Research Practice* M9 [2.1].
26 Wendy Larcombe, Towards an Integrated, Whole-School Approach to Promoting Law Student Wellbeing' (Chapter 2 this volume).
27 Paul Ricoeur, *Freud and Philosophy* (Denis Savage trans, Yale University Press, 1970); Orford, above n11, 36; Donna M Orange, *The Suffering Stranger: Hermeneutics for Everyday Clinical Practice* (Routledge, 2011) 26–31.
28 Orford, above n11, ch 2.
29 Orange, above n27, 35.
30 The entire discipline of community psychology is dedicated to this goal: Orford, above n11, xii–xiv.
31 Molly Townes O'Brien and Stephen Tang, 'Law School Too Hard? Why the Struggle Could Be a Good One', *The Conversation* (23 September 2013) <https://theconversation.com/law-school-too-hard-why-the-struggle-could-be-a-good-one-17989>.
32 Rachael Field, James Duffy and Anna Huggins, *Lawyering and Positive Professional Identities* (LexisNexis, 2014) 477; Molly Townes O'Brien, 'Connecting Law Students to Health and Wellbeing' (Chapter 12, this volume); Isaac Prilleltensky and Dennis R Fox, 'Psychopolitical Literacy for Wellness and Justice' (2007) 35 *Journal of Community Psychology* 1.
33 Donald D Price, Damien G Finniss and Fabrizio Benedetti, 'A Comprehensive Review of the Placebo Effect: Recent Advances and Current Thought' (2008) 59 *Annual Review of Psychology* 565.
34 World Health Organization, *Mental Health Policy, Plans and Programmes* (revised ed, 2005). Often a third level, policy, is included, but may be unnecessary in our smaller context. For a good example of strategy and programmes, see Law Institute of Victoria, *Mental Health and the Legal Profession: A Preventative Strategy* (2014).
35 Edward L Deci and Richard M Ryan, 'Hedonia, Eudaimonia, and Well-Being: An Introduction' (2008) 9 *Journal of Happiness Studies* 1.
36 Carol D Ryff and Burton H Singer, 'Know Thyself and Become What You Are: A Eudaimonic Approach to Psychological Wellbeing' (2009) 9 *Journal of Happiness Studies* 13.
37 Kim S Cameron, Jane E Dutton and Robert E Quinn, *Positive Organizational Scholarship* (Berrett-Koehler, 2003); P Alex Linley and Stephen Joseph (eds), *Positive Psychology in Practice* (Wiley, 2004).
38 Tang and Ferguson, above n23, 42.
39 TJMF Guidelines, above n9.
40 See, e.g., Anthony Jorm et al, *A Guide to What Works for Depression* (beyondblue, 2nd ed, 2013) and Nicola Reavley et al, *A Guide to What Works for Anxiety Disorders* (beyondblue, 2010). For what does not work, see Scott O Lilienfeld, 'Psychological Treatments that Cause Harm' (2007) 2 *Perspectives on Psychological Science* 53.
41 Simon Dennis and Walter Kintsch, 'Evaluating Theories' in Robert J Sternberg, Henry L Roediger III and Diane F Halpern (eds), *Critical Thinking in Psychology* (Cambridge University Press, 2007) 143.
42 This is especially true for transdiagnostic models which seek to explain multiple forms of psychological distress or disorder: Susan Nolen-Hoeksema and Edward R Watkins, 'A Heuristic for Developing Transdiagnostic Models of Psychopathology: Explaining Multifinality and Divergent Trajectories' (2011) 6 *Perspectives on Psychological Science* 589.
43 Hubert JM Hermans, 'On the Integration of Nomothetic and Idiographic Research Methods in the Study of Personal Meaning' (1988) 56 *Journal of Personality* 785.
44 Rachael Field, 'Promoting Law Student Well-Being through the Curriculum' (Final ALTC Teaching Fellowship Report, Office for Learning and Teaching, 2014); Anna Huggins, 'Autonomy Supportive Curriculum Design: A Salient Factor in Promoting Law Students' Wellbeing' (2012) 35 *UNSW Law Journal* 683.

45 Alex Steel and Anna Huggins, 'Law Student Lifestyle Pressures' (Chapter 4, this volume).
46 Margaret Thornton, 'Deregulation, Debt and the Discipline of Law' (2014) 39 *Alternative Law Journal* 213, 215–16.
47 Adele J Bergin and Nerina L Jimmieson, 'Australian Lawyer Well-Being: Workplace Demands, Resources and the Impact of Time-Billing Targets' (2014) 21 *Psychiatry, Psychology and Law* 427.
48 Foley and Tang, 'On Being, Not just Thinking Like, a Lawyer: Connections between Uncertainty, Ignorance and Wellbeing' (Chapter 10, this volume).
49 Kennon M Sheldon and Lawrence S Krieger, 'Understanding the Negative Effects of Legal Education on Law Students: A Longitudinal Test of Self-Determination Theory' (2007) 33 *Personality and Social Psychology Bulletin* 883.
50 An 'unknown known': see Foley and Tang, above n49.
51 O'Brien, Tang and Hall, above n23, 168–80.
52 This is, however, the primary 'technique' of many humanistic psychotherapies: Carl Rogers, *On Becoming a Person: A Therapist's View of Psychotherapy* (Houghton Mifflin, 1995).
53 Rick Budd and Ian Hughes, 'The Dodo Bird Verdict: Controversial, Inevitable and Important: A Commentary on 30 Years of Meta-Analyses' (2009) 16 *Clinical Psychology and Psychotherapy* 510; Jürgen Barth et al, 'Comparative Efficacy of Seven Psychotherapeutic Interventions for Patients with Depression: A Network Meta-Analysis' (2013) 10 *PLoS Medicine* e1001454.
54 Bruce E Wampold, 'The Research Evidence for the Common Factors Model: A Historically Situated Perspective' in Barry Duncan et al (eds), *The Heart and Soul of Change: Delivering What Works in Therapy* (APA Books, 2nd ed, 2010) 49.
55 Arthur C Bohart, 'The Client is the Most Important Common Factor: Clients' Self-Healing Capacities and Psychotherapy' (2000) 10 *Journal of Psychotherapy Integration* 127.
56 Ibid. 132.
57 Ibid. 145.
58 Tang and Ferguson, above n23, 50.

2 Towards an Integrated, Whole-School Approach to Promoting Law Student Wellbeing

Wendy Larcombe[*]

Introduction

It is now well established that law students in Australia experience high rates of psychological distress. While US studies identified more than 25 years ago that legal education has a negative impact on student wellbeing,[1] it was thought for some time that 'the Australian situation is quite different'.[2] The research undertaken by the Brain and Mind Research Institute (BMRI) in 2008 dispelled conclusively that vain hope. Thirteen Australian universities participated in the BMRI study, which found that one in three law students experienced 'high' or 'very high' levels of psychological distress as measured by the Kessler Psychological Distress Scale (K10).[3] Using a different instrument, the Depression Anxiety and Stress Scales (DASS-21), studies at the Australian National University (ANU, 2010) and the University of Melbourne (UOM, 2011 and 2012) produced similar findings: approximately 30 per cent of the law students (LLB and JD) who participated in the ANU and UOM studies reported experiencing 'moderate' to 'extremely severe' levels of depressive symptoms, and a similar proportion recorded moderate to extremely severe anxiety symptoms.[4] At these levels, students' daily functioning is likely to be negatively impacted and this, in turn, impairs academic achievement.[5]

The empirical data on law student distress is now robust, putting law schools on notice that they have a serious problem to redress. Moreover, if law schools are to support all students to realize their academic potential, student wellbeing must be addressed as a learning and teaching issue, not only as a matter for student services professionals. As Field and Kift have noted in the Australian context, promotion of law student mental health must be, or become, the responsibility of the entire Australian legal academic community.[6] That responsibility is currently being accepted and met by a range of initiatives in diverse law schools, as evidenced by this collection.[7] Positive strategies to enhance student wellbeing include those that foster resilience, 'vitality' or life-balance, self-management, reflection, peer engagement and positive professional identities. Positive psychology[8] and Self-Determination Theory (SDT)[9] have provided sound theoretical frameworks for such programmes, and empirical research into the factors that contribute to and those that mitigate law student psychological distress provides additional direction.[10]

Many of the initiatives being developed to promote student mental health in law schools target students directly with programmes and activities to build their 'mental health literacy'[11] and emotional intelligence,[12] thereby enabling them to better self-identify and manage stress, and to seek appropriate support when indicated. However, such programmes have implications beyond the individual level. For example, some student wellbeing initiatives challenge long-held assumptions about the skills required to be a lawyer and what it means to 'think like a lawyer'. As with the long-standing movement to 'humanize' legal education and legal practice in the United States,[13] many recent innovations to promote student wellbeing and resilience in Australian law schools give priority to intrinsic values and social service goals rather than the 'extrinsic' measures of success that have conventionally informed legal education and professional life.[14] The introduction of revised learning and teaching standards for legal education in Australia (under the Australian Qualifications Framework) provides further opportunities for reformulation of the skills and values promoted within legal education.[15] In sum, mental health is not only being promoted within law schools currently; a number of activities to improve students' mental wellbeing are also considering and addressing the ways that law schools and the law curriculum contribute to or inhibit student wellbeing.

The present chapter takes up the school-level implications of the movement to promote law students' mental wellbeing and considers how student wellbeing strategies, such as those showcased in the present collection, can be conceptualized and embedded – and thereby become sustainable – within an integrated, whole-school approach. Guidance for developing such an approach is found in the World Health Organization's Charter for Health Promotion ('the Ottawa Charter'), which underpins the Healthy Universities framework,[16] and also the Australian national mental health initiatives for primary and secondary schools: KidsMatter and MindMatters.[17] The components of these initiatives and their guiding principles are briefly outlined below before considering their application to mental health promotion activities and processes in law schools. I suggest that actions to promote law student wellbeing are usefully conceptualized into five domains, in line with the Ottawa Charter. In addition, a five-step process for initiating, enabling and implementing effective interventions is outlined, drawing on the 'whole-school' approach. Combined, these activities and processes ensure a comprehensive framework for mental health promotion that is coordinated, evidence-based and sustainable.

Conceptualizing (Mental) Health Promotion

The World Health Organization adopted the Ottawa Charter in 1986, defining health promotion as 'the process of enabling people to increase control over, and to improve, their health', where 'health' is defined as 'a state of complete physical, mental and social well-being'.[18] The Charter further notes that 'health is created and lived by people within the settings of their everyday life' so that these settings are themselves enriched by and become determinants of individuals' health and collective health-promoting actions. Now known as the 'healthy settings approach',[19] this ecological model of public health recognizes that the triggers and impacts of ill-health are community based. More specifically, health is understood as a product of the interactions between an individual's resources – personal, physical, social, economic and emotional – and the protective and risk factors in their social and physical settings. The health promotion framework advocates a comprehensive approach to improving health outcomes that seeks not only to change individual behaviour but also to change the environmental risk and protective factors – the 'settings' – in which everyday life is lived to ensure that they contribute to good health. In short, it seeks to ensure that the settings of people's lives are actively 'health-promoting'.

Within this framework, the Ottawa Charter identifies five key areas of health promotion activity.[20] First, Building Healthy Public Policy encompasses action to ensure that health enablers and outcomes are considered in public policy development – in both health and non-health sectors. Second, creating Health Supportive Environments encompasses actions by governments, organizations and individuals to ensure that living and working environments are 'safe, stimulating, satisfying and enjoyable'. Strengthening Community Actions is the third domain or focus for action, acknowledging that health promotion works through effective community involvement in setting priorities and in planning and implementing strategies for better health – especially given that health is an outcome of being able to take decisions and have control over one's life circumstances and actions. Developing individuals' Personal Skills through access to information and education is the fourth domain, noting that health information needs to be sensitive and adapted to diverse cultural and community needs. Finally, reorienting Health Services to combine prevention and early intervention (primary and secondary interventions) with clinical services (tertiary response) is an essential strategy for health promotion.

The healthy settings approach and the five domains for action outlined in the Charter have informed development of established public health programmes such as Healthy Cities, Healthy Schools and the Healthy Universities initiative.[21] The latter comprises a network of universities that aim 'to create a learning environment and organisational culture that enhances health, wellbeing and sustainability of its community and enables people to achieve their full potential'.[22] Importantly, the initiative is about continual improvement, not league tables: 'a health-promoting university is not one that has achieved a particular level of health; it is one that is conscious of health and striving to improve it'.[23] An example of a health-promoting university advancing actions within the five domains of the Ottawa framework is provided in Australia by the University of the Sunshine Coast.[24] However, to date, the Healthy Universities initiative has not received the level of government commitment and funding extended to Healthy Schools programmes.[25] The Australian government has recently invested in an extensive, schools-based mental health initiative at both primary and secondary levels of education: KidsMatter and MindMatters respectively. The comprehensive resources developed to support this initiative – including curriculum materials, guidance for school leaders and online skills development modules for both students and staff – provide further insight into the elements and enablers of a 'whole-school' approach to mental health promotion in the higher education sector.[26] The next section of this chapter considers how this approach and these resources can be adapted and applied to support the development of health-promoting law schools.

A Whole Law School Approach to Mental Health Promotion

Given the prevalence of psychological distress among law students, and the range of associated individual and contextual factors, it is almost certain that no single measure or intervention will redress the problem.[27] A comprehensive, multi-level approach to prevention and intervention is needed to reduce the rates of distress and promote law student mental wellbeing. Isolated or one-off measures designed to promote mental wellbeing may be undermined by other practices within a law school, or forgotten when a particular individual leaves the school. An institutionalized and sustainable approach to mental health promotion is needed. This is a considerable challenge and one likely to benefit from collective effort and collaboration within and across law schools.[28] This chapter suggests that the healthy settings framework outlined in the Ottawa Charter and further developed through the Health-Promoting Schools and Universities initiatives provides useful guidance for developing a whole-school approach to promoting law students' mental health. In short, a whole-school or settings approach ensures that mental health is not only promoted *in* the law curriculum and law school activities but also promoted *by* the law curriculum and law school activities.

Activities

The Ottawa Charter's five domains of health promotion activity, slightly adapted, provide a useful tool or checklist for conceptualizing and planning mental health promotion activities[29] within law schools. Note that it is not essential for each school to undertake all suggested activities. It is, however, important to a 'healthy settings' approach that each school undertake activities in each of the five identified domains, as the domains are mutually reinforcing or enabling (Figure 2.1).

Health-Promoting Policies in Law Schools

Activities in this domain include:

- Consulting relevant national good practice guidelines for mental health promotion in law, such as those developed for law schools by the Council of Australian Law Deans (CALD)[30] as well as the Tristan Jepson Memorial Foundation's *Best Practice Guidelines for the Legal Profession.*[31]
- Reviewing anti-discrimination obligations as they relate to mental illness and psychological health
- Developing a discrete mental health policy at the law school level.[32]

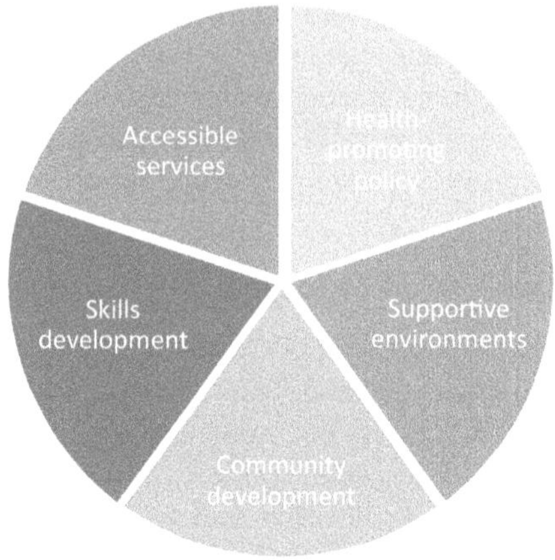

Figure 2.1 Areas of health-promotion activity

- Ensuring that policies governing special consideration in assessments and arrangement of academic accommodations include students experiencing mental health difficulties.
- Auditing school policies on confidentiality and privacy in relation to student health information, guidelines for record-keeping, and procedures governing access to and use of recorded student health information to ensure they do not discourage disclosure.
- Reviewing crisis incident management procedures to ensure that they consider mental health difficulties as both a trigger for an incident and as a potential consequence of an incident.
- Auditing and enhancing staff knowledge of relevant policies and guidelines.

Supportive Student Environments

Activities in this domain include:

- Auditing curriculum workloads and assessment requirements within subjects/units and across the program to ensure reasonable expectations, flexibility and recognition of student diversity.
- Auditing co-curricular and professional development opportunities such as internships and clinical placements to ensure they are inclusive and accessible to all students.
- Auditing and adjusting school and classroom level communications, activities and examples to ensure that they consistently recognize and value social and cultural diversity, affirm and enable varied forms of contribution and engagement, and promote intrinsic goals and diverse careers.
- Auditing and enhancing student facilities and spaces to ensure access to: healthy food options and food preparation/storage equipment; bicycle

storage; quiet spaces for reflection; spaces for social interaction; sporting facilities and/or spaces for yoga or meditation classes.
- Increasing opportunities for students to experience autonomy, competence and relatedness to others within the classroom and the broader teaching and learning environment.[33]
- Building social relationships and promoting a sense of belonging – for example, fostering peer networking and creating opportunities for students to take elective subjects with an academic mentor.
- Drawing on positive psychology to inform teacher interactions with students and feedback on assessment tasks.[34]

Community Development

Activities in this domain include:

- Building partnerships with student societies and student groups at risk of isolation or discrimination – for example, by appointing liaison officers for indigenous students; students with disabilities; international students; LGBTIQ students; and 'mature age' students.
- Developing partnerships with mental health professionals and other health service providers in the university and the local community, and drawing on their expertise to inform school activities.
- Conducting surveys, focus group discussions and other processes of information gathering to build an accurate profile of the student body, their backgrounds, interests and needs, and their suggestions and ideas for improving the student experience and wellbeing.
- Involving students in developing and delivering a programme of activities to promote student mental health and wellbeing at key points during the academic calendar such as orientation, interim assessment, revision periods (swot vac) and exams.
- Joining relevant professional networks such as the Wellness Network for Law[35] and funding school representatives (staff and students) to attend relevant workshops and seminars.

Skills Development for Students and Staff

Activities in this domain include:

- Providing opportunities for students to learn health-promoting knowledge and skills – such as mindfulness, resilience, conflict resolution, emotional intelligence, time and task management and to 'give voice to values' – within the formal curriculum, through co-curricular activities and through institution-wide learning management systems.[36]
- Collaborating with health professionals to offer workshops or develop curriculum materials on relevant topics.

- Developing and publishing online and print resources for students on ways to maintain mental health and wellbeing in law school, such as the booklets written by US Law school Professor Larry Krieger.[37]
- Developing curriculum and co-curricular offerings that expand students' access to experiential learning and clinical opportunities in order to build students' sense of competence in diverse contexts.[38]
- Developing curriculum and co-curricular offerings that build students' understanding of the professional roles and values engaged within diverse forms of legal practice as well as students' ability to identify roles consistent with their own values and strengths.[39]
- Providing workshops and individualized academic skills support for students needing assistance to develop writing, communication, analytical or research skills.
- Organizing, funding and promoting mental health training for key professional and academic staff as well as student leaders involved in peer support programmes.

Accessible Services for Students Experiencing Mental Health Difficulties

Activities in this domain include:

- Auditing and developing appropriate print and online guides to available school, university and community-based services (health and non-health) that may be relevant to students experiencing psychological distress – such as counselling, medical services, financial aid, childcare, chaplaincy, international student services, disability support, indigenous programmes, LGBTIQ networks and so on.
- Making contact with staff within these services and ensuring they have an accurate understanding of the law student body and students' mental health needs.
- Developing strategies to ensure that relevant law school staff are familiar with the available services, and confident that they know when and where to refer a student who may be experiencing mental health difficulties.
- Developing strategies to ensure that law students are familiar with the available services, and confident that they know when and where to refer a friend who may be experiencing mental health difficulties.
- Ensuring that school-based mental health services and information can be accessed discreetly so that use of such services does not require disclosure of a health difficulty to third parties.
- Ensuring that there is a dedicated academic member of staff to counsel and advise students unsure about making disclosures regarding mental health issues, or incidents or allegations of breaching academic integrity when applying for admission to practise law.

- Ensuring that confidentiality and privacy policies as well as anti-discrimination obligations are understood and observed by all staff providing services to students.
- Ensuring that service providers are involved in reviewing and evaluating student services, and also in development of information for students about such services.

Processes

The mental health promotion activities outlined above will not occur spontaneously, and many require a significant commitment of financial and human resources. Again drawing on the Healthy Universities and MindMatters initiatives, the elements and sequence of a sustainable process for establishing a health-promoting law school can be mapped as shown in Figure 2.2.[40]

Mental health promotion in law schools will not be effective or sustainable at a whole-school level without high-level executive commitment and endorsement; dedicated resources; a steering group involving key stakeholders; and project coordination (undertaken by an individual or small team with appropriate skills and qualifications).[41] Thus, the first step in developing a whole-school approach to promoting student mental health is identification and recruitment of the people who will undertake these various roles, including some relatively senior academic staff, student representatives and professional staff in key executive roles (such as a faculty general manager, director of career services and student experience manager). An advance meeting schedule and secretarial support are helpful. Some level of funding is also needed, if only to print pamphlets or cover the cost of yoga mats. Of course, the more funding, the more that can be done in some respects. This is one reason why high-level executive

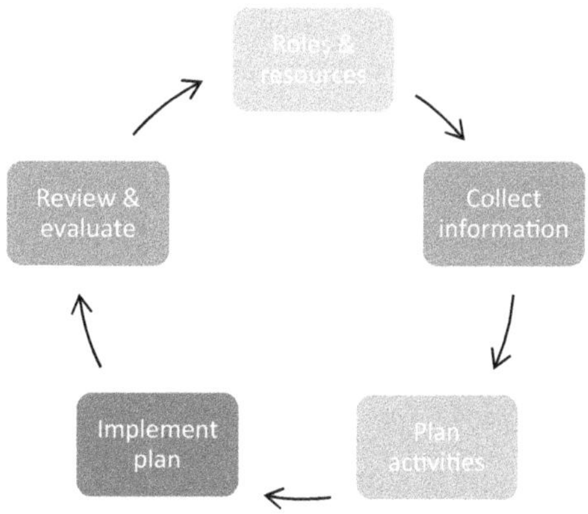

Figure 2.2 Steps in the health promotion process

commitment is essential: 'student wellbeing activities' needs to become a permanent line-item in the school budget.

Once a project team or Wellbeing Working Group has been established and resourced, step two involves this group collecting as much information as possible about students' characteristics, aspirations, course experience and levels of mental wellbeing; protective and risk factors in the school environment and curriculum; current initiatives; potential partners; support services and so on. A literature review to ensure that the team is up to date with the latest research and good practice examples will also be useful. However, examples from other law schools will need to be adapted to the local conditions and context, considering policy goals and priorities as well as resource constraints. This can be done as a 'SWOT analysis'[42] – systematically identifying strengths, weaknesses, opportunities and threats within the particular school that can assist or impact a mental wellbeing promotion project. This type of analysis – whether using a formal process or not – will also help ensure that issues such as looming funding cuts, work overload and other factors that might generate resistance[43] are identified and considered in the next step – planning activities.

Step three requires the development of a wellbeing activities plan. This may be annual or cover a longer time frame if appropriate review and adjustment are built in. Each of the five domains of health promotion activity outlined above should be covered if possible; however the choice of activities within each area can be determined by the individual law school's priorities, strengths, resources and access to local services (as identified in stage two). As well as determining *what* will be done in a given time frame, it is essential that the plan identifies *who* will do it. Once the plan has been developed, costed and approved, implementation is the next step.

Looking ahead to step five – review and evaluation of activities – it is important to document and seek feedback on activities as they are being delivered. Collection of feedback should be an element of step four (implementation). It is useful to review this feedback at the conclusion of activities, and for those involved to make timely notes about any improvements for future administration. In addition, it is essential that the entire project team engages in a process of review and evaluation at the end of the year (or period of the plan), reflecting on the 'hits' and 'misses' of the activities as implemented, lessons learned, future needs and so on. This evaluation then informs the next cycle of activity, which may also require renewal of the project team membership and reconsideration of other resource requirements. The review process may also identify needs for further information, expertise or support in other forms. It will always be valuable to have experts in mental health – from the university or the wider community – participate in the review and evaluation process.

Conclusion

The Good Practice Guidelines for Promoting Student Wellbeing adopted by the Council of Australian Law Deans (CALD) in 2013 were an important first step in assisting law schools to adopt a comprehensive, evidence-based approach to mental health promotion.[44] The framework outlined in this chapter offers further guidance for planning student wellbeing activities and, more importantly, for developing health-promoting law schools. Conceptualizing key areas of health promotion activity, and undertaking that activity within a project planning and review cycle, will ensure an integrated and sustainable whole-school approach to mental health promotion. Moreover, communication of that approach to students will signal that their mental health is an issue of serious concern to their law teachers and the school as a whole. And the good news is that research suggests that this, in itself, is a positive step towards promoting student wellbeing.

Notes

* Dr Wendy Larcombe, Associate Professor, Melbourne Law School, University of Melbourne, Victoria 3010, Australia. E: w.larcombe@unimelb.edu.au; T: +61 3 83441005. I would like to thank Rachael Field, Stephen Tang and Kath Hall for useful comments on an earlier version of some material included in this chapter. Thanks also to James Duffy and Colin James for careful editing and helpful suggestions.

1 For an overview of the early US research, see Matthew M Dammeyer and Narina Nunez, 'Anxiety and Depression among Law Students: Current Knowledge and Future Directions' (1999) 23(1) *Law and Human Behaviour* 55. Legal education as a contributing factor to student psychological distress was specifically investigated in an early study by G Andrew et al, 'The Role of Legal Education in Producing Psychological Distress among Law Students and Lawyers' (1986) 11 *American Bar Foundation Research Journal* 225.

2 Norm Kelk, Sharon Medlow and Ian Hickie, 'Distress and Depression among Australian Law Students: Incidence, Attitudes and the Role of Universities' (2010) 32 *Sydney Law Review* 113, 113.

3 Norm Kelk et al (Brain and Mind Research Institute), *Courting the Blues: Attitudes towards Depression in Australian Law Students and Lawyers* (2009) 12, http://www.cald.asn.au/docs/Law%20Report%20Website%20version%204%20May%2009.pdf. The Kessler Psychological Distress Scale (K10) was used to assess participants' risks of experiencing depression. Results showed that 35.4 per cent of law students reported high or very high levels of distress, compared with only 13.3 per cent of a general population sample aged 18–34. See also Kelk, Medlow and Hickie, above n2, 115–16.

4 Molly Townes O'Brien, Stephen Tang and Kath Hall, 'Changing Our Thinking: Empirical Thinking on Law Student Wellbeing, Thinking Styles and the Law Curriculum' (2011) 21 *Legal Education Review* 149 reports the ANU 2010 study. Wendy Larcombe et al, 'Does an Improved Experience of Law School Protect Students against Depression, Anxiety and Stress? An Empirical Study of Wellbeing and the Law School Experience of LLB and JD Students' (2013) 35 *Sydney Law Review* 407 reports the UOM 2011 study. Wendy Larcombe and Katherine Fethers, 'Schooling the Blues? An Investigation of Factors Associated with Psychological Distress among Law Students' (2013) 36(2) *UNSW Law Journal* 390 reports the UOM 2012 study.

5 O'Brien, Tang and Hall, above n4, 165. Confirming this, Stallman's study involving 6,479 students from two Australian universities found that students experiencing very high levels of psychological distress reported increased 'days out of role' as well as significantly lower grade point averages (GPAs) than other students: Helen M Stallman, 'Psychological Distress In University Students: A Comparison with General Population Data' (2010) 45(4) *Australian Psychologist* 249.

6 Rachael Field and Sally Kift, 'Addressing the High Levels of Psychological Distress in Law Students through Intentional Assessment and Feedback Design in the First Year Law Curriculum' (2010) 1 *International Journal of the First Year in Higher Education* 65, 67.

7 See also the articles collected in the recent special issue on Wellness for Law: (2014) 14 (1) *QUT Law Review*.

8 See, especially, James Duffy, Chapter 11 this collection; Martin EP Seligman, Paul R Verkuil and Terry H Kang, 'Why Lawyers are Unhappy' (2005) 10 *Deakin Law Review* 49; Martin EP Seligman, *Authentic Happiness: Using the New Positive Psychology to Realize Your Potential for Lasting Fulfillment* (Free Press, 2002).

9 See especially Richard M Ryan and Edward L Deci, 'Self-Determination Theory and the Facilitation of Intrinsic Motivation, Social Development, and Well-Being' (2000) 55 *American Psychologist* 68; Kennon M Sheldon et al, 'Applying Self-Determination Theory to Organizational Research' (2003) 22 *Research in Personnel and Human Resources Management* 357, 362, 366–8 ('Applying SDT'); Kennon M Sheldon, 'The Self-Concordance Model of Healthy Goal Striving: When Personal Goals Correctly Represent the Person', chapter 3 in Edward L Deci and Richard M Ryan (eds), *Handbook of Self-Determination Research* (University of Rochester Press, 2004) 65, 70–74.

10 See, in particular, Kennon M Sheldon and Lawrence S Krieger, 'Does Legal Education Have Undermining Effects on Law Students? Evaluating Changes in Motivation, Values, and Well-Being' (2004) 22 *Behavioral Sciences and the Law* 261; Kennon M Sheldon and Lawrence S Krieger, 'Understanding the Negative Effects of Legal Education on Law Students: A Longitudinal Test of Self-Determination Theory' (2007) 33 *Personality and Social Psychology Bulletin* 833; Larcombe and Fethers, 'Factors Associated with Distress', above n4; Wendy Larcombe, Ian Malkin and Pip Nicholson, 'Law Students' Motivations, Expectations and Levels of Psychological Distress: Evidence of Connections' (2012) 22 *Legal Education Review* 71.

11 See, generally, Claire M Kelly, Anthony F Jorm and Annemarie Wright, 'Improving Mental Health Literacy as a Strategy to Facilitate Early Intervention for Mental Disorders' (2007) 187(7) *Medical Journal of Australia* S26; The Desk, University of Queensland, 2014, https://www.thedesk.org.au/about.

12 See, especially, Colin G James, 'Lawyer Dissatisfaction, Emotional Intelligence and Clinical Legal Education' (2008) 18 *Legal Education Review* 123.

13 See, e.g., resources for law students and teachers on the Humanizing Law School website, http://www.law.fsu.edu/academic_programs/humanizing_lawschool/humanizing_lawschool.html.

14 See, e.g., Molly Townes O'Brien, Chapter 12 this collection; Rachael Field, James Duffy and Anna Huggins, *Positive Professional Identities and Lawyering* (LexisNexis, 2014). See also Lawrence S Krieger and Kennon M Sheldon, 'What Makes Lawyers Happy? Transcending the Anecdotes with Data from 6200 Lawyers' (2014) FSU College of Law, Public Law Research Paper No 667, http://papers.ssrn.com/sol3/papers.cfm?abstract_id=2398989.

15 See, e.g., Anna Huggins, Sally Kift and Rachael Field, 'Implementing the Self-Management Threshold Learning Outcome for Law: Some Intentional Design Strategies from the Current Curriculum Toolbox' (2011) 21(2) *Legal Education Review* 183.

16 See Agis D Tsouros et al (eds), *Health Promoting Universities: Concept, Experience and Framework for Action* (World Health Organization, 1998); the Healthy Universities website: http://www.healthyuniversities.ac.uk/; Mark Dooris et al, *Healthy Universities: Concept, Model and Framework for Applying the Healthy Settings Approach Within Higher Education in England: Final Project Report* (Healthy Universities, March 2010).

17 See Australian Government Department of Health, *KidsMatter: Growing Healthy Minds*, http://www.kidsmatter.edu.au/; Australian Government Department of Health, MindMatters, http://www.mindmatters.edu.au/; also Johanna Wyn et al, 'MindMatters: A Whole-School Approach Promoting Mental Health and Wellbeing' (2000) 34 *Australian and New Zealand Journal of Psychiatry* 594.
18 The Ottawa Charter for Health Promotion, First International Conference on Health Promotion, Ottawa, 21 November 1986, http://www.who.int/healthpromotion/conferences/previous/ottawa/en/index2.html.
19 See Mark Dooris and Sharon Doherty, 'Healthy Universities: Current Activity and Future Directions – Findings and Reflections from a National-Level Qualitative Research Study' (2010) 17(3) *Global Health Promotion* 6, 7.
20 'Health Promotion Actions Means', Ottawa Charter 1986, http://www.who.int/healthpromotion/conferences/previous/ottawa/en/index1.html.
21 Dooris and Doherty, above n19.
22 Healthy Universities website, above n16.
23 Tsouros et al, above n16, 129.
24 University of the Sunshine Coast, Healthy University Initiative, http://www.usc.edu.au/study/support-and-services/health-and-wellbeing/healthy-university-initiative.
25 Dooris and Doherty, above n19, 8.
26 See above n17.
27 Larcombe and Fethers, above n4; Sheldon and Krieger, 'Negative Effects of Legal Education', above n10.
28 The Australian Wellness Network for Law, initiated by Australian Learning and Teaching Council (ALTC) fellow Rachael Field, is an important facilitator of such collaboration in Australia: http://wellnessforlaw.com/.
29 Of course, mental health is a subset of overall health, and it may become artificial in time to maintain a specific focus on mental health promotion. In the short term, however, a specific strategy to promote mental wellbeing is an important means of responding to the empirical data on law student psychological distress.
30 Council of Australian Law Deans (CALD), *Promoting Law Student Well-Being: Good Practice Guidelines for Law Schools* (March 2013), http://www.cald.asn.au/resources.
31 Tristan Jepson Memorial Foundation, *TJMF Psychological Wellbeing: Best Practice Guidelines for the Legal Profession*, http://www.tjmf.org.au/raise-the-standard/.
32 An example of such a policy, developed at Melbourne Law School, can be obtained from the author on request.
33 See, especially, Anna Huggins, 'Autonomy Supportive Curriculum Design: A Salient Factor in Promoting Law Students' Wellbeing' (2012) 35(3) *University of New South Wales Law Journal* 683; Huggins, Kift and Field, above n15.
34 See, especially, Duffy, Chapter 11 this collection.
35 http://wellnessforlaw.com/.
36 See, especially, chapters in this collection by Judith Marychurch, Colin James, Molly Townes O'Brien, Penelope Watson, Prue Vines and Patricia Morgan, and Helen Stallman and James Duffy.
37 *The Hidden Sources of Law School Stress* and *A Deeper Understanding of Your Career Choices* can be ordered through http://www.law.fsu.edu/academic_programs/humanizing_lawschool/booklet2.html. See also Kate van Hooft, 'Mindfulness Resources for Law Students', Melbourne Law School, http://www.law.unimelb.edu.au/lasc/support-for-wellbeing/mindfulness-resources.
38 See, especially, Judy Bourke and Maxine Evers, Chapter 7 this collection.
39 See, especially, Rachael Field, Chapter 14 this collection; Field, Duffy and Huggins, above n14.
40 See also The JED Foundation and EDC Inc, *A Guide to Campus Mental Health Action Planning* (2011), www.jedfoundation.org/CampusMHAP_Web_final.pdf.

41 Tsouros et al, above n16, 130.
42 http://en.wikipedia.org/wiki/SWOT_analysis.
43 See, e.g., Kath Hall, 'Do We Really Want to Know? Recognising the Importance of Student Psychological Wellbeing in Australian Law Schools' (2009) 9(1) *QUT Law and Justice Journal* 1.
44 Above n30.

3 The Persistence of Distress

Paula Baron[*]

Abstract

The high levels of distress, mental illness and addiction amongst law students and the practising profession are now well documented. Since the results of US studies were largely replicated in Australia by the BMRI report, there has been a significant amount of literature that has sought to find ways of reducing law student distress. This literature proposes a range of solutions, from curriculum innovation through to pastoral care initiatives, to the application of self-determination theory and positive psychology. Much of this literature is immensely valuable for proposing long-overdue changes to law school culture and pedagogical practices.

At the same time, the reasons for the high levels of distress remain largely speculative and, despite changes in law schools and in the profession aimed at addressing distress, the problem persists. This chapter seeks to contribute to the discussions on law student well-being by providing some insights from Lacanian psychoanalytic theory as to the potential causes of the distress of law students and lawyers, and the remarkably resilient and persistent character of this distress.

> I have . . . been undissuaded by the common observation that law student distress results from the current lack of employment prospects for new graduates, or from the grading system at the college, or from other designated stressors in the current educational and professional environments. After all, my classmates and I were saying the same things in 1971, in a time of completely different hiring opportunities, at a school with a different grading system. Research indicates that even during the 1980's, the purported 'Golden Age' of hiring for new law graduates, law student and lawyer distress was inordinately high. Furthermore, there is the persistence of distress among lawyers, who are no longer competing for grades or for their first job. It seems irresponsible for us, perhaps the most powerful and intelligent group in society, to be looking 'elsewhere' for the causes of our personal and professional distress.
>
> Larry Krieger (refs omitted)[1]

Introduction

Mental distress, in the forms of anxiety and depression, are widespread in advanced western nations; and there is a considerable body of literature that analyses incidence, cause, consequences and treatment. Even in the context of the ubiquitous nature of this distress among the general population, law students and the legal profession stand out for the remarkably high incidence of such distress. This phenomenon has been documented and well known for at least the last 25 years in the US,[2] and more recent studies in Australia reveal similar findings.[3]

These studies have led to a wealth of literature and practical solutions aimed at addressing the problem. These initiatives are valuable, particularly for the changes they have introduced or proposed to law school culture and pedagogy. At the same time, the cause(s) of distress remain largely speculative and, despite changes in law schools and in the profession aimed at addressing distress, the problem persists. Hence, Krieger's observations in the opening quotation which highlight the ubiquity of this phenomenon: why should the high levels of distress persist across different jurisdictions, different economic circumstances, different law schools and across a highly diversified profession?

This chapter seeks to understand the persistence of distress, utilizing insights from Lacanian psychoanalysis. This is significant for two reasons: firstly, there is relatively little literature which addresses the issue of lawyer distress from a psychoanalytic perspective,[4] although there is a body of literature from a psychoanalytic perspective more generally on anxiety, depression and burn-out among professionals.[5] Secondly, although there is a wealth of literature on lawyer and law student distress, there is relatively little literature that seeks to understand the *persistence* of this phenomenon. The Lacanian analysis provides a number of intriguing insights that, in most cases, supplement and reinforce, rather than replace or contradict, our existing knowledge of lawyer distress. The most significant point of difference, however, is that in the Lacanian schema depression is not characterized as an illness – as is the case, explicitly or implicitly, in much of the existing literature.

This chapter begins by briefly outlining the phenomenon of lawyer distress. It then provides a basic outline of Lacanian theory, before applying a Lacanian analysis to the phenomenon of lawyer distress.

The Phenomenon of Law Student and Lawyer Distress

Research conducted over the last 25 years in the US showed high distress levels amongst American law students. When compared to other student cohorts, law students are more likely to suffer from stress, anxiety and depression.[6] Further studies have suggested that this distress does not decrease significantly as the law degree progresses, or even into the first few years of legal practice.[7] Distress often persists into legal practice.[8] Lawyers suffer higher levels of unhappiness in their careers than other trades and professions[9] and have a greater tendency to develop depression.[10] Such high rates of distress have serious consequences. Studies have found high rates of substance abuse among lawyers.[11] Suicide ranks among the leading causes of premature death among lawyers; and male lawyers, in particular, have a much higher tendency than the general population to commit suicide.[12] One study found that lawyers are at a much greater risk because they are more likely to act on their suicidal thoughts and more likely to succeed.[13]

Although studies of the issue of mental distress in law students were known in Australia, it was not clear whether similar problems existed there. In particular, there are significant differences in legal education between the US and Australia, making it questionable as to whether Australian law students faced the same problems.[14] However, a report published in 2009 by the Brain and Mind Research Institute, *Courting the Blues* (hereafter the BMRI Report),[15] found that some 41 per cent of law students report symptoms of psychological distress severe enough to indicate clinical assessment. The BMRI Report also revealed high levels of psychological distress and substance abuse among the legal profession itself.

The BMRI measure was a self-report of particular symptoms; and there is a possibility that participating law students and lawyers might have overestimated their symptoms. However, research in Australian universities appears to confirm the problem amongst law students.[16] Other studies have confirmed the problem within the profession. For instance, the Legal Services Commissioner for Queensland has estimated that emotional distress features in 30 per cent of the disciplinary matters dealt with by the Commission.[17] A 2011 study by Beaton Consulting,[18] which engaged with over 25 professional associations, 100 professional service firms and a pro bono partner, found that lawyers were the most likely professional group to have experienced symptoms of depression (49 per cent), but were not the most likely to be diagnosed with depression. Lawyers were also the most likely of the professions studied to have suffered symptoms of anxiety. At the same time, lawyers were significantly more likely to think their organization would react negatively to someone experiencing depression or an anxiety disorder within the workplace.

The Elusive Nature of Cause

The general literature on depression and psychological distress identifies a wide range of factors that are potentially causative. Life events are known to both contribute to depression and predispose individuals to depression.[19] In particular, the emotional meaning of the event for that individual and their personal, prior vulnerabilities are significant factors. Experiences of loss, humiliation and entrapment are associated with greater risk of depression.[20]

The general literature also identifies two main types of depression: a category of depression arising from feelings of loss; and a category of depression associated with feelings of failure.[21] Some theorists argue that the quality of interpersonal relations in childhood, adolescence and adulthood contribute to the formation of these two types of depression.[22] It has been found that depressed and non-depressed individuals alike have relatively extensive beliefs about the causes of depression comparable to those held by clinical psychologists. However, depressed individuals tend to favour biological explanations of the causes of depression to a greater extent than clinical psychologists, who place more emphasis upon unconscious processes and childhood vulnerability factors.[23]

Why the incidence of distress in *lawyers* should be so high, however, is unclear. The BMRI Report observed that the precise cause of the phenomenon remain unknown.[24] A number of potential causes have been identified, however. In relation to the high incidence of distress amongst law students, US researchers have argued that the law school is a significant causative factor in this distress[25] – and this would seem consistent with the findings that distress begins in the first year of law school.[26] However, the BMRI notes that present understandings cannot identify whether it is the law school that generates distress or whether law students possess certain attributes that predispose them to problems during law school. If law school is a causative or contributing factor to student psychological distress, a number of characteristics of legal education may be responsible. The BMRI, again consistent with the US literature, points to the competitive and adversarial nature of legal education and legal culture. Low levels of engagement have been identified as potentially problematic,[27] as have lack of autonomy[28] and lack of intrinsic motivation.[29] Heavy workload; the need to be in 'survival mode'; incivility in classroom instruction; peer pressure to compete and an inability to handle mediocrity; uncertainty about progress and feelings of inadequacy; lack of feedback; the fact that many students study law for the 'wrong reasons'; unrealistic salary goals; and debt, unemployment, indecision as to careers; and delaying the move from school to work have also been implicated.[30] In relation to the legal profession and law students, potentially causative factors relating to inherent personality factors have been identified, such as tendencies toward perfectionism, competitiveness[31] and pessimism.[32] In relation to the legal profession, factors such as cultivation of a professional demeanour that suppresses 'alarm, fear, disgust, abhorrence and boredom'[33] have been implicated. Some commentators point to lawyer ego as the cause of the problem;[34] and, of course, stress is considered a causative factor.[35] Despite distress, it seems that many lawyers are adept at concealing the problem. Thus, for instance, many high-functioning alcoholic lawyers 'are often able to maintain employment, project an acceptable outward image in spite of the inner turmoil, sustain interpersonal relationships, and "work the system" in dealing with legal problems resulting from the addiction'.[36]

Perhaps the most curious aspect of this issue is that the high incidence of distress amongst law students and lawyers appears to be remarkably persistent. The phenomenon of distress seems consistent across very different law schools and student cohorts and teaching methods,[37] both in the US and Australia. It also appears consistent across very different external environments, as Krieger points out; and persists beyond law school into professional practice, despite the increasing diversification of the membership of the legal profession, and changes in practice. The persistence of distress suggests an underlying, systemic problem. I turn now to psychoanalytic theory to provide some insights into what this problem might be.

A Psychoanalytic Perspective on the Persistence of Distress

Some Introductory Remarks

By way of introduction to the application of psychoanalysis to the issue of lawyer distress, some introductory comments are warranted. Firstly, psychoanalysis is not a unitary theory. There are many psychoanalytic theories, and it has been said that it is difficult to find any analyst conversant with more than one approach. This is in part because '[t]he literature of each school is extensive and each clinical sensibility finely honed, presenting a challenging prospect to any single analyst attempting to digest it all'.[38] The approach taken in the remainder of this chapter is specifically based upon the work of Jacques Lacan.

A second observation is that the tenets of psychoanalysis are very different from those of psychology, which is usually relied upon in discussions of law student and lawyer distress. Some of these differences are worth noting. Firstly, the notion of 'normality' is challenged by psychoanalysis. 'Normality' in psychoanalysis (particularly Lacanian analysis) has been described as 'a convenient fiction', the relationship between abnormal and normal being more complex and more problematic.[39] In this way, psychoanalysis tends to humanize mental illness, and serves to counter 'culturally endorsed projective systems that seek to view those suffering from distress as fundamentally "other", "not like us" '.[40] Secondly, Lacanian psychoanalysis does not emphasize happiness as a therapeutic goal; nor does it expect the individual to think positively – and it does not view the individual as an object, a number or item.[41] An emphasis upon subjectivity is essential to psychoanalysis.[42] Largely as a consequence of this emphasis upon subjectivity, psychoanalysis sets itself in opposition to the medicalized view of depression. For orthodox medicine, the symptom is a sign of disease, its cause organic and foreign to the subject. For psychoanalysis, the symptom is a sign of subjectivity itself, and indicates a psychic conflict within the subject. For Lacan, the symptom is subordinated to the laws of language. It is a metaphor: that is, a signifier that stands in for another signifier which has been repressed.[43]

Accordingly, unlike the views of much contemporary psychology and psychiatry, from the psychoanalytic perspective an individual is not merely a passive recipient of their illness, but somehow actively involved in their disorder.[44] Psychoanalysis thus takes its lead from philosophy to view depression as a manifestation of being.[45] As we will see, anxiety and depression in the Lacanian schema are neither illnesses nor, indeed, symptoms. In order to better understand this, it is necessary to outline some fundamental concepts of Lacanian theory.

Lacan 101

Lacanian theory is extremely rich and complex, so it is only possible to sketch some core concepts relevant to this discussion:

- the three registers of experience;
- the notion of desire and its relationship to lack;

- the distinction between desire and *jouissance*;
- the distinction between the other and the Other; and
- the distinction between normal functioning and depression.

Lacan maintained that reality is made up by three registers of experience: the Real, the Imaginary and the Symbolic. These three registers are also developmental, in the sense that the 'normal' (the neurotic, in Lacanian terms) individual passes through them. Thus the child is born into the Real, a state characterized by need. At around 18 months, the child enters the 'mirror stage', the point at which she recognizes herself in the mirror and so is ushered into the Imaginary, a register characterized by demand – specifically, the demand to be loved. At a later point, the child moves into the symbolic order – the realm of language, law and culture – by passing through the Oedipal process. This register is characterized by desire, a longing for that which will make us complete.

At the core of Lacanian theory are the notions of desire and the divided self, a fundamental splitting and alienation in the psyche:

> We are alienated insofar as we are spoken by a language that functions in certain respects, like a machine . . . with a life of its own; insofar as our needs and pleasures are organized and channelled into socially acceptable forms by our parents' demands . . . and insofar as our desire comes into being as the Other's desire.[46]

The mirror stage gives us the allure of unity, but it alienates us from our mirror image, so there is, in reality, no unified subject. There is only an illusion of unity taken from the image in the mirror, or the image of others: 'The subject is no one. It is decomposed, in pieces. And it is jammed, sucked in by the image, the deceiving and realized image, of the other, or equally by its own specular image. That is where it finds its unity.'[47]

The distinction between the Imaginary and the Symbolic orders gives rise to a distinction in Lacanian theory between the other and the Other. The other exists primarily in the Imaginary register. The 'other' is our rival: not only our peers, but also our alienated counterpart in the mirror. The Other (with a capital 'O'), might be 'another person in their essentially enigmatic dimension; or it might be the assumed virtues, morals and ideals of our culture and upbringing'.[48] The Other exists primarily in the Symbolic dimension. For the law student, their own mirror image and other law students might constitute the small 'o' other and subject to feelings of rivalry and competition, while Law itself, parental expectations, the law school and language are instances of the large 'O' Other.

Lacan also makes an important distinction between desire and *jouissance*. Desire is not only sexual desire, but also 'what we broadly conceive as our ability to chart out a life that is our own'.[49] But the notion of our 'own' desire is complex. Desire is always intersubjective, and always exists within the parameters of social law: 'to desire is to answer the question 'What does the Other desire?' 'When we call our desires our own what we really mean is only that we have succeeded in seeking out the gaps in the desire of the Other, and carving out a space for ourselves there'.[50] Because the Other's desire is always enigmatic and unknowable, it can never be satisfied.[51]

Jouissance, on the other hand, is often translated as 'enjoyment' in English, but it is a particular kind of enjoyment. It is the pleasure in the unpleasurable; the satisfaction in dissatisfaction. It is a pleasure that is excessive, resulting in feelings of disgust or overwhelm.[52] It exceeds the limits of social rule and restraint, going beyond pleasure – even, in some cases beyond self-preservation.[53] Excesses of alcohol, drugs, sex are all examples of *jouissance*.

So-called 'normal' functioning, then, operates in this way in the Lacanian schema: the individual pursues desire. This is always the desire of the Other, and is enigmatic and unknowable. As a desiring subject, the individual accepts that she lacks; and this acceptance causes her to pursue desire creatively within social bounds, and so leads to individuation. In some cases, however, desire goes astray and, as we will see, anxiety is a warning sign of this. Desire goes astray when the individual is subject to the relentless demand of the other. This leads to anxiety and an attempt to cover up or fill the lack. This leads to an accumulation of *jouissance* and a loss of desire, as the individual stops being a desiring subject and becomes the object of demand.

Desire Gone Astray

From a Lacanian perspective, then, distress – in the form of anxiety and depression – is a sign that desire is going, or has gone, astray, because of the relentless demand of the Other. Gueguen observes that depressive phenomena generally are linked to the promotion of ideals (norms of health, beauty, social status, image, social integration, success in every part of sexual and intellectual life).[54] At an individual level, depression is more severe where the individual's ideals are high and she cannot find substitute satisfaction.[55]

Distress is thus driven by external and by internal pressures. Externally, the individual suffers from the weight of demand: she is a 'mere puppet at the mercy of an omnipresent Other'.[56] Depression is a defence against being crushed under the weight of this Other.[57] But demand, particularly parental demand, is also internalized, so that the individual is driven by the superego. The superego is an internal voice that comments on the difference between how one is (ego) and how one could have been (ideal ego). It turns the idea of how one could have been into an imperative of how one *should* have been and accentuates the subject's failures. The superego is 'senseless', 'blind', 'tyrannical';[58] is 'the law and its destruction'.[59] Unlike Freud's notion of the superego as an agent of prohibition, however, Lacan's superego is a command or imperative to enjoy. Enjoyment at once fuels the superego – and promotes guilt.[60] At the command of the ferocious superego, the subject looks for and finds a stop-gap in order to defend herself against lack; that is, she renounces the path of desire in exchange for the accumulation of *jouissance*.[61] But renouncing the path of desire generates guilt.

This, then, would provide a psychoanalytic explanation for the persistence of distress: law students and lawyers are particularly subject to the demand of the Other. Distress is thus likely to result, regardless of jurisdiction, law school, teaching methods and so on. For those of us who teach in law schools, this explanation is likely to accord with experience. Those of our students who are school-leavers are generally high-achieving – indeed, often overachieving – students, driven to succeed. They tend to be 'good' children who become 'good' university students and go on to be 'respected' members of the profession. Quite a number undertake law studies on the advice – or explicit demand – of their parents, who tend to have high expectations of their children. Universities exhort law students to excel; and, in turn, the profession makes explicit its own high expectations of conduct and achievement. Lawyers are thus particularly subject to the demand of the Other, in terms of ideals and expectations. Of course, other professions can be subject to the demand of the Other, but it is likely that, for lawyers, duties abound and substitute satisfaction is difficult to find.

Importantly, from a psychoanalytic viewpoint, depression is not an illness. Much of the literature, and the rhetoric around the issues of lawyer distress, characterizes depression as an illness or a biochemical imbalance. In the Lacanian schema, however, depression is the sign of inner conflict:

> depression is to be considered not as an illness, but as the result of a debate between the subject and his own duties (the supposed ones, the imposed ones, the unconscious ones and the conscious possibilities he has at hand in order to respond to them).[62]

Lacan, controversially, described depression as a moral issue: it is the failure to be 'well-spoken'.[63] For Lacan, to be 'well-spoken' is for the individual 'to know, to decipher, to express himself in his own words and find an ethics based on the desire to exist'.[64]

Nor is depression a symptom. A depressed state is an indication of the position of the subject in relation to his *jouissance*.[65] Unique to each subject, *jouissance* is both outside meaning and inside the subject. But once this experience has occurred, it tends to repeat.[66] In the depressive state, the subject is said to be 'petrified' by their *jouissance*, having no desire, no movement, no will; and characterized by self-devaluation, self-accusation and the masochism of the death drive.[67] The depressed individual:

> tends to recoil from desire to seek refuge in the silence of the death drive, in the stillness of apathy, to the bed of inertia, all of which denote the object's position[68] with characteristics of waste and emptiness.[69]

In this schema, anxiety occupies a particular place. Anxiety and depression are distinct but related phenomena. Like depression, anxiety is a sign, not a symptom. Unique to the Lacanian schema, anxiety is not generated by lack but 'lack of lack'. Many psychoanalytic theories relate anxiety to loss or separation. Lacan, however, rejects this notion:

> What is most anxiety provoking for the child is precisely when the relation on which he founds himself, from the lack that produces desire, is disturbed, and

> it is most disturbed when there is no possibility of lack, when the mother is on his back all the time, specially to wipe his bottom, as a model of the demand, of the demand that could never falter.[70]

Anxiety is not the response to lack but to the *lack* of lack. Thus, the primary source of all anxiety is that of being invaded by the 'demand of the Other': '[t]he anxiety in face of the demand of the Other is the anxiety of being captivated by the mirror image that the Other holds up to the subject through his *presence* alone' (in other words, ideals).[71]

Importantly, anxiety functions as a warning of a fading subjectivity,[72] the threat of confusion between *jouissance* and desire that threatens the complete loss of desire.[73] In the Lacanian schema, anxiety thus occupies the gap between desire and *jouissance*.[74] Anxiety is generated by the overwhelming presence of objects (which, in Lacanian theory, must first be lost and thus lacking in order for a subject to be generated). Without lack and without desire, all that is experienced is relentless demand from the Other:[75] '[t]he anxiety in face of the demand of the Other is the anxiety of being captivated by the mirror image that the Other holds up to the subject through his presence alone'.[76]

In Quinet's view, as signs, rather than symptoms, neither depression nor anxiety 'deceives'. Rather, they reveal 'the subject's position as an object, cast aside by the representation of the signifier, displaced from its chain of desire'.[77]

For the law student, then, anxiety is a warning sign that law schools need to take seriously. It may augur the descent into depression, as the student becomes overwhelmed by demand and, in consequence, loses their own desire.

Tentative Conclusions

The psychoanalytic explanation for the persistence of distress, then, is that lawyers (both lawyers-in-training and lawyers-in-practice) tend to be 'weighed down' by the demands of others, trying to live up to ideals that are initially externally, and later internally, imposed – and, in doing so, lose their own desire. This tendency would exist across jurisdictions, different law schools and regardless of different teaching methodologies. On this view, psychoanalysis appears to be supportive of the propositions in the literature that perfectionism and competition amongst law students and lawyers contribute to the development of distress. The psychoanalytic perspective is also supportive of the importance of intrinsic motivation as preventative of distress, at least so far as intrinsic motivation corresponds to the individual's desire rather than the weight of the Other's demand.[78]

For those of us in law schools who are concerned about law student distress, the Lacanian viewpoint carries certain implications. The first is that law schools (and later the profession) tend to reinforce, rather than challenge, internalized (parental and cultural) ideals. This may be particularly problematic in the current climate where law is increasingly perceived as vocational and commercial (rather than professional), employment opportunities are highly competitive and the messages given to students, explicitly and implicitly, urge them to excel. Law schools can counter such messages by helping students explore the range of options available to them through their law degrees by offering clinical experiences and by helping students find and pursue their *own* desire, whether that be in legal practice, in addition to legal practice or outside legal practice. The second is that law schools should be cognizant of the imposition of their own demands upon law students and, in particular, be aware that student anxiety should always be taken seriously: it is a warning that, potentially, the individual is being overwhelmed by demand and may be on a path to depression.

Notes

* Paula Baron, La Trobe Law; p.baron@latrobe.edu.au.

1 Lawrence S Krieger, 'What We're Not Telling Law Students – and Lawyers – That They Really Need to Know: Some Thoughts-in-Action toward Revitalizing the Profession from Its Roots' (1998) 13(1) *Journal of Law and Health* 1, 6–7.

2 See, for instance, Stephen B Shanfield, G Andrew and H Benjamin, 'Psychiatric Distress in Law Students' (1985) 35 *Journal of Legal Education* 65; G Andrew et al, 'The Role of Legal Education in Producing Psychological Distress among Law Students and Lawyers' (1986) 11(2) *Law and Social Inquiry* 225.

3 Norm Kelk et al, *Courting the Blues: Attitude towards Depression in Australian Law Students and Lawyers* (Brain and Mind Research Institute, 2009).

4 One notable exception is the first chapter of Peter Goodrich's book *Oedipus Lex* (University of California Press, 1995), in which Goodrich takes a Freudian perspective on lawyer depression.

5 See, for instance, Antonio Quinet, 'Depression and Melancholy' (2002) 11 *Analysis* 1; James S Grotstein, 'Nothingness, Meaninglessness, Chaos and the Black Hole in Psychoanalysis' (1990) 26(2) *Contemporary Psychoanalysis* 257; Pierre-Gilles Gueguen, 'The Ethics of Depression' (1995) 6 *Analysis* 99; Stijn Vanheule and Paul Verhaeghe, 'Professional Burnout in the Mirror' (2005) 22(2) *Psychoanalytic Psychology* 285; Stijn Vanheule and Paul Verhaeghe, 'Identity through a Psychoanalytic Looking Glass' (2009) 19 *Theory and Psychology* 291.

6 Jennifer Jolly-Ryan, 'Promoting Mental Health in Law School: What Law Schools Can Do for Law Students to Help Them Become Happy, Mentally Healthy Lawyers' (2009–2010) 48 *U Louisville L Rev* 95, 97.

7 Rachael Field and James Duffy, 'Better to Light a Single Candle than to Curse the Darkness: Promoting Law Student Well-Being through a First Year Law Subject' (2012) *Qld U Tech L & JJ* 133, 140.

8 Jolly-Ryan, above n6, 100.

9 Nancy Levit and Douglas O Linder, 'Happy Law Students, Happy Lawyers' (2008) 58 *Syracuse Law Review* 351, 351–2, citing Tom W Smith, *Job Satisfaction in the United States* (2007).

10 Yvette Hourigan, 'Chasing' (2011) *Bench and Bar* 16.

11 Jolly-Ryan, above n6, 101.

12 Hourigan, above n10, 17.

13 Ibid.

14 Judy Allen and Paula Baron, 'Buttercup Goes to Law School' (2004) 29(6) *Alternative Law Journal* 285.

15 Kelk et al above n3.

16 See, for example, work done at UNSW: Massimilano Tani and Prue Vines, 'Law Students' Attitudes to Education: Pointers to Depression in the Legal Academy and the Profession?' (2009)19(1) *L Ed Rev* 3; University of Melbourne: Wendy Larcombe et al, 'Does an improved Experience of Law School Protect Students against Depression, Anxiety and Stress? An Empirical Study of Wellbeing and the Law School Experience of

LLB and JD students' (2013) 35(2) *Syd L Rev* 407; and at ANU: Molly Townes O'Brien, Stephen Tang and Kath Hall, 'Changing our Thinking: Empirical Research on Law Student Wellbeing, Thinking Styles and the Law Curriculum' (2011) 21 *L Ed Rev* 149, 149.

17 John Briton, 'Lawyers, Emotional Distress and Regulation' (2009) 1, paper presented at the Bar Association Queensland Conference, March 2009, available at http://www.lsc.qld.gov.au/__data/assets/pdf_file/0006/106197/lawyers-emotional-distress-and-regulation.pdf.

18 Beaton Consulting and Beyond Blue, 'Mental Health in the Workplace' (2011), available at http://www.beatonglobal.com/pdfs/Anxiety_and_depression_in_the_workplace.pdf.

19 Daniel McQueen, 'Depression in Adults: Some Basic Facts' (2009) 23(2) *Psychoanalytic Psychotherapy* 225, 232, citing a study by Brown and Harris, 1978.

20 McQueen, above n19, 232, citing studies by Brown et al, 1995; Kendler et al, 2003.

21 McQueen, above n19, 229, citing studies by Blatt, 1998; Keller and Nesse, 2005, 2006.

22 Sidney J Blatt and Celine Maroudas, 'Convergences among Psychoanalytic and Cognitive-Behavioural Theories of Depression' (1992) 9(2) *Psychoanalytic Psychology* 157, 184, citing Bowlby (1980, 1988a, 1988b); Arieti and Bemporad (1978, 1980); Beck (1983).

23 Willem Kuyken et al, 'Causal Beliefs about Depression in Depressed Patients, Clinical Psychologists and Lay Persons' (1992) 65(3) *British Journal of Medical Psychology* 257.

24 Kelk et al, above n3, 43.

25 See, for instance, Andrew et al, above n2; Lawrence S Krieger, 'Institutional Denial about the Dark Side of Law School, and Fresh Empirical Guidance for Constructively Breaking the Silence' (2002) 52 *J Legal Ed* 112.

26 See, for instance, G Andrew H Benjamin, Elaine J Darling and Bruce Sales, 'The Prevalence of Depression, Alcohol Abuse and Cocaine Abuse among United States Lawyers (1990) 13 *International Journal of Law and Psychiatry* 233, 234; Krieger, above n25; KM Sheldon and LS Krieger, 'Understanding the negative Effects of Legal Education on Law Students: A Longitudinal Test of Self-Determination Theory' (2007) 33(6) *Personality and Social Psychology* 883.

27 Rachael Field and Sally Kift, 'Addressing the High Levels of Psychological Distress in Law Students through Intentional Assessment and Feedback Design in the First Year Law Curriculum' (2010) 1(1) *International Journal of the First Year in Higher Education* 65.

28 Sheldon and Krieger, above n26, 883.

29 Krieger, above n25; Tani and Vines, above n16, 3.

30 Jolly-Ryan, above n6, 104–13.

31 Susan Daicoff, 'Lawyer, Know Thyself: A Review of Empirical Research on Attorney Attributes Bearing on Professionalism' (1997) 46 *American University Law Review* 1337, 1418.

32 Martin EP Seligman, Paul R Verkuil and Terry H Kang, 'Why Lawyers are Unhappy' (2001) 23 *Cardozo Law Review* 33.

33 Hourigan, above n10, 16; Sofia Yokren, 'Lawyer as Emotional Laborer' (2008–09) *U Mich JL Reform* 141. Emotion management at work has been shown to have negative effects when it increases the individual's estrangement from their feelings and authenticity: Melissa M Sloan, 'Emotion Management and Workplace Status: Consequences for Well-Being' (2008) 2(3) *Int J Work Organisation and Emotion* 236.

34 Hourigan, above n10, 16; Leonard L Riskin, 'The Contemplative Lawyer: On the Potential Contributions of Mindfulness Meditation to Law Students, Lawyers and their Clients' (2002) 7(1) *Harvard Negotiation Law Review* 1, 8.

35 Hourigan, above n10, 17; Susan Saab Fortney, 'Soul for Sale: An Empirical Study of Associate Satisfaction, Law Firm Culture, and the Effects of Billable Hour Requirements' 69 *UMKC L Rev* 239, 271–3.

36 Hourigan, above n10, 19.
37 Christine Pedigo Bartholomew and Johanna Oreskovic, 'Normalizing Trepidation and Anxiety' (2010) 48 *Duquesne Law Review* 349, 359.
38 Bruce Fink, 'What's So Different about Lacan's Psychoanalysis?' (2011) 98(6) *Psychoanalytic Review*, 843, 844, quoting Mitchell and Black.
39 David Bell, 'Psychiatry and Psychoanalysis: A Conceptual Mapping' in Alessandra Lemma and Matthew Patrick (eds), *Off the Couch: Contemporary Psychoanalytic Applications* (Taylor & Francis, 2010) 176.
40 Ibid.
41 Rene Rasmussen, 'Who Is Afraid of DSM? The Place of the Subject in the Society of Therapy' in Lene Auestad (ed), *Psychoanalysis and Politics: Exclusion and the Politics of Representation* (Karnac, 2012) 139, 148.
42 Jason Glynos and Yanni Stavrakakis, 'Lacan and Political Subjectivity: Fantasy and Enjoyment in Psychoanalysis and Political Theory' (2008) *Subjectivity* 256, 256.
43 Quinet, above n5, 6.
44 Bell, above n39.
45 Quinet, above n5, 7.
46 Bruce Fink, *The Lacanian Subject: Between Language and Jouissance* (Princeton University Press, 1995) xi.
47 Jacques Lacan, *The Seminar of Jacques Lacan: Book II: The Ego in Freud's Theory and in the Technique of Psychoanalysis, 1954–1955*, Jacques-Alain Miller, ed, Sylvana Tomaselli trans (Norton, 1991) 54.
48 Owen Hewitson, 'What Does Lacan Say about. . . . Desire?, quoting Lacan, *Ecrits*. Available at http://www.lacanonline.com/index/2010/05/what-does-lacan-say-about-desire/comment-page-1/ [last accessed 18 October 2015].
49 Drucilla Cornell, 'Autonomy Re-Imagined' (2003) 8(1) *Journal for the Psychoanalysis of Culture and Society*, 144.
50 Hewitson, above n48.
51 Fink, above n46, xiii.
52 Ibid, xii.
53 Jean Wyatt, 'Jouissance and Desire in Michael Hanake's *The Piano Teacher*' (2005) 62(4) *American Imago* 453, 453.
54 Gueguen, above n5, 101.
55 Ibid, 102.
56 Pierre Skriabine, trans. Jack W Stone, 'Some Moral Failings Called Depression', available at http://www.lacan.com/depression.htm.
57 Ibid.
58 Jacques Lacan, *The Seminar. Book I: Freud's Papers on Technique, 1953–54*, John Forrester, trans (Cambridge University Press, 1988) 102.
59 Ibid.
60 See further, Slavoj Zizek, 'Ego Ideal and Superego: Lacan as Viewer of *Casablanca*', available at http://www.lacan.com/zizraphael.htm.
61 Skriabine, above n56.
62 Gueguen, above n5, 102.
63 Jacques Lacan, *Television: A Challenge to the Psychoanalytic Establishment* (Norton, 1990) 22.
64 Quinet, above n5, 11.
65 Ibid, 6.
66 Megan Williams, 'Anxiety in the Gap' (2000) *Analysis* 158, 160.
67 Quinet, above n5, 9.
68 As opposed to a subject's position – that is, the individual becomes an object, rather than a subject.
69 Quinet, above n5, 10.

70 G Diatkine, 'Lacan' (2007) 88 *International Journal of Psychoanalysis* 643, 649 quoting Lacan, Seminar X: Anxiety, 2004, 67.
71 Ibid.
72 Williams, above n66, 158; Roberto Harari, *Lacan's Seminar on Anxiety: An Introduction* (Other Press, 2001) 36.
73 Harari, above n72, 36.
74 Williams, above n66.
75 Ibid, 158.
76 Diatkine, above n70, 649.
77 Quinet, above n5, 8.
78 The movement from intrinsic to extrinsic motivation in law students is discussed by Kennon M Sheldon and Lawrence S Krieger, 'Does Legal Education Have Undermining Effects on Law Students? Evaluating Changes in Motivation, Values, and Well-Being' (2004) 22 *Behavioral Sciences and the Law* 261. For an excellent discussion of intrinsic and extrinsic motivation and wellbeing, see Edward L Deci and Richard M Ryan, 'Facilitating Optimal Motivation and Psychological Wellbeing across Life's Domains (2008) 49(1) *Canadian Psychology* 14.

4 Law Student Lifestyle Pressures

Alex Steel and Anna Huggins[*]

Introduction

One significant factor influencing student wellbeing is the degree to which their studies are subject to external lifestyle pressures. These pressures are relieved or exacerbated by choices students make around their approaches to study, and the amount of time they devote to work and leisure. This chapter considers results from a 2012 survey of law students at the University of New South Wales (UNSW), Sydney, Australia. Those results are compared to results from a similar US law student survey, and comparable data from the UK and Australia more broadly. In addition, the UNSW study compares key lifestyle choices of undergraduate (LLB) and graduate (JD) law students.

The UNSW survey was based on the Law School Survey of Student Engagement (LSSSE). LSSSE is a national survey of US law schools run annually since 2004.[1] The 2012 UNSW survey was the first time LSSSE had been conducted outside of North America. Slight modifications were made to the wording of some items to ensure consistent meaning.[2] Beyond this, the items were left identical to the US version to enable direct comparisons between the UNSW and US results.

In this chapter we examine student responses to questions regarding the amount of time spent reading and preparing for class and assessments; the amount of paid and volunteer work students do outside of the classroom; the extent to which they have family caring responsibilities; and the time they devote to leisure activities. Importantly, whilst many other studies on law students' wellbeing have focused on students' course-based experiences,[3] recent research has cast doubt on whether improvements in students' course experiences reduce law students' distress levels.[4] This highlights the desirability of better understanding the range of lifestyle patterns and pressures beyond students' course-based experiences that may be impacting their sense of balance and wellbeing during their time at law school.

The survey data allows us to draw comparisons between LLB and JD students at UNSW, and with average US JD students' results.[5] Additionally, for some questions comparable data is available from other Australian surveys and from a 2013 UK survey. These comparisons provide important context for understanding the similarities and differences between trends in Australian law students' wellbeing and those of law students in other education systems. The body of Australian research on law students' elevated distress levels is relatively small and recent,[6] particularly compared to the long-documented and extensive literature on this phenomenon amongst American law students.[7] As evidenced in the discussion in other chapters in this book,[8] American research has thus played a crucial role in informing recent Australian research on these issues. To better appreciate the utility and limits of drawing on findings from other education systems to inform research about Australian law students' experiences, it is important that the contextual variations influencing students' experiences are more fully understood.

The Basis for Comparison

There are a number of similarities between the US and Australian legal education systems, including a predominant focus on 'doctrinal legal theory and analysis'; emphasis on 'thinking like a lawyer;[9] and privileging of academic grades and honours as the chief predictors of subsequent success.[10] However, significant differences between the two education systems have led to criticisms of attempts to transfer broad student engagement surveys from one educational culture to another. In particular, criticisms have been made of the use of the US National Survey of Student Engagement (on which LSSSE is based) as a basis for an Australian and New Zealand university survey – the Australian Survey of Student Engagement.[11] Hagel et al. have pointed out that there are significant differences between Australian universities and US colleges, including that:

- the average size of Australian universities is four times that of US colleges;
- Australian universities are overwhelmingly public rather than private;
- Australian students are much more likely to live at home and commute to university rather than live on campus; and
- Australian students undertake more paid work off campus while studying.[12]

Similar differences exist between US and Australian law schools and students.

Such differences mean that it is likely that many direct comparisons between US and UNSW law students would be quite tenuous if it was claimed that the results were able to objectively measure comparative student engagement, or other aspects of students' experiences. However, the aim of this chapter is not to comparatively examine engagement levels, but rather to compare the external environment within which students study. As such, while the different educational environments would be important to analyse in order to understand how study-related pressures have come about, and in order to effect real change in the student experience, they are not necessary for a comparative stocktake of the pressures themselves. Such a stocktake provides important background to contextualize the issue of law students' wellbeing.

Profile of the UNSW LSSSE Survey Respondent Sample

The UNSW LSSSE survey achieved overall response rates of 31% of all JD students, and 20% of LLB students. The JD respondents represented a similar proportion of students across all three years,[13] whilst for the LLB students, across the five years of enrolment the response rate rose from 16% of 1st year to 33% of final year students (a combination of those in their 5th or 6th year of study).[14] While these response rates are lower than the US average of around 50%,[15] the rates are significant enough to be indicative of student preferences. Some caution is needed in interpreting the responses from the early years of the LLB given the lower response rates, but tentative trends across those years may be deduced.[16]

While enrolment patterns by gender approximate parity in the law school, almost two-thirds of LLB *respondents* were female. There was gender parity in the JD responses. In the LLB there are different numbers of students enrolled in each concurrent degree programme. As some concurrent programmes have small enrolment numbers, the programmes were collapsed into three categories – Arts/Law, Business/Law, and Science and Engineering/Law. On this basis, the response rate exhibited a bias in favour of Arts/Law students (45% of responses compared to 34% of total enrolments), and against Business/Law (48% of responses compared to 57% of total enrolments). Numbers in Science and Engineering were too small to be significant (both in terms of responses and total enrolments).

There was also a potential bias in the respondents' reported average grades. Amongst both the JD and LLB respondents, 50% saw themselves as Distinction students and 40% as Credit students.[17] This is likely to be a higher percentage of better performing students than in the total law student population.[18]

In summary, the response levels appear to be significant enough to be indicative of student attitudes. This is also true for analysis of the students by year cohort – other than the early years of the LLB, and by Arts or Business co-degree. There are potential biases in the LLB responses on the basis of gender, co-degree and on overall grade averages.[19]

Learning Habits

In determining the types and extent of external pressures on UNSW law students, it is necessary to first understand how much time students spend preparing for class.

The data provided by the survey allows for some comparative examination of the time and effort students put into their studies and assessment. The LSSSE questions ask for time spent preparing for class; how often students skip their readings; and how many drafts they complete before handing in assignments.

Level of Preparedness for Class

Law is taught, both at UNSW and in the US, on the basis that students complete assigned readings before coming to class, and thus class discussion can proceed on an assumption that the material has been read and understood. However, the practice of teaching at UNSW may not consistently require that degree of conscientiousness from students. One of the LSSSE questions asked students to nominate how often they failed to complete readings (Figure 4.1).

The responses indicate that UNSW students are more likely not to have completed their readings than their US counterparts. The level of pre-class reading by UNSW students in comparison to students in other Australian law schools is unknown, but one partial comparator is available from Larcombe et al.'s study of Melbourne University Law School students.[20] That study found that, in response to the statement 'I regularly come to class without completing readings or assigned work', 72% of LLB survey respondents either agreed or were neutral, and 46% of JD respondents agreed or were neutral.[21] When compared to the percentages in the LSSSE surveys responding 'often' or 'very often', this suggests that a significantly higher proportion of UNSW students read for class than in a comparable Australian law school.[22]

While reading levels begin quite high, the data indicates that UNSW students are increasingly likely not to conscientiously prepare for class as their degree progresses. The fact that by the final year of the LLB degree 60% of respondents often do not read for class suggests that there is a strong sense that one can pass courses without significant ongoing preparation. This is strikingly different to the much smaller 31% of 3rd year JD students who often do not complete readings.

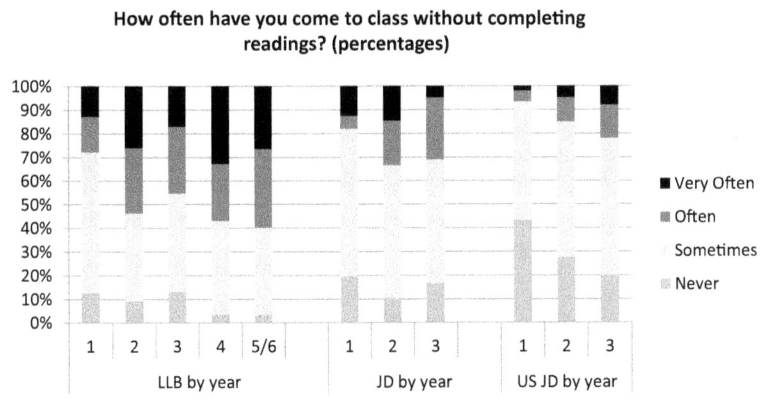

Did not read for class(%)	LLB by year						JD by year				US JD by year		
	1	2	3	4	5/6		1	2	3		1	2	3
Never	12.8	9.3	13.2	3.4	3.4		19.6	10.4	16.7		43.2	27.5	19.9
Sometimes	59.6	37.0	41.5	39.7	36.8		62.5	56.3	52.4		50.3	57.5	58.0
Often	14.9	27.8	28.3	24.1	33.3		5.4	18.8	26.2		4.6	10.2	14.1
Very Often	12.8	25.9	17.0	32.8	26.4		12.5	14.6	4.8		1.9	4.9	7.9

Figure 4.1 How often have you come to class without completing readings? (%)

It could be expected that undergraduate law students would be comparatively more relaxed about their study habits than their postgraduate counterparts.[23] LLB students predominantly come straight from high school and are experiencing the freedoms of adulthood for the first time. They are likely to have fewer family responsibilities and less sense of a financial debt being created as part of achieving their degree. Early in their degree they may not even be certain they wish to be lawyers.[24] It is therefore not surprising that reading for class might drop if such reading is not required to achieve high grades. By contrast, JD students are likely to have made significant sacrifices to come back to university; they are likely to be more aware of the financial costs and debt involved, and many will be paying full tuition fees. Consequently, it can be assumed that JD students would be more independently motivated to prepare for class. Thus, the extent to which UNSW JD students do not prepare for class is much more likely to be due to other workload and lifestyle pressures, discussed below.

The significantly higher rate of students who never fail to read for class in the US, particularly in their first year, may also be a reflection of teaching practices that cause deep embarrassment for students who are unable to answer questions in Socratic dialogue due to lack of pre-reading.[25] However, when compared to the UNSW JD 1st year cohort, another possibility arises. Whereas US JD students are likely to have moved cities and live on campus in their first year, UNSW JD students are overwhelmingly from Sydney and remain in their previous accommodation, and often employment, in their first year. Given the seriousness of the step to enrol in the JD, the extent to which UNSW JD students do not read as conscientiously as US JD students may very well be because of lifestyle pressures, discussed below.

Increasing the extent to which students prepare for class is likely to be complicated. Direct attempts to examine students on their preparation and understanding, if not undertaken in a supportive manner, could well lead to the deleterious effects of student stress and fear of humiliation that have been documented with extreme forms of Socratic teaching.[26] However, exploring methods where the expectation to have prepared for class comes from student peers rather than from teacher expectations has the potential to be effective.[27]

Time Spent Preparing for Class and Studying

Both LLB and JD students at UNSW also spend less time preparing for class and studying than US students. Relevant LSSSE questions ask for both the time spent reading set materials and on other preparation such as studying, writing, doing homework etc. in an average week. For the purposes of this analysis, student responses indicating the time spent on these types of activities were merged.

In order to determine how much time conscientious students spend preparing for class, the responses to this question were split into those respondents who also answered that they either ‘never’ or ‘sometimes’ failed to do the reading (those who ‘mostly read’) and respondents who either ‘often’ or ‘very often’ failed to do the reading (those who ‘mostly didn’t read’). The mean scores for each group across year cohorts are set out below. Additionally, data from a recent survey of British law students has been included for further comparison.[28]

When one looks at the means for the conscientious students, it becomes clear that across both UNSW degrees the amount of reading increases with each year, but for the US it decreases each year (Figure 4.2). Despite that decrease, US students still spend more time preparing for class than UNSW students. UNSW JD students also spend more time preparing than LLB students.

One possible explanation for this difference may lie in the teaching methods at UNSW. Because readings are discussed in class, there is an expectation that students are not set readings in excess of what is able to be discussed in a two-hour class. If a degree of student discussion and interaction is expected, the amount of reading is necessarily limited. UNSW has a policy guideline stating that 'students are expected to do between 1 and 2 hours of reading for every hour taught, but no less than 1 hour of reading for every hour taught'.[29] That would equate to a range of 16–32 hours of reading per week for a full-time load, with a nominal average of 24 hours. Conscientious UNSW JD students meet or exceed that mark. The mean reading time in the final year of 32 hours may suggest that later year electives are setting higher reading requirements than compulsory courses.[30]

The much lower LLB hours spent on largely the same reading requirements imposed on the UNSW JD students reinforce the impressions discussed earlier of cultural differences in approaches to study between students in both degrees.

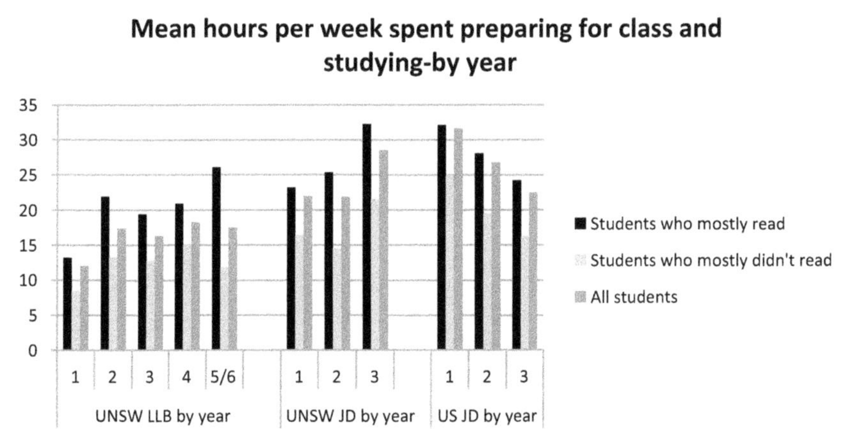

Preparedness for class (%)	UNSW LLB by year					UNSW JD by year			US JD by year		
	1	2	3	4	5/6	1	2	3	1	2	3
Students who mostly read	13.18	21.88	19.38	20.88	26.03	23.15	25.32	32.21	32.06	28.04	24.22
Students who mostly didn't read	8.46	13.34	12.79	15.03	11.83	16.40	14.50	21.54	24.97	19.53	16.20
All students	12.06	17.36	16.30	18.20	17.52	21.93	21.83	28.49	31.61	26.80	22.47

Figure 4.2 Mean hours per week spent preparing for class and studying – by year

A United Kingdom comparison is also available for the overall means for students across all years of the degree (Figure 4.3).[31] UNSW LLB students fall below the preparation levels of both US and UK students. If UNSW students are on average spending more time preparing for class than other Australian law students, it that suggests Australian undergraduate students are less prepared for class than their international counterparts. This may be evidence of a cultural attitude that places less weight on preparation.

Time Spent on Assessment

In addition to time spent preparing for class, students spend significant time completing assignments. The LSSSE questions do not ask students how long they spend on these assignments, but it does ask whether they prepare multiple drafts of assignments (Figure 4.4).

The data from the survey confirms that UNSW students are less likely to do multiple drafts than is the norm in the US. Again, the likelihood of multiple drafts is higher for UNSW JD respondents than LLB respondents. But the data does suggest that UNSW students are more likely to do multiple drafts as they progress through the later years of their degree, in contrast to US students. This raises the interesting notion that UNSW students put less effort into their reading but more into assignments as their degree progresses. This might be evidence of strategic approaches to learning.[32] If final examinations are not set for subjects, and there is little to no graded class participation, it would be likely that students with competing time pressures, and a lower level of interest in the subject, would spend less time preparing for classes.

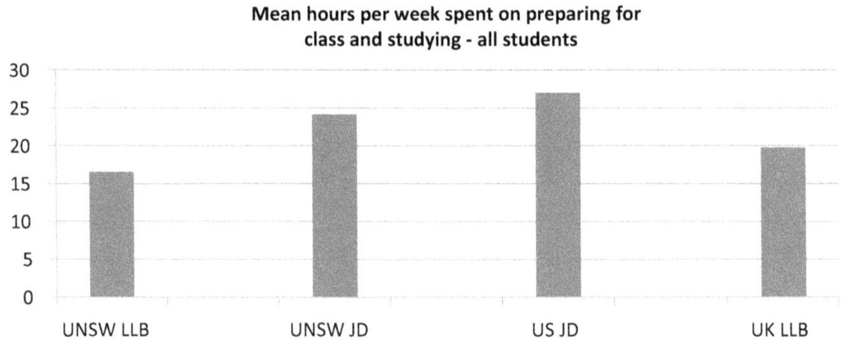

	UNSW LLB	UNSW JD	US JD	UK LLB
Preparing for class and studying (hours/week)	16.53	24.13	26.99	19.74

Figure 4.3 Mean hours per week spent on preparing for class and studying – all students

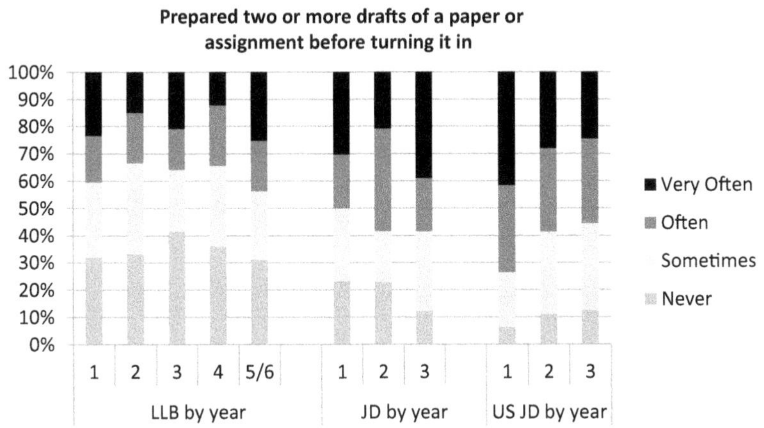

Preparing multiple drafts (%)	LLB by year					JD by year			US JD by year		
	1	2	3	4	5/6	1	2	3	1	2	3
Never	31.9	33.3	41.5	36.2	31.0	23.2	22.9	12.2	6.3	11.1	12.4
Sometimes	27.7	33.3	22.6	29.3	25.3	26.8	18.8	29.3	20.1	30.3	32.0
Often	17.0	18.5	15.1	22.4	18.4	19.6	37.5	19.5	32.0	30.5	31.0
Very Often	23.4	14.8	20.8	12.1	25.3	30.4	20.8	39.0	41.6	28.1	24.6

Figure 4.4 Prepared two or more drafts of a paper or assignment before turning it in

Lifestyle Impacts

UNSW students also appear to have busier lives away from study than is the norm for US students. These impacts are examined below under the categories of home, work, volunteering and relaxation.

Home: Commuting

Where a student lives and their responsibilities within the home can have a significant impact on their educational experience. US students are likely to move cities to study and thus live closer to campus. By contrast, many UNSW LLB students continue to live at home, and rely on public transport to attend university. Commuting thus has a significant time impact on these students (Figure 4.5). UNSW JD students seem to be less impacted. This suggests that JD students choose to live closer to the university than is the norm for LLB students.

Family Responsibilities

UNSW JD students have the highest levels of family responsibilities, with an overall mean of 6.14 hours per week compared to 2.49 hours for LLB students

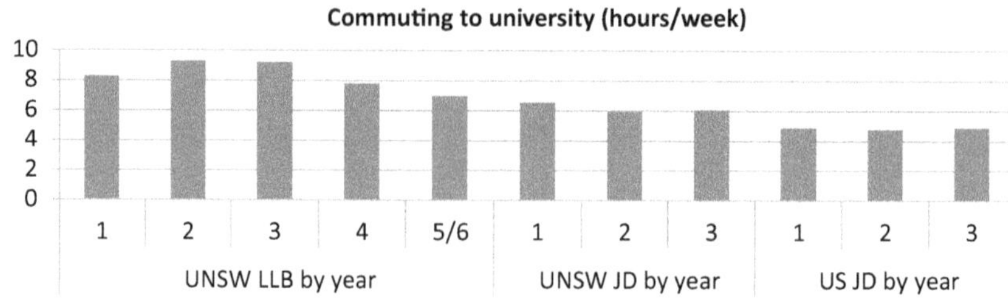

	UNSW LLB by year						UNSW JD by year				US JD by year		
	1	2	3	4	5/6		1	2	3		1	2	3
Weekly commute (hours)	8.26	9.29	9.19	7.79	6.98		6.55	5.94	6.07		4.88	4.78	4.87

Figure 4.5 Commuting to university (hours/week)

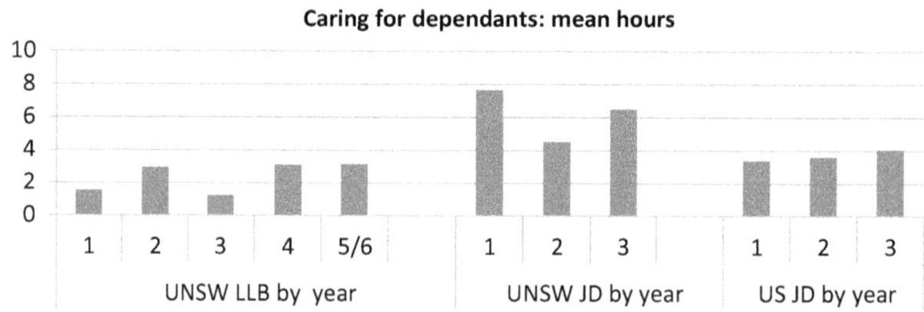

	UNSW LLB by year						UNSW JD by year				US JD by year		
	1	2	3	4	5/6		1	2	3		1	2	3
Caring for dependants (hours/week)	1.54	2.93	1.21	3.1	3.15		7.66	4.52	6.48		3.39	3.59	4.05

Figure 4.6 Caring for dependants (mean hours)

and 3.72 for US JD students (Figure 4.6). In terms of the overall impact on the student body, 45% of UNSW JD respondents had caring responsibilities, compared to only 30% of US JD students and 39% of UNSW LLB respondents. The UNSW figures are comparable to those reported by Larcombe et al. in a 2008 survey of Melbourne University law students.[33] That study found that 37% of commencing JD respondents had family responsibilities, compared to 34% of LLB respondents. By comparison, the UNSW LSSSE figures for 1st years were 41% for JD respondents, compared to 27% for LLB respondents.

These figures tend to further support the idea that because metropolitan Australian law students are overwhelmingly from the city of their law school, they carry greater family responsibilities than interstate students would. Importantly, the much higher levels of responsibility reported by UNSW JD students indicate that this is likely to be a significant trigger of student stress.

Paid Work

UNSW students work significantly longer hours per week than US students, and, importantly, most of those hours are in non-legal work. A recent survey of UK students also reported that those studying law in the UK worked even less hours – a mean of 3.19 hours per week.[34]

This suggests that there is strong pressure on UNSW students to earn income alongside studying. Earning an income may be for lifestyle reasons for many LLB students, but is likely to be an economic necessity for most UNSW JD students. The JD figures in Figure 4.7 should be treated with caution as UNSW JD students are able to enrol on a part-time basis. However, an analysis of those commencing students enrolled on a full-time or close to full-time load indicates that around 30% work more than 16 hours per week. In the 2008 study of paid work by commencing students at Melbourne University Law School, while the spread of hours worked by LLB students was comparable to that of the UNSW LSSSE respondents, only 15% of commencing JD students worked 16 hours or more. Further research is needed to determine whether JD students continue to maintain the hours of paid work they are doing when they enter law school, and what impact that amount of work has on their grades and wellbeing.

Just as striking is a comparison of the percentage of students in no paid work (Figure 4.8). It is clear that for most US students law school is an all-encompassing

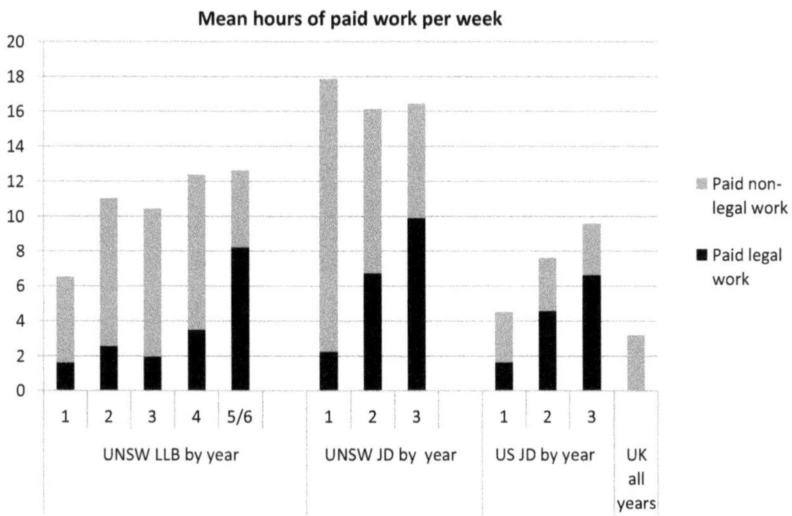

	UNSW LLB by year						UNSW JD by year				US JD by year				UK
	1	2	3	4	5/6		1	2	3		1	2	3		All years
Paid legal work (hours/week)	1.63	2.56	1.98	3.5	8.22		2.25	6.73	9.91		1.65	4.58	6.63		3.19
Paid non-legal work (hours/week)	4.9	8.45	8.45	8.86	4.4		15.6	9.4	6.52		2.86	3.02	2.97		

Figure 4.7 Mean hours of paid work per week

undertaking, and UK students do even less paid work.[35] By contrast, most UNSW law students undertake paid work at a rate that is higher than national student employment figures. Nationally, around 75% of all later year Australian university students are in paid work,[36] whereas approximately 90% of final year UNSW LLB students and JD students were in paid work.

UNSW students also have a greater likelihood of being employed by law firms than US law students, with the percentage of those not employed as paralegals falling to 42% for LLB and 37% for JD students in their final years (Figure 4.9).

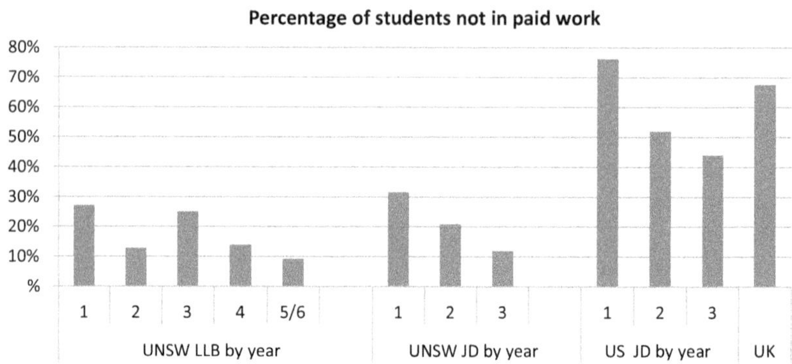

	UNSW LLB by year						UNSW JD by year				US JD by year				UK
	1	2	3	4	5/6		1	2	3		1	2	3		All years
Students not in paid work (%)	27.1	12.7	25.0	13.8	9.1		31.6	20.8	11.9		76.1	51.9	44.0		67.4

Figure 4.8 Percentage of students not in paid work

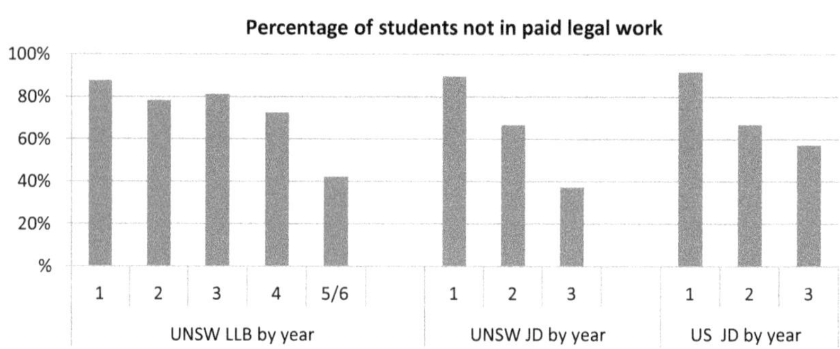

	UNSW LLB by year						UNSW JD by year				US JD by year		
	1	2	3	4	5/6		1	2	3		1	2	3
Students not in paid legal work (%)	87.5	78.2	81.1	72.4	42.0		89.5	66.7	37.2		91.5	66.9	57.0

Figure 4.9 Percentage of students not in paid legal work

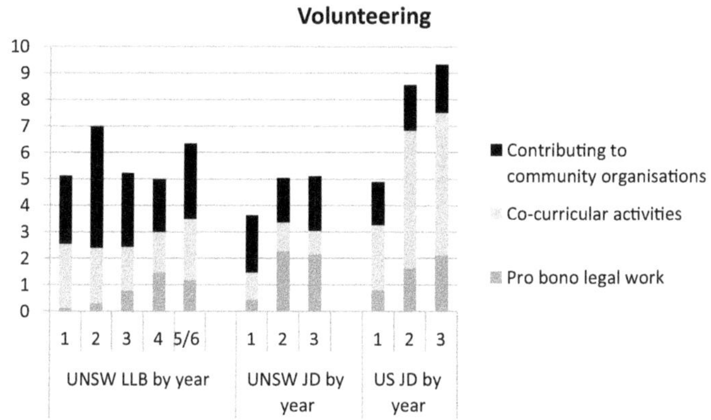

Volunteering (hours/week)	UNSW LLB by year						UNSW JD by year				US JD by year		
	1	2	3	4	5/6		1	2	3		1	2	3
Pro bono legal work	0.13	0.31	0.78	1.47	1.17		0.45	2.27	2.14		0.81	1.62	2.12
Co-curricular activities	2.42	2.09	1.66	1.53	2.31		1.02	1.08	0.9		2.45	5.21	5.38
Contributing to community organisations	2.55	4.58	2.77	1.98	2.85		2.15	1.69	2.07		1.63	1.71	1.81

Figure 4.10 Volunteering

Employment as a paralegal is increasingly seen as a more certain path to graduate legal employment in Australia.

These figures underline the increasing demands on law students' time as they progress through their degree.

Unpaid Work and Community Involvement

Three other questions sought information about the amount of time spent on non-paid volunteer work – whether legal, university or community related (Figure 4.10). The data suggests that UNSW students are more strongly engaged with community volunteering than US students – perhaps because they predominantly still live in their local communities. US JD students are more engaged with university activities, but UNSW JD students undertake more pro bono work.

Relaxation

Finally, three questions in the LSSSE provide an indication of the amount of time students spend relaxing (Figure 4.11). Personal reading – that is reading unrelated to study, and somewhat quaintly described in the relevant LSSSE question as 'Reading on your own (not assigned) for personal or academic enrichment'[37] – begins at a low level with 1st year LLB respondents but increases throughout the degree, and also increases throughout the JD. Later year students in both UNSW degrees read more than US students, though the meagreness of a mean of

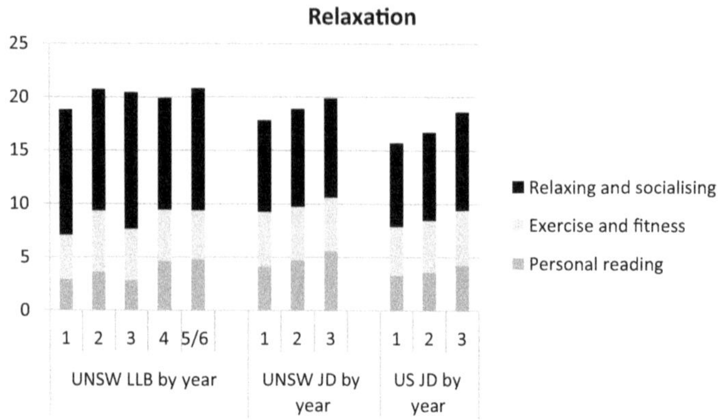

Relaxation (hours/week)	UNSW LLB by year						UNSW JD by year				US JD by year		
	1	2	3	4	5/6		1	2	3		1	2	3
Personal reading	2.88	3.6	2.77	4.63	4.78		4.09	4.7	5.56		3.29	3.58	4.22
Exercise and fitness	4.21	5.76	4.89	4.81	4.6		5.18	5.06	5.07		4.55	4.85	5.17
Relaxing and socialising	11.7	11.4	12.8	10.5	11.4		8.53	9.08	9.21		7.83	8.26	9.17
Total relaxation hrs	18.8	20.7	20.4	19.9	20.8		17.8	18.8	19.8		15.7	16.7	18.6

Figure 4.11 Relaxation

4½ hours a week is most probably testament to the increasing competition reading now faces from electronic entertainment. That reading increases throughout the degree might, however, suggest an increasing development of a reflective turn of mind.

There are no significant differences in the levels of exercise undertaken by UNSW students in both degrees. UNSW LLB students do, however, spend more time relaxing and socializing, perhaps reflecting their earlier stage in life and comparatively lighter family responsibilities.

Conclusions

This chapter suggests that there is much similarity between UNSW law student lifestyle patterns and pressures and those of US law students; but there are also some important differences. UNSW students do not devote as much time and energy to their studies as US students; but, despite this, their overall levels of preparedness appear to increase throughout the degree. UNSW students appear to have high, and possibly unsustainable, work hours outside of university, and this may impact on the degree to which they prepare for class. However, the extent of preparation appears to also be attributable to broader cultural differences – possibly because of the undergraduate setting of the LLB.

Figure 4.12 summarizes the findings discussed in this chapter. It indicates that UNSW students are attempting to 'do it all', and running out of time to do it. While US students might spend more time studying, their days are not significantly busier than UNSW LLB students', and are less so than those of UNSW JD students. The reason is UNSW students' increased time spent commuting, with family and in paid work.

As previously mentioned, some of the limitations of this study include that there were lower response rates for early year LLB students, and there were potential biases in the LLB responses on the basis of gender, co-degree and on overall grade averages. Future cross-sectional studies using the same survey instrument are desirable to test the reproducibility of our results in the absence of these participant demographic issues. Moreover, on the data presented here, it appears to be fruitful to further compare UNSW JD students against UNSW LLB and US JD students, and to obtain more widely based Australian data. A further valuable focus for future research is to investigate possible connections between particular lifestyle pressures experienced by law students with specific symptoms of elevated distress.

The broader significance of the analysis in this chapter for understanding law students' wellbeing is that comparing American and Australian law students' lifestyle patterns provides insights into significant contextual variation between both groups, which is important to bear in mind when comparing American and Australian research on law students' wellbeing, and appreciating the limits of such comparisons. Significantly, much of the wellbeing literature to date has focused on course-based stressors;[38] but in light of Larcombe et al.'s research indicating that improvements in students' course-based experiences may not have a direct

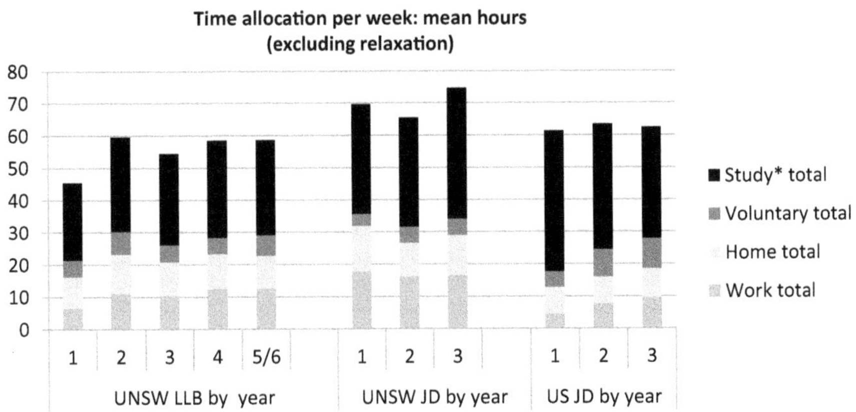

Figure 4.12 Time allocation per week: mean hours (excluding relaxation)

* In this chart Study combines mean preparation hours of class preparation and a nominal 12 hours of class time per week. One course at UNSW would be 3–4 hours. In years 1–3 of the LLB students are also studying other courses.

effect on law students' elevated levels of psychological distress,[39] it is important to understand the broader life pressures and stressors that may be impacting law students' wellbeing.

Notes

* Anna Huggins is a Senior Lecturer in the Queensland University of Technology School of Law; E: a.huggins@qut.edu.au. Alex Steel is a Professor in the Faculty of Law, University of New South Wales; E: a.steel@unsw.edu.au.

1 For an overview, see Carole Silver and Lindsay Watkins, 'The Law School Survey of Student Engagement: Helping Law Schools Understand What's Working (and What's Not)' (2012) 81(2) *Bar Examiner* 14. The data from the LSSSE surveys is increasingly being used to identify issues and trends in US legal education. See e.g. Carole Silver et al, 'Gaining from the System: Lessons from the Law School Survey of Student Engagement about How Students Benefit From Law School' (2013) *University of St Thomas Law Review*; Carole Silver, Amy Garver and Lindsay Watkins, 'Unpacking the Apprenticeship of Professional Identity and Purpose : Insights from the Law School Survey of Student Engagement' (2011) 17 *Journal of the Legal Writing Institute* 373.

2 For example, 'faculty' was altered to 'academic staff members'. In Australia, 'faculty' refers to the organizational body, rather than the people who constitute it.

3 See, e.g. the overviews provided in Penelope Watson and Rachael Field, 'Promoting Student Wellbeing and Resilience at Law School' in Sally Kift et al (eds), *Excellence and Innovation in Legal Education* (LexisNexis, 2011) 389, 392–3, and Kennon M Sheldon and Lawrence S Krieger, 'Understanding the Negative Effects of Legal Education on Law Students: A Longitudinal Test of Self-Determination Theory' (2007) 33 *Personality and Social Psychology Bulletin* 883, 883–4.

4 Specifically, Larcombe et al.'s recent research at Melbourne Law School found that 'improved levels of course satisfaction and engagement did not result in reduced levels of depression, anxiety and stress', which indicates that 'various program features that improve students' experience of law school do not automatically result in improved levels of student well-being': Wendy Larcombe et al, 'Does an Improved Experience of Law School Protect Students Against Depression, Anxiety and Stress? An Empirical Study of Wellbeing and the Law School Experience of LLB and JD Students' (2014) 35 *Sydney Law Review* 407, 409, 432.

5 The 2012 US LSSSE collected over 25,000 student responses from 81 US law schools. Data reported on in this chapter represents the mean scores across that full set of data: Law School Survey of Student Engagement (LSSSE) (2012) <http://www.lssse.iub.edu/pdf/2012/LSSSE_2012_AnnualReport.pdf>.

6 The first major study to provide empirical evidence that Australian law students are at increased risk of psychological distress compared to the general population was Norm Kelk et al, *Courting the Blues: Attitudes Towards Depression in Australian Law Students and Lawyers* (Brain and Mind Research Institute, 2009) <http://www.cald.asn.au/docs/Law%20Report%20Website%20version%204%20May%2009.pdf>.

7 Key studies include G Andrew et al, 'The Role of Legal Education in Producing Psychological Distress Among Law Students and Lawyers' (1986) 11 *American Bar Foundation Research Journal* 225; Matthew M Dammeyer and Narina Nunez, 'Anxiety and Depression Among Law Students: Current Knowledge and Future Directions' (1999) 23 *Law and Human Behavior* 55; Mary E Pritchard and Daniel N McIntosh, 'What Predicts Adjustment Among Law Students? A Longitudinal Panel Study' (2003) 143 *The Journal of Social Psychology* 727; Kennon M Sheldon and Lawrence S Krieger, 'Does Legal Education Have Undermining Effects on Law Students? Evaluating

Changes in Motivation, Values, and Wellbeing' (2004) 22 *Behavioral Sciences and the Law* 261; Sheldon and Krieger, above n3.

8 See, e.g., Anna Huggins and Alex Steel, 'The Relationship Between Class Participation and Law Students' Learning, Engagement and Stress: Do Demographics Matter?', Chapter 5 this collection.

9 There has, however, been an increasing emphasis in recent decades on teaching generic skills in Australian legal education. For an overview, see Sally Kift, '21st Century Climate for Change: Curriculum Design for Quality Learning Engagement in Law' (2008) 18(1) *Legal Education Review* 1.

10 Colin James, 'Seeing Things as We Are: Emotional Intelligence and Clinical Legal Education' (2005) 8 *International Journal of Clinical Legal Education* 123, 127.

11 Erik Brogt and Keith Comer, 'Interpreting Differences Between the United States and New Zealand University Students' Engagement Scores as Measured by the NSSE and AUSSE' [2012] *Assessment and Evaluation in Higher Education* 1; Pauline Hagel, Rodney Carr and Marcia Devlin, 'Conceptualising and Measuring Student Engagement Through the Australasian Survey of Student Engagement (AUSSE): A Critique' (2012) 37 *Assessment and Evaluation in Higher Education* 475.

12 Hagel, Carr and Devlin, above n11, 508.

13 The respondents represented 29% of 1st year students (>48 units of credit/UOC; 51/176); 28% of 2nd year students (>96 UOC; 46/167); and 28% of 3rd years (>144 UOC; 38/135).

14 The respondents represented 16% of 1st year students (48/306); 16% of 2nd year students (55/352); 18% of 3rd year students (54/301); 19% of 4th year students (58/310); and 33% of 5th/6th years (86/257).

15 The average was 48% in 2013 and 46% in 2012: LSSSE Annual Report (2013) <http://www.lssse.iub.edu/pdf/2012/LSSSE_2012_AnnualReport.pdf>.

16 The method for determining what year cohort respondents were in varied between degrees. For US respondents, the cohort was supplied by their law school. A small percentage of law schools had a four-year JD. In this analysis, JD 4th year students' responses have been discarded. For UNSW students, ethics restrictions meant we were required to rely on the students' self-reporting of their year of study. LLB students reported their year of enrolment. Because some dual degrees take six years to complete, responses indicating students were in year 5 or 6 cohorts were recorded as a combined 5th/6th year cohort. As UNSW JD students can enrol in less than a full-time load, they were asked to report the nominal year they would be in by indicating the relevant number of units of credit they had completed. Thus, <48 UOC is equivalent to 1st year, <96 UOC to 2nd year and <144 UOC to final year. The responses of students who responded 'Other' were discarded.

17 In the JD 3rd year, the proportion of respondents who identified themselves as Distinction students jumped to 70%.

18 The precise extent of this variation is difficult to determine as the question asks for student impressions of their grades overall, and we have statistical records only of the overall average grades. Thus some students who consider themselves to be Distinction students might well have only 50% of their grades as Distinction. Such a mix of grades might well see them with an overall average mark in the Credit range.

19 These biases have not been fully accounted for in this chapter, which amounts to a preliminary analysis.

20 Larcombe et al, above n4.

21 Ibid. 421. The survey involved students across Melbourne's transition from an LLB to a JD programme.

22 While the change at Melbourne from a lecture/tutorial LLB degree to a seminar-based JD programme significantly increased the degree of pre-reading, this rise was not to the extent reported by UNSW students.

23 This is not intended to downplay the very real stresses undergraduate students can face, nor the range of significant life stresses individual students may face, and which are explored in this book.
24 In their 2009 study, Tani and Vines found that, relative to students from nine other faculties, UNSW law students were, inter alia, more likely to have chosen their degree for external reasons, including to please their parents, and were less motivated by learning and less intrinsically interested in the content of their degree than students from other disciplines: Massimiliano Tani and Prue Vines, 'Law Students' Attitudes to Education: Pointers to Depression in the Legal Academy and the Profession?' (2009) 19(1) *Legal Education Review* 3, 12–25.
25 See e.g. Elizabeth Mertz, *The Language of Law School: Learning to Think Like a Lawyer* (Oxford University Press, 2007).
26 Ibid.
27 Alex Steel, Julian Laurens and Anna Huggins, 'Class Participation as a Learning and Assessment Strategy in Law: Facilitating Students' Engagement, Skills Development and Deep Learning' (2013) 36(1) *University of New South Wales Law Journal* 30.
28 Derived from underlying data available from the Higher Education Policy Institute (HEPI) and Which, 'Student Academic Experience Survey' (2013) <http://www.hepi.ac.uk/455–2154/2013-Student-Academic-Experience-Survey-produced-jointly-by-HEPI-and-Which.html>.
29 UNSW Faculty of Law, Law School Assessment Policy, 2009.
30 The school policy pre-dates a reduction in the teaching hours of electives to 3 hours per week. If this policy were applied correctly in the final year, students would only be expected to do 26 hours of reading per week.
31 See above n28.
32 See, e.g., Graham Gibbs, 'Using Assessment Strategically to Change the Way Students' Learn' in Sally Brown and Angela Glasner (eds), *Assessment Matters in Higher Education: Choosing and Using Diverse Approaches* (SRHE and Open University Press, 1999) 42.
33 Wendy Larcombe, Pip Nicholson and Ian Malkin, 'Commencing Law Students Interests and Expectations: Comparing Undergraduate and Graduate Cohorts' (2008) *Journal of Australasian Law Teachers Association* 9.
34 See above n28. This figure was derived from the underlying data set for students who selected Law as their subject group.
35 These means are derived from responses to the question: 'In an average week during term-time, roughly how many hours have you spent in paid employment unrelated to your course?'
36 Hamish Coates, 'Working on a Dream: Educational Returns from Off-Campus Paid Work' (2011) 8 *AUSSE Research Briefing*.
37 The use of the word 'enrichment' may have led to underreporting.
38 See above n3.
39 Larcombe et al, above n4, 409.

5 The Relationship Between Class Participation and Law Students' Learning, Engagement and Stress

Do Demographics Matter?

Anna Huggins and Alex Steel

Introduction

Student participation in the classroom has long been regarded as an important means of increasing student engagement and enhancing learning outcomes by promoting active learning.[1] However, the approach to class participation common in US law schools, commonly referred to as the Socratic method, has been criticized for its negative impacts on student wellbeing.[2] A multiplicity of American studies have identified that participating in law class discussions can be alienating, intimidating and stressful for some law students,[3] and may be especially so for women[4] and students from minority backgrounds.[5] Using data from the Law School Student Assessment Survey (LSSAS) conducted at UNSW Law School in 2012, this chapter provides preliminary insights into whether assessable class participation (ACP)[6] at an Australian law school is similarly alienating and stressful for students, including the groups identified in the American literature. In addition, we compare the responses of undergraduate Bachelor of Laws (LLB) and graduate Juris Doctor (JD) students.

The LSSAS is, we believe, one of only two empirical studies[7] to gauge Australian law students' perceptions regarding the potential benefits of ACP; their satisfaction with their levels of engagement in class discussions; and their self-reported anxiety and confidence levels in relation to participating in class. Although differences in the survey instruments used limit the direct comparability of the LSSAS survey results with the findings of American studies, they provide a preliminary indication of how Australian students' experiences of law class discussions both align with and differ from American law students'.

The LSSAS findings indicate that most respondents recognize the potential learning and social benefits associated with class participation in legal education,[8] but remain divided over their willingness to participate. Further, in alignment with general trends identified in American studies,[9] LLB students,[10] women, international students and non-native English speakers perceive they contribute less frequently to class discussions than JD students, males, domestic students and native English speakers, respectively. Importantly, the LSSAS indicates that students are more likely to be anxious about contributing to class discussions if they are

LLB students (compared to their JD counterparts), and if English is not their first language (compared to native English speakers). There were no significant differences in students' self-reported anxiety levels based on gender, which diverges from the findings of American research.[11]

Class Participation and Law Students Distress

The focus of this chapter is on assessable class participation, which for the purposes of this chapter will be described as:

> [A]n active learning technique, based on social learning theory principles, which seeks to promote students' learning and understanding through interactions with their peers within the physical or virtual classroom. . . . As such, ACP is sharply distinguished from many traditional forms of summative assessment as being directed primarily at achieving a peer-based attainment of competency and awareness, rather than the essentially private assessment of work by the teacher.[12]

This definition of ACP represents the ethos underpinning the approach to ACP at UNSW Law.[13] In a 1976 UNSW Law document, the rationale behind ACP was described as follows:

> Courses at this Law School are based on the discussion method of teaching where students are encouraged to take an active role in the classroom.
>
> 'It was thought that there was an educational advantage in a system that encouraged students to think for themselves, formulate ideas and develop skills in argument. . . .'
>
> To facilitate class discussion, the assessment of students' participation was introduced. The allocation of marks for participation in class emphasizes the importance of the classroom as a source of learning and development of skills. It motivates students to prepare for classes, and encourages students to contribute to discussion.[14]

Although it is of course recognized that ACP at UNSW Law is not monolithic, and is influenced by differences in individual law teachers' interpersonal and teaching styles, as well as varying class dynamics, the responses of the students who completed the LSSAS will nonetheless reflect their experiences at a law school for which this model of ACP is 'central' to the educational model.[15]

This chapter examines whether key trends identified in American literature on the Socratic method may be applicable in an Australian legal education context. The transferability of these trends should not be assumed a priori as there are salient differences in the approaches to class participation in America and Australia. For example, the Socratic method utilized in US law schools – which involves students, who may be cold-called, answering a string of questions about legal issues and reasoning and their application to hypothetical fact scenarios,[16] – is regarded as a 'signature pedagogy' of American legal education,[17] and has been identified as a contributing factor to elevated distress levels amongst law students.[18] By contrast, the Socratic method is only used in modified form, if at all, in Australian legal education.[19] As described above, ACP is the preferred approach to class discussions at UNSW Law, and anecdotal evidence suggests that other Australian law schools facilitate class discussions in ways that are more analogous to ACP than the pure Socratic method.

Prior American research 'strongly suggests' that the Socratic approach to class participation contributes to many law students becoming 'depressed, anxious, and disengaged'.[20] In particular, women[21] and students from non-English speaking and other minority backgrounds[22] may find participating in class more stressful and anxiety-provoking,[23] and may therefore be less likely to participate in class discussions than other students. In some cases, students who struggle with class participation begin to doubt their fitness for the study and practice of law, despite strengths in other legal skills.[24] Some Australian commentators have suggested that similar effects exist in Australia.[25]

This chapter will make a preliminary contribution to this debate by providing empirical evidence of different types of students' reactions to various aspects of ACP in the LSSAS. It is important to recognize that law students are taught in a range of methods throughout Australia – including lectures, distance education and seminar-style classes. At UNSW Law, introductory first year courses are taught in interactive seminar-style classes of fewer than 30 students, whilst the majority of classes later in the degree are in groups of around 44. This study only considers the effects on student wellness of assessing class participation in a smaller class environment.

The 2012 LSSAS

In 2012, all UNSW LLB and JD students were invited to participate in the UNSW Law School Student Assessment Survey.[26] The LSSAS was administered online via Survey Monkey, and students were invited to participate via email on a voluntary and anonymous basis. The survey questions were deliberately written in more colloquial, rather than formal, language with the aim of enhancing students' engagement with the survey. Accordingly, the questions in relation to ACP were not intended to be formal or rigorous psychological self-assessment measures, but rather to provide an environmental scan of the types of student preferences, resistances and stresses in relation to ACP, and their perspectives on its utility for learning and skills development. The data were analysed using SPSS Statistics software.

A Profile of UNSW Law Courses

UNSW Law offers both an undergraduate combined LLB degree, in which students study law simultaneously with a degree from another discipline, and a graduate JD degree, both of which qualify students for legal practice in Australia. Due to practitioner admission requirements, two-thirds of both degrees are comprised of compulsory doctrinal courses required for admission to legal practice,[27] and courses are taught using a similar interactive, seminar-style approach, meaning that there is substantial similarity, and hence comparability, between the teaching methodologies of both degrees.

The combined LLB degree is structured so that students complete fewer law courses while they simultaneously complete the bulk of their non-law degree in the first three years; and in the fourth, fifth and in some cases sixth years of the dual degree programme, the balance shifts to predominantly law courses. The most popular combinations in 2012 were with Business (57%) and Humanities (37%).[28] As the JD is a graduate degree, JD students have already completed an undergraduate degree in another discipline, and most have also had experience in the workforce. Thus, the survey responses reflect the attitudes of both school-leavers and mature graduate law students.[29]

B Data and Coding

A total of 317 LLB and JD students started the survey and, of these, 295 answered the questions on ACP that are the focus of this chapter. LLB students accounted for 200 survey participants (67.8%), representing the views of approximately 12.4% of 2012 LLB students; 95 JD students (32.2%) participated, constituting approximately 20% of 2012 JD students.[30] Based on demographic information provided by each of the respondents to the LSSAS, responses were coded to reflect respondents:

1 degree (LLB or JD)
2 gender (male, female or other)
3 student residency status (domestic or international)
4 first language spoken (English or other than English)
5 other degree (commerce-related or other)
6 year of degree (1–6 LLB, 1–3 JD).

The demographics of respondents to the LSSAS are reported in Table 5.1.

The analysis that follows is based on students' responses to eight questions that were asked in the LSSAS that pertained to students' views on the potential benefits of ACP; their satisfaction with their levels of engagement in class discussions; and their self-reported anxiety and confidence levels in relation to participating in class.[31] These questions – and the number and proportion of respondents who strongly disagreed, disagreed, agreed or strongly agreed with each – are shown in Table 5.2. Respondents' comments in relation to each question, except for question 8, were coded using a 4-point Likert scale where 4 = strongly agree, 3 = agree, 2 = disagree and 1 = strongly disagree. In relation to Q8, where students were asked to rate the quantity of their ACP compared with other students, the following 4-point Likert scale was employed: 4 = I am usually one of the most talkative; 3 = I participate as much as most people; 2 = I participate less than most people; 1 = I am one of the least talkative.

Table 5.1 Demographics of respondents

Categories of Respondents	*Demographics of Respondents*	*Number of Respondents (n = 295)*		
Degree	LLB	200		
	JD	95		
Gender	Female	170		
	Male	116		
	Other	9*		
Student residency status	International	29		
	Domestic	266		
First language spoken	English	219		
	Other than English	76		
Other degree	Commerce	121		
	Other	174		
Year of degree		LLB	JD	Total
	1st year	46	36	82
	2nd year	39	30	69
	3rd year	30	25	55
	4th year	35	2**	37
	5th year	39	2**	41
	6th year	11	0	11

* These nine responses were coded 0 for gender (as female = 1), and sensitivity tests excluding these responses revealed similar results.

** The JD is a three-year degree; perhaps these four students who indicated they were in the fourth or fifth year undertook a part-time study load or needed to repeat failed subjects.

C Model Specification

In order to identify significant differences between various demographic sub-groups in relation to each of the relevant survey questions on ACP, we ran a series of linear regressions and cross-tabs. The model specification for the regressions was:

> *Response to questions* = f(*LLB, female, international students, English not first language, other degree commerce(-related), year of degree*)

where LLB, female, international students, English not first language, other degree commerce(-related) = 1 if included in this group respectively, 0 otherwise, and year of degree is a continuous variable coded 1–6.[32] Each of these independent variables was chosen as, based on the trends identified in the abovementioned US literature and anecdotal evidence,[33] they were perceived as being more likely to be associated with students' negative reactions to ACP. Multicollinearity tests indicated that multicollinearity was not an issue for this model.

Analysis of Students' Responses

Do Students Value the Potential Benefits of ACP?

There were three questions (Q1–3) that attempted to gauge the extent to which students recognized the potential benefits of ACP pertaining to deep learning,

Table 5.2 Descriptive statistics

	Strongly Disagree	*Disagree*	*Agree*	*Strongly Agree*	*Total (n = 295)*
Q1: Overall, CP enhances my learning.	27 (9.2%)	80 (27.1%)	127 (43.1%)	61 (20.7%)	295
Q2: Overall, CP makes classes more interesting.	25 (8.5%)	67 (22.7%)	135 (45.8%)	68 (23.1%)	295
Q3: Overall, CP helps me to improve my oral communication skills.	22 (7.5%)	69 (23.4%)	149 (50.5%)	55 (18.6%)	295
Q4: Overall, I am happy with my level of involvement in CP.	19 (6.4%)	91 (30.8%)	144 (48.8%)	41 (13.9%)	295
Q5: I often feel anxious about contributing to class discussions.	45 (15.3%)	91 (30.8%)	107 (36.3%)	52 (17.6%)	295
Q6: I feel confident about expressing myself orally in English for law assessments.	11 (3.7%)	45 (15.3%)	147 (49.8%)	92 (31.2%)	295
Q7: I would prefer to sit and listen instead of participating in class discussions.	32 (10.8%)	121 (41.0%)	97 (32.9%)	45 (15.3%)	295
Q8: In general, how would you rate the quantity of your participation in class compared with other students?	I am one of the least talkative. 31 (10.5%)	I participate less than most people. 67 (22.7%)	I participate as much as most people. 126 (42.7%)	I am usually one of the most talkative. 71 (24.1%)	295

engagement and skills development.[34] Overall, 63.8% of students agreed or strongly agreed that ACP enhances their learning (Q1). Non-native English speaking students were less likely to perceive the benefits of ACP for their learning than native English speakers ($t = -2.160$, $p < 0.05$). Further, the more years respondents had been enrolled, the more likely they were to agree with this statement ($t = 2.562$, $p < 0.05$). Additional analysis separating out the first year students to examine the difference between first year students and students in later years did not indicate significant results, suggesting that students' appreciation of the learning benefits of ACP increases as they progress through their degrees.

Overall, 68.9% of respondents agreed or strongly agreed that ACP makes classes more interesting (Q2), and an almost identical proportion of respondents (69.1%) agreed or strongly agreed that ACP helps them improve their oral communication skills (Q3). Female students were slightly less likely to agree with the latter proposition than males ($t = -1.888$, $p < 0.10$), and respondents' year of degree also slightly influenced results ($t = 1.943$, $p < 0.10$).

In another survey question (Q9), which was not included in the regression analysis or Table 5.2 as the responses did not correspond with a 4-point Likert scale, students were also asked what percentage of their final grade should be based on class participation, and a response of 0% was permitted. In other words, they were asked if they believed ACP should be summatively assessed. Significantly, 91.6% of LLB respondents felt it should be assessed, as did 81.6% of JD respondents, although students' views on its appropriate weighting varied. This evidences a very high level of support for the continued inclusion of ACP as an integral component of the assessment regimes of UNSW Law courses.

Students' Responses to Their Level of Involvement in ACP

Three questions (Q4, 7 and 8) related to students' perceptions of their level of involvement in ACP. Question 8 provides an appropriate starting point to contextualize the following discussion. In relation to this question, which asked students to 'rate the quantity of [their] participation in class compared with other students', 42.7% of respondents indicated that they 'participate as much as most people', and 24.1% of respondents identified themselves as 'usually one of the most talkative'. Significantly, LLB, female, non-native English speaking and international students were less likely to rate their quantity of participation highly compared to JD ($t = -2.307$, $p < 0.05$), male ($t = -2.252$, $p < 0.05$), native English speaking ($t = -2.906$, $p < 0.01$) and domestic students ($t = -3.687$, $p < 0.01$), respectively. These results appear consistent with the findings of American research indicating that women and students from minority backgrounds do not participate in class discussions as frequently as others.[35]

Two related questions pertained to whether students were 'happy with [their] level of involvement in ACP' (Q4), and whether they would 'prefer to sit and listen' than actively engage in class discussions (Q7). Overall, 62.7% of respondents agreed or strongly agreed with the former statement, and 48.2% agreed or strongly agreed with the latter. Similarly to the results for Q8, LLB and female students were significantly less likely to be happy with their level of involvement in ACP compared with JD ($t = -2.223$, $p < 0.05$) and male students ($t = -2.035$, $p < 0.05$). The year of degree was also significant ($t = 2.002$, $p < 0.05$), indicating that students' contentment with their involvement in ACP increased as they progressed through their degrees. Female, non-native English speakers and international students were also more likely to prefer to sit and listen than male ($t = 1.747$, $p < 0.10$), native English speaking ($t = 1.948$, $p < 0.10$) and domestic students ($t = 2.529$, $p < 0.05$), respectively.

Students' Anxiety and Confidence Levels in Relation to ACP

The survey question of highest salience in terms of assessing the stress students experience as a result of participating in ACP is question 5, where students were asked to rate the extent to which they 'often feel anxious about contributing to class discussions'. The majority of respondents (53.9%) agreed with this statement, with 17.6% of these strongly agreeing.

When regressions were run based on demographic sub-groups, LLB respondents and students for whom English is a second language demonstrated far stronger support for the statement in Q5 than their JD ($t = 3.450$, $p < 0.01$) and native English-speaking counterparts ($t = 3.086$, $p < 0.01$). This indicates that the most important variables accounting for law students' self-assessed anxiety about contributing to ACP are their status as LLB students, which may be further equated with relative youthfulness and inexperience in tertiary studies compared to JD students, and a lack of native proficiency with English – which makes intuitive sense given the rapid pace and sophistication of some of the oral exchanges in law school classrooms. Interestingly, female respondents' agreement with this statement did not differ significantly from male respondents' agreement levels. To this extent, our results differ from previous American research cited above.[36]

Despite the high levels of anxiety reported, a significant majority of students (81.0%) agreed or strongly agreed that they felt confident expressing themselves in English for law assessments (Q6). Mirroring the results of Q5, compared to JD students and native English-speaking students, LLB students ($t = -3.678$, $p < 0.01$) and non-native English-speaking students ($t = -2.432$, $p < 0.05$) were more likely to disagree with this statement.

Significant correlations also existed between those who would prefer to stay silent in class (Q7) and those who were anxious about contributing (Q5) (Pearson's $r = 0.545$ for LLB and 0.424 for JD students, both at the 0.01 level of significance (2-tailed)). As percentages, 41.6% of LLB respondents and 28.7% of JD respondents agreed that they were both often anxious (Q5) and preferred to stay silent (Q7). There was also a strong negative correlation between levels of contribution (Q8) and anxiety (Q5) in class (Pearson's $r = -0.597$ at the 0.01 level of significance (2-tailed)), with 95.9% of those who participated less than most people and 91.7% of the least talkative in the LLB, and 84% and 100% respectively in the JD, agreeing that they experienced anxiety surrounding ACP. Further, there were significant negative correlations between the extent to which respondents were happy with their levels of contribution (Q4) and the extent to which they felt anxious (Q5) (Pearson's $r = -0.527$ at the 0.01 level of significance (2-tailed)). These correlations existed across both degree programmes and in each year.

Interestingly, the existence of anxiety around contributing in class does not necessarily impact negatively on student learning. Of the 53.9% of respondents who agreed that they were often anxious when contributing in class (Q5), 48.8% still considered that ACP enhanced their learning (Q1), and 56.8% indicated it made classes more interesting (Q2). When these responses were combined, 37% found ACP neither enhanced learning nor made classes more interesting, which corresponds to 20.3% of all respondents. Of that 20%, there was no significant gender difference (51% female), two-thirds had English as a first language (66.7%) and most were local students (85%), suggesting that anxiety and negativity towards ACP were not linked to demographic factors. Further, of that 20% of respondents, only 33.3% thought ACP should not form part of a final grade (that is, 7% of all respondents). This suggests that despite broad levels of anxiety, most respondents still find learning benefits associated with ACP and wish it to be retained as a form of assessment.

Discussion and Conclusion

This chapter has reported empirical findings from an Australian law school regarding students' perceptions of the benefits of ACP, and self-assessments of their levels of engagement and anxiety in relation to in-class participation. It provides evidence that law students, even in an environment of smaller class teaching, are evenly split over whether they would prefer to speak in class or remain silent. This is a significantly high degree of resistance to class participation that teachers will need to bear in mind. There are also relatively high levels of anxiety associated with contributions in class. Again, roughly 50% of respondents reported that they often felt anxious in class; however, contrary to our expectations based on prior US research, the reported anxiety levels of male and female respondents were comparable. What this study does not capture is the level of anxiety that students are suffering, or how great this anxiety is in comparison to other forms of learning and assessment approaches.

Although differences between the demographic groups of interest varied for each of the eight questions analysed, the cumulative evidence suggests that, like in the US, the students that are most likely to find ACP challenging and stressful in various ways are women, non-native English speakers and international students. Additionally, LLB students expressed more concern than JD students, indicating that age and relative experience mediate students' perceptions and experiences of ACP. However, there was no clear demographic pattern for those students who did not value the potential learning outcomes associated with ACP. Further, one variable that did not account for significant differences in students' responses on the questions pertaining to their engagement or anxiety and confidence levels was the discipline of their other degree, suggesting that prior or concurrent tertiary experiences do not predict reactions to ACP.

Whilst prima facie these results might suggest comparability with US studies on the negative effects of the Socratic method, the results of our survey – which asked a series of more specific questions around student attitudes to ACP – paint a more complex picture. Specifically, our results suggest that for most students ACP is a positive experience overall, despite elevated anxiety levels. There are high levels of student acceptance that ACP makes student learning more effective and the classroom environment more interesting (and, by implication, more engaging). Our findings indicate that there is a group of approximately 20% of respondents who are both anxious and find little learning benefit in ACP. Yet, of those respondents, most would still prefer ACP to be a component of the final grade. This may suggest that for this small group of students, ACP is a lesser evil than other forms of assessment, and/or that these students prefer a broad mix of assessments.

The overwhelming indication that respondents want participation to be assessed suggests that ACP is viewed as a positive component of the assessment suite, and that many students would be strongly opposed to its removal, even on grounds of student anxiety. Further research is thus needed to determine whether the negative impacts experienced by certain sub-groups of students can be linked to particular forms of participation, and the impact that different teaching and marking styles have.[37]

Our results thus draw into question whether ACP is a significant contributing factor to Australian law students' elevated distress levels as has been 'strongly suggested' by the research on the Socratic approach in the US.[38] Interestingly, recent research by Larcombe et al. at Melbourne Law School indicates that there are other variables, beyond students' course experiences, that may be the most salient contributing factors to law students' elevated distress levels.[39] This raises further questions about whether students' stress about ACP may be relatively insignificant compared to other stressors, which constitutes a valuable opportunity for further research.

Notes

1 For an overview see Alex Steel, Julian Laurens and Anna Huggins, 'Class Participation as a Learning and Assessment Strategy in Law: Facilitating Students' Engagement, Skills Development and Deep Learning' (2013) 36 *University of New South Wales Law Journal* 30.

2 For an overview of this literature, see, e.g., Robert Schuwerk, 'The Law Professor as Fiduciary: What Duties Do We Owe to Our Students?' (2004) 45 *South Texas Law Review* 753, 771 at n42; James B Levy, 'As a Last Resort, Ask the Students: What They Say Makes Someone an Effective Law Teacher' (2006) 58(1) *Maine Law Review* 50, 54 n14.

3 Michael Hunter Schwartz, Sophie Sparrow and Gerald F Hess, *Teaching Law by Design: Engaging Students from the Syllabus to the Final Exam* (Carolina Academic Press, 2009) 92.

4 For an overview of this literature, see Jennifer L Rosato, 'The Socratic Method and Women Law Students: Humanize, Don't Feminize' (1997) 7 *Southern California Review of Law and Women's Studies* 37, 37 at nn3–5.

5 For an overview of the American literature on the silencing and other negative effects of the Socratic method on minority students, see Elizabeth Mertz, *The Language of Law School: Learning to 'Think Like a Lawyer'* (Oxford University Press, 2007) 178–85.

6 We adopt the term assessable class participation and the abbreviation 'ACP' from the work of Merilyn Armstrong, 'Assessing Students' Participation in Class Discussion' (1978) 3 *Assessment in Higher Education* 186.

7 The other survey, conducted by the UNSW Tertiary Education Research Centre (TERC) in 1976, also examined UNSW Law student attitudes to class participation: Merilyn Armstrong, 'The Assessment of Class Participation in the University of New South Wales Law School' (University of New South Wales, 1976) 45.

8 For an outline of these benefits, see Steel, Laurens and Huggins, above n1.

9 See above nn3–5.

10 As American legal education is based on a graduate system, there is no comparable US data examining the perceptions of undergraduate and graduate law students.

11 See above n4.

12 Steel, Laurens and Huggins, above n1, 32 (citations omitted).

13 For an overview of the history of and approach to ACP at UNSW Law, see ibid. 33–5.

14 Armstrong, above n6, 1 (citations omitted).

15 Steel, Laurens and Huggins, above n1, 34.

16 Jeffrey D Jackson, 'Socrates and Langdell in Legal Writing: Is the Socratic Method a Proper Tool for Legal Writing Courses?' (2007) 43 *California Western Law Review* 267, 272–3.

17 William M Sullivan et al, *Educating Lawyers: Preparation for the Profession of Law* (Jossey-Bass, 2007) 23–4.

18 See above n2.
19 Steel, Laurens and Huggins, above n1, 51.
20 Hunter Schwartz, Sparrow and Hess, above n3, 92.
21 See above n4.
22 See above n5. Although the LSSAS did not ask students questions pertaining to their ethnic background, students were asked if they are native English speakers and/or international students. Although it is recognized that such demographic groupings do not necessarily align with the concept of 'minority students' as discussed in the American literature, these are the closest proxies we have based on the data available from the LSSAS.
23 These types of anxiety can range from 'standard low-grade nerves' to 'severe public speaking anxiety': Heidi K Brown, 'The "Silent But Gifted" Law Student: Transforming Anxious Public Speakers into Well-Rounded Advocates' (2012) 18 *Journal of the Legal Writing Institute* 291, 293.
24 Jennifer Jolly-Ryan, 'Promoting Mental Health in Law School: What Law School Can Do for Law Students to Help Them Become Happy, Mentally Healthy Lawyers' (2009) 48 *University of Louisville Law Review* 95, 124.
25 See, e.g., James and Field, who state: '[T]he way law and its culture are taught and . . . the isolated, competitive environment that can exist at law school, are factors contributing to Australian law students' high levels of distress': Nickolas James and Rachael Field, *The New Lawyer* (Wiley, 2012) 348.
26 The survey contained 81 items spanning six areas of law school assessment: (1) class participation; (2) group work; (3) legal problem questions; (4) essays; (5) examinations; and (6) general assessment and feedback questions. The items were a mixture of forced-choice Likert scale responses to statements, open-ended text-based answers to questions, and multiple choice single-answer questions, and were developed based on a literature review and the investigators' hypotheses of likely student issues. A related article analysing survey responses to the questions on group work in this survey is Alex Steel, Anna Huggins and Julian Laurens, 'Valuable Learning, Unwelcome Assessment: What LLB and JD Students Really Think about Group Work' (2014) 36(2) *Sydney Law Review* [291], 321. The survey, which had ethics approval (no 12 058), formed part of UNSW Law's contribution to a university-wide Assessment Project, and helped to inform aspects of the Law School's 2011–2013 Curriculum Review.
27 Consultative Committee of State and Territory Law Admitting Authorities, 'Schedule 1: Prescribed Areas of Knowledge' (1992) <http://www.lawcouncil.asn.au/shadomx/apps/fms/fmsdownload.cfm?file_uuid=30440CF8–1C23-CACD-222E-59CF362D9B5A&siteName=lca>.
28 Business includes both Commerce/Law and Economics/Law. Humanities includes Arts/Law, International Studies/Law, Social Science/Law, Criminology and Criminal Justice/Law, Media/Law and Social Work/Law.
29 Steel, Huggins and Laurens, above n26.
30 At the time of the survey there were 1,612 LLB students (cohorts of 381, 372, 320, 316 and 223 students in each of the five years, noting that fifth and sixth year cohorts have been combined) and 488 JD students (cohorts of 204, 153, 131 in each of the three years). Across the year cohorts, the LLB responses averaged 9% for years 1–4 and jumped to 21% for the fifth year. The JD cohorts averaged a response rate of 20% across the three years. The representativeness of our study, particularly for LLB students, constitutes one of the limitations of our research.
31 There were 26 questions on ACP in the LSSAS, but we are limiting the focus of our regression analysis to the eight questions that pertain to these issues of relevance for this chapter. An additional question, Q9, is also discussed below, but was not included in the regression or in Table 5.2 as the responses did not correspond with a 4-point Likert scale.

32 The year of respondents' degree has been coded as both a continuous variable and as a dummy variable – where first year = 1, 0 otherwise – to isolate whether first year students' responses were skewing results. Such potential skewing may result from first year law students having done relatively few law courses before they answered the LSSAS at the end of semester 1, 2012, and having only had experiences in smaller classes of around 30 students. Additional sensitivity analysis using the dummy variable 'first year' (not reported, except in relation to Q1 where the 'year' variable was significant) did not reveal any significant differences compared to the continuous variable 'year', indicating that first year students' responses did not skew the results.

33 It should be noted that it was expected that students whose other degree was commerce-related might be more likely to have negative reactions to ACP as anecdotal evidence suggests that, compared to their counterparts in other discipline areas, such as the Humanities, they are likely to have less experience of in-class discussions. For similar reasons of relative inexperience, it was predicted that LLB students were less likely to have positive reactions to ACP than JD students.

34 Steel, Laurens and Huggins, above n1, 35.

35 Above nn4 and 5.

36 Above n4.

37 A range of valuable pedagogical strategies for supporting students' diverse needs, learning styles and preferences can be sourced from the extant literature. See, e.g., Steel, Laurens, and Huggins, above n1, 52–4; Stuckey et al, *Best Practices for Legal Education: A Vision and a Road Map* (Clinical Legal Education Association, 2007) 207–25.

38 Above nn2–3.

39 Wendy Larcombe et al, 'Does an Improved Experience of Law School Protect Students against Depression, Anxiety and Stress? An Empirical Study of Wellbeing and the Law School Experience of LLB and JD Students' (2014) 35 *Sydney Law Review* 407.

6 Vitality for Life and Law

Fostering Student Resilience, Empowerment and Well-Being at Law School

*Judith Marychurch**

Introduction

Vitality for Life and Law is an innovative, preventative programme developed in response to the growing awareness of the high levels of psychological distress experienced by law students and legal professionals. This chapter explores the process involved in developing a positive, educative, preventative approach to enable students to develop an understanding of stress and the impacts of stress on their body, mind and emotions, and to equip themselves with a range of techniques to facilitate and support sustained optimal performance in their personal and professional lives. Issues addressed include the need to achieve 'buy-in' from the legal academy in implementing programmes such as *Vitality for Life and Law*, and for a cultural shift in legal education to support integration of student well-being initiatives into the curriculum of Australian law schools. This will lead to a discussion of the key learning outcomes from the pilot and subsequent offerings of the programme, and the implications for the transition to law school and to the legal profession, curriculum development and implementation of *Threshold Learning Outcome (TLO) 6: Self-Management for the Bachelor of Laws*.

The Beginning of the Journey: A Pilot Programme

The planning and preparation for *Vitality for Life and Law* began in 2009, shortly after the release of *Courting the Blues: Attitudes Towards Depression in Australian Law Students and Legal Practitioners*.[1] As Sub-Dean[2] and then Associate Dean: Teaching and Learning, the author knew from personal experience[3] the devastating effect of depression and anxiety-related mental illness on Australian law students. Heartened by the opinion in *Courting the Blues* that 'it is not necessary to be clear about the causes in order to formulate effective strategies'[4] the author took a decision to actively pursue opportunities to provide law students at the University of Wollongong (UOW) with access to appropriate interventions. These strategies were designed to assist students in managing stress; where possible, prevent development of symptoms of depression and anxiety; and to encourage help-seeking behaviour where symptoms of depression and anxiety-related mental illness are present. This required an approach that would be preventative and educative, and that would, initially, need to operate alongside the curriculum rather than as part of it. The author met with Marie Jepson, co-founder and board member of the Tristan Jepson Memorial Foundation ('TJMF'), with a view to facilitating dialogue on how to make such a programme a reality. Jepson organized introductions to Dr Norm Kelk, co-author of *Courting the Blues*, and Holly Kneebone, a former lawyer, now leadership consultant and executive coach.[5] Michael Devitt[6] – a senior lecturer at UOW at the time, and a Wollongong solicitor of long-standing – also joined the author in initial planning meetings in 2009 to decide on the best way to garner support for a student programme and to develop the programme itself.

Initial talks focused on three key aspects: first, the need for regular monitoring of law students over the course of their studies; second, the need for training of staff in mental health first-aid and referral, as well as the need for staff 'champions' of mental health programmes for students; and third (and most critically for the purposes of this chapter), programmes for students to increase their level of social connectedness and self-awareness about their own well-being, particularly the need to distinguish between their personal and professional lives and attain an appropriate balance between them.[7] To achieve and maintain good mental health, students would need to learn lifestyle skills to manage stress and ameliorate the impact of stress on their physical and mental well-being. It was noted that long-term change would require curriculum renewal,[8] but that a pilot to trial content and gauge student and staff perceptions would be necessary as a first stage.

Funding was approved in late 2009 for a pilot programme of *Vitality for Life and Law* during 2010, via UOW's Educational Strategic Development Fund ('ESDF').[9] In preparation for the ESDF funding application, a series of seminars and meetings were held. These were very effective at putting well-being on the agenda of relevant university staff and in garnering support for the pilot. A lunchtime seminar was scheduled for Kelk to present to law academics, professional staff and Academic Services Division staff[10] on the findings of the *Courting the Blues* report. The seminar was followed up with a subsequent series of roundtable meetings with key UOW stakeholders in well-being support, including the Dean of Students, Learning Development staff, Disability Liaison Officers, Counselling and Student Support Advisers, as well as representatives from the Law Students Society and the law student body generally.

The pilot initially targeted first year students specifically to aid academic transition to tertiary study in law and to intervene early in a law student's studies with the hope of preventing a decline in mental health status. Despite extensive promotion at Orientation Day, including short introductory sessions with Kneebone timed to fit around primary activities without adding to the overall length of the day, and a positive focus on thriving at law school and optimizing performance,[11] few students registered for the programme. Follow-up promotion in the early weeks of semester were also unproductive, so the pilot quickly moved to open availability to law students at any point in their studies, with the hope that a mix of year levels among participants would create opportunities for vertical peer support of later year students to early year students. Ultimately, six students completed the six-week, two hours per week pilot programme facilitated by Kneebone. The group was predominantly male, with only one female student. Two staff groups were added, to replace the other two student seminar groups initially planned for Kneebone to run. These staff groups were well attended, with approximately 12 staff members each week averaged across the five weeks for which the seminars ran. Participants included academic and professional staff from Law and staff from other faculties and the Academic Services Division. The staff groups were one of the best aspects of the pilot, and they paid longer-term dividends by encouraging staff to be open to the subsequent promotion of the programme of *Vitality for Life and Law* in their own lectures and seminars, having had the benefit of the sessions themselves. In addition, staff from other faculties and the Academic Services Division started to talk more about well-being issues.[12]

Several key learning outcomes from the pilot influenced the subsequent iteration of *Vitality for Life and Law* in spring/second semester 2010. First, it was apparent that reaching first year students, particularly at the beginning of their first session, was difficult. Students at this point in their studies are typically on a 'high', having achieved well in their prior studies and gained access to (in many cases) their 'dream' degree. While there is evidence that the decline in mental health of law students begins in the first year of law studies,[13] using an extra-curricular programme like *Vitality for Life and Law* to assist students to develop appropriate stress management techniques, even with an emphasis on optimizing performance, at this early stage is unlikely to attract the majority of students. Early intervention strategies must be part of intentional curriculum design,[14] with early stage skills introduced at appropriate points of the curriculum to meet current needs without overwhelming students with information. The difficulty with this in the context of a programme like *Vitality for Life and Law* is that breaking up the content across a multiple year curriculum causes a lack of cohesion and cogency unless there is a very explicit communication strategy and a structured process for students to bring their learning together. A further problem is that one of the critical components of *Vitality for Life and Law* is the nature of delivery, with an emphasis on small group learning and personal reflection. This is best facilitated through regular meetings over a period of weeks rather than periodically over the duration of a course. In this way, the life skills developed in *Vitality for Life and Law* are akin to the professional skills developed in the Bachelor of Laws (LLB) or Juris Doctor (JD) programmes. They need to be taught and learned at a basic level, then further developed and refined over a period of time.

Kneebone's work with students and staff during the autumn 2010 pilot focused on four aspects of wellness: physical, mental, emotional and spiritual – which are common to many approaches to well-being. Rumer Godden refers to this in *A House with Four Rooms*:

> There is an Indian proverb or axiom that says that everyone is a house with four rooms, a physical, a mental, an emotional, and a spiritual. Most of us tend to live in one room most of the time but, unless we go into every room every day, even if only to keep it aired, we are not a complete person.[15]

Students were guided through key concepts within each of these aspects of well-being during the programme, with opportunity to self-reflect and discuss issues within the group. The other key component of each session in the *Vitality* programme led by Kneebone was instruction in Mindfulness Based Stress Reduction (MBSR). These included exercises based on the work of the founder of MBSR, Jon Kabat-Zinn.[16] According to the *Center for Mindfulness in Medicine, Health Care, and Society* founded by Kabat-Zinn in 1995:[17]

> Mindfulness is a way of learning to relate directly to whatever is happening in your life, a way of taking charge of your life, a way of doing something for yourself that no one else can do for you – consciously and systematically working with your own stress, pain, illness, and the challenges and demands of everyday life.

The *Vitality for Life and Law* programme incorporated Kabat-Zinn's raisin exercise[18] and body-scan practice,[19] which are key parts of the eight-week MBSR programmes offered via the Center for Mindfulness in Medicine, Health Care, and Society.[20] In essence, these practices are designed to bring one's conscious awareness to the present moment, rather than the past or future. The raisin exercise is an example of mindful eating, where an everyday necessity of taking in nutritional sustenance becomes a meditational practice by bringing one's mind and senses to focus on the sight, smell and sensations of what one is eating.[21] With the body-scan exercise, one's awareness is taken progressively to different parts of the body while focusing on breathing, noticing any feelings or sensations, such as tightness or pain. *Vitality for Life and Law* participants reported that they found both exercises to be highly beneficial, and that they could practise them at any time themselves.[22]

Subsequent Iterations of Vitality for Life and Law

The spring 2010 *Vitality for Life and Law* programme incorporated several changes to structure and timing in response to feedback from students in the autumn semester. The seminars were reduced in length from two hours to one hour, but extended in the number of weeks of delivery; and they were scheduled for the common lunch hours on Wednesdays and Thursdays to avoid any possibility of a clash with scheduled classes. Students indicated that they could not commit two hours per week to the programme, but would happily commit to more than six weeks once the event was in their diary on a weekly basis, like their classes. Two seminar groups were held, one facilitated by the author and the other by a Disability Liaison Officer at UOW with a background in psychology and injury management. Kneebone provided training via telephone as needed prior to each week's session. Spring registrations for *Vitality for Life and Law* went up dramatically following promotion by one of the students who completed the pilot programme in autumn in lectures and seminars in early spring semester. This was, by far, the most effective advertising of the programme. Promotion by staff who had completed the programme in autumn also assisted; one colleague was heard to say to a student: 'If you think you don't have time to do Vitality, then you need to do Vitality!' Other promotions included a 'Zen passport', where students who attended a session each week had their passport 'stamped', with prizes awarded to students who attended most of the six sessions scheduled, to give students an extra incentive to do the full programme. Prizes had a well-being flavour and were donated by local businesses.[23] While welcome, the prizes were not a huge incentive, and most students would have completed the programme without the Zen passport.

Total registrations for the spring semester were approximately 20 students, with a near equal division between genders, and 13 students going on to complete most of the programme.[24] Attendance patterns in the two groups varied markedly and may be indicative of the importance of community in designing interventions to address the decline in mental health of law students. The group facilitated by the author had higher and more consistent attendance by participants than the other group, led by a facilitator who was not a lawyer. This trend was repeated in autumn 2011, when two streams of *Vitality for Life and Law* seminars were again scheduled, with one group facilitated by a non-lawyer trained in counselling and with a background in leading small group discussions and meditation practices. The value of keeping support within the community, where group-based interventions are made up of people in the same discipline and led or facilitated by appropriately trained people also from that discipline, is worthy of further study given the recent increase in well-being initiatives at a central level within universities, as the success of such interventions may be affected by a disciplinary focus. If the knowledge of the participants that the facilitator is in the same discipline and so likely possesses a level of shared experience with the participants makes them more likely to attend, engage in and complete an intervention programme, this would suggest that delivery of well-being programmes at a central level of a university rather than within a discipline may be less effective than discipline-specific programmes. This would not prevent central coordination of training and delivery of well-being interventions, but would suggest that staff from within the discipline may be more appropriate as facilitators. This poses the additional issue of the sourcing and professional development of appropriate staff to deliver well-being initiatives within the curriculum.

In autumn 2011, 10 students completed the *Vitality for Life and Law* programme. From spring 2011–spring 2012, the author facilitated very small groups of students for *Vitality for Life and Law*, with a total of approximately five students completing the programme. With dwindling numbers and other demands on the author's time due to impending restructure at UOW, the decision was taken to cease offering *Vitality for Life and Law* in its current form at the end of 2012. By this time, nearly 35 students had completed the *Vitality for Life and Law* programme. Out of total enrolments, this is a small proportion and will not lead to sustained, long-term change. However, the students who did complete the programme were overwhelmingly positive about their experience and the impact on their lives. Students who participated in *Vitality for Life and Law* made comments like:[25]

> I paid a lot of attention to my sleeping patterns after *Vitality* and I have been working on developing a healthy diet.
>
> Learning something new each week and checking in with everyone, and being able to just spend an hour of one day concentrating on yourself and tapping into how you were feeling was excellent.
>
> Learning how to not just cope in my studies (and ultimately the profession) but learning how to *thrive* really attracted me.
>
> The people in the group were great; also the content – it was useful, so I wanted to learn more.
>
> I concentrate on my breathing in order to relax – very helpful. I now pay more attention to my physical well-being.

These comments indicate that the students did take on board the different aspects of well-being addressed in the programme, and were consciously paying more attention to their physical well-being in particular. Sleep was a consistent area of concern raised in small group discussions, particularly the number of hours slept on a regular basis. Several students indicated that they slept only 4–5 hours per night, significantly below the recommended 7–9 hours for adults.[26] Given that symptoms of sleep deprivation include poor concentration, emotional problems and mood changes such as irritability,[27] inadequate sleep over the medium to long term may be a contributing factor to the rates of anxiety and depression in law students. This is worthy of further study. The social connectedness within the groups also comes through in student comments. This is indicative of the need for community involvement and group support in addressing mental distress in law students and the legal profession.

Key Learning Outcomes and Their Implications

While the voluntary nature of the programme during this period may have been attractive to students who were already experiencing problems, anecdotal evidence still suggests that interventions like *Vitality for Life and Law* do have the potential to positively influence the well-being of individual students. Several students have kept in regular touch with the author after completing the *Vitality for Life and Law* programme and have gone on to do well in their law studies and to graduate with Honours, reporting that what they learned in the programme had helped them succeed in their studies and lives. In order to achieve sustained and long-term change, life skills like those promoted in *Vitality for Life and Law* need to be incorporated into the curriculum alongside the professional skills our students need to become skilled and employable graduates, so that all of our graduates become self-aware, autonomous decision-makers capable of prioritizing their own health and well-being. This is how we will achieve true cultural change in the long term. In the meantime, it is necessary to identify the key learning outcomes from the pilot and subsequent iterations of *Vitality for Life and Law* and look at what they mean for future development.

Courting the Blues noted that the solutions to the problems of high levels of depression and anxiety-related mental illness need to be based in the community where the problem is based – that is, law schools, law firms and other employers of law graduates.[28] In terms of reaching students, experience with the *Vitality for Life and Law* programme suggests that community is indeed important to addressing issues of mental health; particularly leadership and mentoring by people from within the discipline. As student support and well-being services tend to be located more at the central, university level as opposed to within schools or faculties, understanding the role that facilitators of programmes play in the success of intervention programmes is important and worthy of further study.

In terms of curriculum development and renewal, experience with the *Vitality for Life and Law* programme suggests that integration of life skills within the curriculum is essential in order to ensure that all students are equipped with stress management techniques to minimize its negative impact on their physical and mental health. This is also in line with implementation of *Threshold Learning Outcome 6: Self-Management for the Bachelor of Laws* [TLO 6],[29] as well as the Council of Australian Law Deans (CALD)'s *Promoting Law Student Well-Being Good Practice Guidelines for Law Schools*[30] and *TJMF Psychological Wellbeing: Best Practice Guidelines for the Legal Profession.*[31] Authors such as Huggins, Field and Kift have written extensively on curriculum development to support the development of TLO 6,[32] so comments here are confined to learning from the *Vitality for Life and Law* programme.

The most difficult aspect of the *Vitality for Life and Law* programme to implement in the law curriculum will be the MBSR practices. This is primarily due to resourcing issues. First, incorporating MBSR practice into the curriculum requires special knowledge, skills and attitudes which may not be commonly found amongst law school staff. Second, although the time required for regular MBSR practices need not be extensive, incorporating these into existing face-to-face classes will meet resistance from staff and also likely students in the perception that they are reducing time to address the substantive law required in a law degree to meet the requirements of the 'Priestley 11'.[33] Third, MBSR practices in a large group environment, although feasible, are potentially less effective due to additional distractions brought by a large group in relatively small surrounds in the typical classroom. Although there are a multitude of ways that MBSR practices can be implemented in everyday life, students need a structured introduction to the practices and regular guided sessions in order to begin to feel the benefit of regular, habitual practice and to make it a part of their daily lives. An eight-week programme of MBSR has been shown to have demonstrable beneficial impacts on brain and immune function,[34] and to alter intrinsic functional connectivity in ways that may reflect a more consistent attentional focus, enhanced sensory processing and reflective awareness of sensory experience.[35] Based on experience with *Vitality for Life and Law*, such a programme would be best delivered on a weekly basis over a minimum of eight weeks, targeted at students in their second or third semester of law study. This could be in the form of a stand-alone subject worth a small number of credit points and with a one-hour seminar-based class each week, or could be added to the curriculum of an existing suitable subject. The resourcing issues identified above would need to be overcome to make this a reality.

One of the other benefits of a seminar-based face-to-face programme is social connectedness, identified by Kelk[36] as being important for addressing the distress felt by law students and legal practitioners. The opportunity to share experiences, perceptions and feelings with others can reduce stress by identifying that others have similar issues; facilitate reflection in a group setting as well as self-reflection; and de-stigmatize mental health issues. This requires a safe, supportive, non-competitive environment; so it is critical that facilitators are able to create and, where necessary enforce, such a space. Not all students will be amenable to such intimate sharing of personal feelings; hence the need for skilled facilitators. The importance of social connectedness has been seen in focus group studies of mature-age students in law at UOW, where mature-age students reported that social isolation – particularly when the majority of the Bachelor of Laws peers are students straight from the Higher School Certificate (HSC) – is a key factor impacting on their transition to studying law. Other pressures include:[37]

- time pressures – especially balancing family/carer commitments, work and study;
- financial pressures – balancing work and study financially and in terms of time;
- academic expectations – differences from other areas of study; expectations in terms of marks; learning how to handle legal problem solving based questions and assignments; and
- internal fears and pressures – 'nerves', especially if there has been a big gap in study or lack of previous university experience.

This study may shed further light on pressures faced by law students generally, with implications for both mature-age students commencing law studies and law students direct from secondary/high school.

Reconceiving Vitality for Life and Law: The Way Forward

With the need to integrate measures to combat mental distress in law students in the curriculum empirically well established, it is worthwhile then considering how law schools can effectively provide ongoing monitoring, and encourage self-monitoring, of students. Individual, face-to-face meetings, although absolutely necessary and appropriate in some cases, are not an efficient model from the perspective of law schools, due to the resource-intensive requirements of such a model, or our time-poor students. With law students identifying active barriers to help-seeking behaviour,[38] mechanisms to assist students to self-identify problems at an early stage and to provide strategies for effective self-help are necessary. As with MBSR practices, over a period of time the ability to self-monitor and take appropriate steps to address problems or to change problem behaviour is something that can be learned, particularly if appropriate tools are provided. The need for a mechanism that is time efficient from the point of view of a law school and its students – and that can help students self-reflect on their lives and progress in their studies while also providing appropriate, timely advice on options to address the issues identified – is at the heart of the revised *Vitality for Life and Law* programme.

Utilizing a unique software system developed by WujiTech,[39] the new *Vitality for Life and Law* programme is based on an interactive survey system conducted online, where students are led through a series of questions designed to help them identify how they are feeling at the present time and where problems are occurring, and to get them to appropriate assistance. While very different in content, structure and format of delivery to the previous programme, this new programme has several advantages. First, it is available to students at any time of the day or night and throughout the academic semester.[40] Second, the ability to layer questions to drill down into the reasons for particular behaviours means that students are more likely to be able to identify and address causes of poor performance or lack of progress in their studies. The top layer of questions ask students about how they are feeling generally and about their studies; how their attendance at and participation in class is going; and how they feel about their learning, including after receiving feedback on assessments. Second and third layer questions, provided seamlessly in response to the options selected by students to the top layer questions, prompt students to reflect more deeply on why they responded the way they did to particular questions and to identify what may help them get back on track. The system then sends them an email with a summary of their responses and information on how they might try to turn identified problems around, or where they can find additional opportunities for development of skills or hints from current practitioners, graduates or later year students. Finally, the system is capable of being tailored to suit other disciplines beyond law and other life situations in addition to a tertiary study environment, such as the workplace. This makes the tool potentially attractive to law firms and other employers in addition to tertiary institutions, particularly in light of the recently released *TJMF Psychological Well-Being: Best Practice Guidelines for the Legal Profession.*[41]

Assuming that self-management strategies are learned in the prescribed curriculum,[42] the revised *Vitality for Life and Law* programme encourages ongoing self-reflection and facilitated self-management in relation to problems and problem behaviours. While it is lacking the elements of social connectedness and face-to-face facilitated training in MBSR techniques present in the original programme, the revised programme is capable of reaching a much wider audience and providing referral points to social and well-being activities and services. These include social, cultural and sporting groups, as well as individual and group counselling, well-being and learning development services, offered at the school or faculty level or through central university services. Access to MBSR activities is provided through links to online activities and programmes, or through referral to facilitated MBSR groups.

With repeated use of the *Vitality for Life and Law* survey tool, students will learn how to self-identify potential areas of concern and implement strategies to assist them in bouncing back more quickly and effectively, as well as to be pro-active in managing their studies. Integrating key indicators of potential student attrition with well-being in the survey means that the tool fulfils a dual purpose of enabling the university to provide a self-diagnostic tool and an automatic referral service for students to existing university support services, as well as well-being advice. Such a tool means that all students can have access at any point in time to surveys designed to increase self-awareness and facilitate help-seeking behaviour. The system has an ability to enable students to register a crisis situation via an option to send a direct email for immediate assistance, which gives rise to a duty of care situation; so implementation of such an alert system requires the ability to respond and resource such a situation effectively.[43] While triggers of such a response are likely to be relatively rare, it is necessary for law schools and universities that seek to meet the needs of students across all years and all stages of their studies via such a programme to understand that there is an added burden of quick and appropriate response to a crisis situation. Given that a failure to implement a well-being strategy potentially puts student mental health as well as success and attrition rates of law schools at risk of decline, it may be that the burden of appropriate response to a crisis situation is one worth bearing. From the students' perspective, the programme is empowering in that they control when and how often they complete the survey, with reminders of its availability going to their email inbox; and in that they have ready access to tailored advice that they can act upon as they choose, all without having to see anyone unless they want to do so.[44] It is anticipated that the programme will assist students to develop resilience and self-management skills. The survey tool familiarizes students with the process of self-reflection through guided questions that assist them in identifying symptoms of problems with well-being as well as potential causes. By also providing advice and access to resources on realistic achievable ways to get back on top of their lives and studies, the programme is designed to encourage students to feel more empowered to implement self-help strategies and to access appropriate outside help when needed.

Conclusion

Piloting the *Vitality for Life and Law* well-being programme for law students has been a challenging but exciting experience. It has demonstrated the value of life-skills, particularly self-management, in enabling law students to not just survive their law studies, but to thrive. These life-skills must be incorporated into the curriculum in order to ensure that all students have the opportunity to learn and develop these skills, and to expose them to the benefit of stress-management techniques such as MBSR. Alongside curriculum development, other mechanisms to provide ongoing monitoring and support of students in their studies should be explored. The new, online *Vitality for Life and Law* programme provides a potential model for such support, as well as providing further opportunities for continued research into the well-being issues faced by law students and the legal profession.

Notes

* Judith Marychurch is the Assistant Dean – Teaching and Learning at Melbourne Law School. E: judith.marychurch@unimelb.edu.au.

1 Norm Kelk et al, *Courting the Blues: Attitudes Towards Depression in Australian Law Students and Legal Practitioners* (Brain and Mind Research Institute, 2009), 43.

2 An academic with responsibility for student matters including provision of academic advice, course planning and course progression.

3 Sub-Dean from June 2008 and Associate Dean: Teaching and Learning from late 2009 to end 2013. Mental health issues were more common and more complex than other health issues students came forward to seek advice and assistance with.

4 Kelk et al, above n1, 43.

5 Holly Kneebone of the Breathing Space <http://www.hollykneebone.com.au>. The author would like to express her sincere thanks to Holly for her work on the pilot for *Vitality for Life and Law* and for conducting the 'train the trainer' programme to enable its subsequent delivery.

6 Michael Devitt, accredited specialist in property law. The author would like to thank Mike for his unwavering support of *Vitality* and for the work he has done in promoting well-being issues amongst law students, graduates and practitioners.

7 Norm Kelk, Proposals for work with law schools, attachment via email 23 October 2009.

8 See Rachael Field, 'Promoting Law Student Well-being through the Curriculum' <http://www.olt.gov.au/resource-promoting-law-student-well-being-through-curriculum>.

9 Judith Marychurch, *Vitality for Life and Law: A Preventative Stress Management Program Fostering Development of Effective Coping Strategies and Building Resilience*, large ESDF grant 2010, in the amount of $25,000. The University of Wollongong's ESDF scheme is an internal teaching and learning innovation funding scheme.

10 The Academic Services Division includes learning development staff, librarians, specialist staff in curriculum development and design, and disability liaison officers. Staff from counselling services also attended.

11 The central tenets of the *Vitality for Life and Law* programme as advertised to students included: learning how to support and sustain optimal performance; understanding stress and developing reflective learning skills; strengthening emotional intelligence; and building a supportive environment with other students. The programme was featured in panel presentation at the Tristan Jepson Memorial Foundation Annual Lecture on 2 September 2010, following a presentation from guest speaker Professor Patrick McGorry, 2010 Australian of the Year. See Tristan Jepson Memorial Foundation, Video: 2010 Tristan Jepson Memorial Foundation Annual Lecture <http://www.tjmf.org.au/2010/08/2010-tristan-jepson-memorial-foundation-annual-lecture>.

12 Wellbeing at UOW now has its own identity and some excellent resources; see <http://www.uow.edu.au/student/wellbeing/index.html>.

13 See Kelk et al, above n1, 3; also Wendy Larcombe et al, 'Does an Improved Experience of Law School Protect Students against Depression, Anxiety and Stress? An Empirical Study of Wellbeing and the Law School Experience of LLB and JD Students' (2013) 35 *Sydney Law Review* 407 at 408, referring to Molly Townes O'Brien, Stephen Tang and Kath Hall, 'Changing Our Thinking: Empirical Thinking on Law Student Wellbeing, Thinking Styles and the Law Curriculum' (2011) 21 *Legal Education Review* 149; Anthony Lester, Lloyd England and Natalia Antolak-Saper, 'Health and Wellbeing in the First Year: The Law School Experience' (2011) 36 *Alternative Law Journal* 47; G Andrew H Benjamin et al, 'The Role of Legal Education in Producing Psychological

Distress among Law Students and Lawyers' (1986) 11 *American Bar Foundation Research Journal* 225; Kennon M Sheldon and Lawrence S Krieger, 'Understanding the Negative Effects of Legal Education on Law Students: A Longitudinal Test of Self-Determination Theory' (2007) 33(6) *Personality and Social Psychology Bulletin* 883.

14 See Rachael Field and Sally Kift, 'Addressing the High Level of Psychological Distress in Law Students through Intentional Assessment and Feedback Design in the First Year Curriculum (2010) 1 *International Journal of the First Year in Higher Education* 65.

15 Rumer Godden, *A House with Four Rooms* (William Morrow, 1989). See also Gretchen Rubin, *The Happiness Project* (HarperCollins, 2009).

16 Jon Kabat-Zinn, *Full Catastrophe Living: Using the Wisdom of Your Body and Mind to Face Stress, Pain, and Illness* (Delta Trade Paperbacks, 1991).

17 University of Massachusetts, Center for Mindfulness in Medicine, Health Care, and Society, Stress Reduction programme <http://www.umassmed.edu/Content.aspx?id=41252>.

18 Kabat-Zinn, above n16, 27–9.

19 Ibid. 75–93.

20 Center for Mindfulness in Medicine, Health Care, and Society, above n17.

21 This exercise was used by the author as part of a presentation on *Vitality for Life and Law* to demonstrate mindfulness practice at the Law Associate Deans Network meeting of 29 November 2011 held at Bond University.

22 One student reported that they had adapted the mindful eating (raisin) exercise to use a mint they had with them while waiting in the foyer of a law firm to be called in for a clerkship interview, and went into the interview feeling centred and focused.

23 The Zen passport was an initiative of Susan Boyd, marketing officer in the Faculty of Law at the time. The author would like to acknowledge and express her thanks to Susan for her wonderful efforts in promoting *Vitality for Life and Law* and liaising with students.

24 Three students attended all sessions, and the remainder missed typically between one and three sessions.

25 All student comments included here were provided voluntarily by students and are used with their permission.

26 Sleep Health Foundation, Good Sleep Habits <http://www.sleephealthfoundation.org.au/information-home/187-good-sleep-habits.html>; Australian Centre for Education in Sleep <http://www.sleepeducation.net.au/sleep%20facts.php>.

27 Better Health Channel <http://www.betterhealth.vic.gov.au/bhcv2/bhcarticles.nsf/pages/Sleep_deprivation>.

28 Kelk et al, above n1, 43.

29 Sally Kift, Mark Israel and Rachael Field, *Learning and Teaching Academic Standards Project: Bachelor of Laws Learning & Teaching Academic Standards Statement December 2010*, Australian Learning and Teaching Council (December 2010) <http://www.altc.edu.au/system/files/altc_standards_LAW_110211.pdf>. On implementation of TLO 6: Self-Management, see Judith Marychurch, *Good Practice Guide: Threshold Learning Outcome 6: Self-Management* (2011) <http://www.tjmf.org.au/wp-content/uploads/2011/10/Marychurch_Good_Practice_Guide_TLO6.pdf>. For an assessment rubric for self-management in the LLB, see Judith Marychurch, Graduate Capabilities Assessment Rubric for Self-Management Standards in the Bachelor of Laws <http://ro.uow.edu.au/cgi/viewcontent.cgi?article=1162&context=lawpapers>.

30 Council of Australian Law Deans, *Promoting Law Student Well-Being Good Practice Guidelines for Law Schools* (March 2013) <http://www.utas.edu.au/__data/assets/pdf_file/0005/422969/Promoting-Law-Student-Well-Being-Good-Practice-Guidelines-for-Law-Schools1.pdf>.

31 Tristan Jepson Memorial Foundation, *TJMF Psychological Wellbeing: Best Practice Guidelines for the Legal Profession* (May 2014) <http://www.tjmf.org.au/raise-the-standard>.

32 See, for example, Rachael Field and Sally Kift, 'Addressing the High Levels of Psychological Distress in Law Students through Intentional Assessment and Feedback Design in the First Year Law Curriculum' (2010) 1(1) *International Journal of the First Year in Higher Education* 65; Anna Huggins, 'The Threshold Learning Outcome on Self-Management for the Bachelor of Laws Degree: A Proposed Focus for Teaching Strategies in the First Year Law Curriculum' (2011) 2(2) *International Journal of the First Year in Higher Education* 23.

33 This can be countered via the necessary focus on abilities and skills needed to demonstrate achievement of the Threshold Learning Outcomes for a Bachelor of Laws or Juris Doctor degree, which reflect the requirements of the Australian Qualifications Framework. However, law schools vary in the extent and method of delivery of the skills of professional practice. It is anticipated that this will be an area of development as law schools address the Council of Australian Law Deans *CALD Standards for Australian Law Schools*; see <http://www.cald.asn.au/docs/CALD%20-%20standards%20project%20-%20final%20-%20adopted%2017%20November%202009.pdf> as well as institutional curriculum reviews and continuing professional accreditation requirements. The 'Priestley 11' refers to the subject areas that candidates for admission to practise as legal practitioners in Australia must successfully complete, namely: administrative law, civil procedure, company law, constitutional law, contracts, criminal law and procedure, equity (including trusts), ethics and professional responsibility, evidence, property and torts.

34 Richard J Davidson et al, 'Alterations in Brain and Immune Function Produced by Mindfulness Meditation' (2003) 65 *Psychosomatic Medicine* 564, 570.

35 Lisa A Kilpatrick et al, 'Impact of Mindfulness-Based Stress Reduction Training on Intrinsic Brain Connectivity' (2011) 56(1) *NeuroImage* 290.

36 Kelk, above n7.

37 Focus groups were conducted during 2012, with follow-up quantitative analysis in 2013. Results of this study are currently being prepared for publication. The study has implications for transition and support of mature-age students and for well-being issues.

38 Kelk et al., above n1, 40 and 42.

39 The author has been working with founder of WujiTech, Francesco Garri Garripoli, and also Elizabeth Denley, to make this initiative a reality; and she would like to express her sincere thanks to them for their assistance, patience and wisdom. WujiTech delivers social and management software for tracking and measuring cognitive response and emotional well-being. By providing new capabilities for understanding an individual's state of mind, it enables innovative approaches to market research, wellness programmes and education: see <http://www.wujitech.com>.

40 As is Helen Stallman's Learning Thermometer – see <https://www.learningthermometer.com.au> – which is also designed to assist students in reflecting on their learning and identify strategies to support their learning, and to help staff develop their teaching and subjects to better support student learning.

41 Tristan Jepson Memorial Foundation, above n29.

42 See Rachael Field, James Duffy and Anna Huggins, *Lawyering and Positive Professional Identities* (LexisNexis Butterworths, 2014).

43 See also Jane Foster et al, 'An SMS a Day Keeps Attrition at Bay: Preliminary Findings from an Intervention Using SMS with First Year Students from a Regional Australian University', International First Year in Higher Education Conference, 7–10

July 2013, Te Papa Tongarewa, Museum of New Zealand, Wellington <http://fyhe.com.au/past_papers/papers13/7A.pdf>.

44 The advice generated contains referral points for in-person contact with academic advisers and other student support staff, such as learning developers, student support advisers and counsellors.

7 Resilience and Wellbeing Programmes

The Practical Legal Training Experience

*Judy Bourke and Maxine Evers**

Research concerning the need for resilience education and wellbeing programmes for law students and lawyers is well established. The impact for law schools in responding to this need has meant, in part, a move away from entrenched teaching methods. Traditionally, legal education focused on disciplinary knowledge. In more recent times, the development of skills – and, most recently – the introduction of resilience and wellbeing training followed.

Legal education leading to admission to practise law includes a final component of practical legal training (PLT).[1] Although the duration of PLT is significantly shorter than academic study,[2] the role of PLT is an important one. Here students build on their legal knowledge, skills and values to transition from student to practitioner. This chapter discusses the role of PLT in legal education, with reference to wellbeing programmes developed by two PLT providers.[3]

Practical Legal Training (PLT) Programmes

PLT programmes provide a nexus between substantive law and its application in practice.[4] Substantive law courses consist of undergraduate[5] and postgraduate[6] programmes. Law degrees include mandated knowledge areas (the subject names vary according to law schools) that are referred to as the Priestley 11.[7] PLT provides the second component to legal education leading to admission, and is often referred to as the Priestley 12.[8] Unlike the doctrinal theoretical focus of academic legal education, PLT is practice-based and outcomes-focused.[9]

In 1973, PLT was established in New South Wales by the College of Law. Since then, the College has established programmes in other Australian States and New Zealand. In 1996, the University of Technology (UTS) was the first Sydney-based university to establish a PLT programme. PLT is currently delivered by private providers, by universities –(either as a stand-alone or integrated programme) or by partnerships – for example, the Law Society of South Australia and the University of Adelaide.

PLT programmes are based on Competency Standards, or 'Competencies', as they are referred to. In 2002, the Law Admissions Consultative Committee (LACC) and the Australasian Professional Legal Education Committee (APLEC),[10] building on earlier work, introduced Competencies as the PLT requirement in the 2002

Admission Rules.[11] The Committees' objective was to draft minimum standards to embed training in several skills,[12] practice areas[13] and values[14] relevant to an entry-level lawyer in general legal practice.

PLT Competencies: Initial Recognition of Personal and Professional Skills

PLT addresses features of practice relevant for many newly admitted lawyers, including supervision by a senior practitioner; management of clients' and employer's expectations; and development of a professional reputation. Entry-level lawyers also face challenges such as achieving a work/life balance; identifying and resolving ethical issues; and satisfying their post-law school expectations about the legal practice. Wellbeing is a significant factor in these features and challenges. Tang and Ferguson highlight the fact that if PLT graduates enter the profession with psychological ill-health, this has an impact on the profession as a body of practitioners, as well as the individual lawyer.[15]

The 2002 Competencies in *Values* and *Skills* recognized, to an extent, the demanding and adversarial practice environment.[16] The *Values* requirement of 'Ethics and Professional Responsibility' states that 'an entry-level lawyer should act ethically and demonstrate professional responsibility and professional courtesy in all dealings with clients, the courts, the community and other lawyers'. Under the element of 'Reflecting on Wider Issues' entry-level lawyers should be able to 'demonstrate an awareness that mismanagement of living and work practices can impair the lawyer's skills, productivity, health and family life'.[17] The *Skills* required in 'Work Management and Business Skills' are described thus:

> An entry-level lawyer should be able to manage workload, work habits, and work practices in a way that ensures that clients' matters are dealt with in a timely and cost-effective manner.[18]

Since 2000, there has been significant debate in the legal education sector about the structure, content and delivery of courses, including the role of skills training in education.

The Academic Programme and Recognition of Skills

The 2002 Competencies introduced a focus on skills that, at the time of drafting, was largely absent from the academic course. Skills development as a necessary and valuable component of legal education was recognized in the 2007 Carnegie Report from the United States, *Educating Lawyers: Preparation for the Profession of Law*.[19] In Australia, the inclusion of skills in legal education was driven by the Australian Learning and Teaching Council (ALTC)'s project on *Learning and Teaching Academic Standards* for undergraduate law.[20] In 2010, Threshold Learning Outcomes (TLOs) were developed by Professors Sally Kift and Mark Israel and Associate Professor Rachael Field. The focus of the six TLOs[21] was to articulate what graduates were expected 'to know, understand and be able to do as a result of their learning'.[22] Assessment in a practical context, articulated in the TLOs, is similar to the competency-based assessment undertaken in PLT.

In particular, the Self-Management TLO recognizes the 'interface' between the academic law course, PLT and Continuing Legal Education (CLE), with life-long learning and ongoing professional development 'as a key aspect of legal professional competence and performance'.[23] Drawing on the University of Sydney Brain and Mind Institute's *Courting the Blues* report[24] in identifying the high number of law students and lawyers who had experienced depression and anxiety, Self-Management also highlights the importance of 'personal awareness and coping skills'.[25] This TLO was a significant influence in the addition of resilience, wellbeing and self-management to the new Competencies drafted in 2012 discussed later in the chapter.

Background to Resilience@law and the Catalyst for Change

The 2006 inaugural lecture of the Tristan Jepson Memorial Foundation (TJMF) was an important event for the law profession in Australia.[26] The Foundation was set up in memory of Tristan Jepson, a young lawyer who suffered from depression and took his own life. The annual lectures were created to provide a forum for the legal community to discuss the issues faced by the profession regarding depression and anxiety.

In 2006 the prevailing view from North American research was that law students and members of the profession exhibited higher levels of psychological distress and depression than community members of a similar age and sex.[27]

Feedback from a workshop for law academics at the University of New South Wales (UNSW) challenged the North American research referred to by Mamta Gautam with the claim that it was not relevant to the Australian situation. The TJMF approached the Brain and Mind Research Institute (BMRI) to conduct evidence-based research to show how prevalent the problem was in Australia. The results of the first reported study of its kind in Australia revealed:[28]

> [H]igh levels of psychological distress and risk of depression in the law students and practicing lawyers who participated, when compared with Australian community norms and other tertiary groups. . . .
>
> [A]ttitudes and behaviours which imply a general reluctance to seek help for mental health issues [including] negative attitudes and stigmatizing views towards mental illness. . . .

The findings suggested that educational and professional organizations should institute changes to increase awareness of mental health issues in the workplace and in educational settings.[29] Following the study, there was recognition within the profession and evidence from Australian research of the problem and of the need for change. One initiative from the BMRI report involved five large national law firms which formed a Depression and Anxiety Working Group (DAWG) to address the growing incidence of depression and anxiety among lawyers.[30]

The inaugural TJMF lecture and subsequent annual lectures galvanized some College lecturers to ask an important question: If the College is training law graduates in preparation for legal practice then is it incumbent upon the College to include training on good mental health and mental health literacy?[31]

In 2009 the College invited a range of stakeholders and other interested parties from the legal, medical and social science professions to a meeting.[32] The meeting's purpose was to consider the training needs of the College's PLT students; and the role of the College in relation to lawyers' mental health, and to seek ideas on the content, form and delivery of such a component. There was support and encouragement for the view that law students be provided with mental health training, and that the College's PLT programme was an appropriate vehicle for this training. College lecturers also used the APLEC annual conferences as a forum to raise awareness of the problem, generate discussion and present their developing ideas as to the best way forward.

In 2009, the College was invited to join DAWG and be involved in the final design and production of a short film on mental health in the profession in Australia, entitled Resilience@law.[33] The film records the stories of real lawyers struggling with common mental illness through law school and into careers which have, in some case cases, reached partnership in national firms. In 2010 the College agreed to design and implement a component on lawyers' mental health in the PLT programme which would also incorporate the short film. This component would be a compulsory part of the programme and would be rolled out nationally in 2011.

Resilience and Wellbeing for Lawyers in the College Programme

PLT training is undertaken at a pivotal point in a law graduate's life, preparing for admission with all the associated benefits, responsibilities and challenges the role will bring. It is therefore appropriate to address the issues around the 'emerging evidence that law students are particularly prone to depressive illness and that depression is widespread within the legal profession'.[34] Lecturers advocating for the inclusion of a new mental health component in the programme took the view that it should be compulsory so all students would benefit and not be required to self-select for attendance.

It was also essential that any new component align with the Competencies.[35] As discussed earlier, the Competencies include standards for Ethics and Professional Responsibility and Work Management and Business Skills. The inclusion of a new mental health component was viewed as consistent with these standards. As any mental health component was regarded as 'new ground', the College decided to collaborate with a professional mental health educator on its design and implementation.[36] The design considerations were many and varied:

- What format would be used?
- What content would be included?
- How would the content be supported?
- Who would deliver the training?

- Would the training be assessable?
- What would it be called?

As the subject matter was mental health and self-care, there was a strong view that it should be taught face to face in a small group of up to 20 students. A non-threatening and supportive environment was important; and, therefore, it was decided that attendance and satisfactory participation by a student would be sufficient for a pass grade.

The objectives of the workshop were aligned with those of TJMF and included awareness and education, removing the stigma which surrounds mental illness, self-care strategies, support and resources for mental health concerns.

The content of the workshop, which is timetabled for 2.5 hours, is set out in a student workbook and is divided into several areas, including:

- introduction and context
- resilience – preparing for challenge, responding to challenge, understanding stress
- when resilience is not enough – responding to mental illness
- what does mental illness and recovery look like at work?
- the short film – Resilience@law
- depression, anxiety and substance misuse – what it might look like
- how to talk about mental health concerns
- getting help for a mental health concern.

At the outset, lecturers acknowledge that students may have prior experience of mental health problems in themselves, family, friends or colleagues – and that no personal information need be disclosed in the workshop. Lecturers give a normalizing message to students that they should be prepared to have a conversation about a mental health concern at some time, given the significant incidence of mental health problems in the community and the even greater incidence in the profession. Lecturers acknowledge there are concerns about workplace environments, which can be stressful due to long working hours, billing practices and a lack of autonomy. These factors are however outside the control of educational institutions.

In order to gain a greater understanding about mental health generally some lecturers completed a Mental Health First Aid (MHFA) course.[37] This course was designed so that mental health training could be delivered by (trained) non-health professionals to non-health professionals. The aim was to make it a broad-based course which could reach significant numbers of the community while still maintaining appropriate mental health standards. The way that MHFA training was delivered meant that it was possible for lecturers to be trained appropriately to deliver mental health information to students from a non-health background.

It was decided that lecturers who deliver the workshop must first complete an MHFA course, a one-day in-house training programme and observe a workshop delivered by an experienced lecturer.

College lecturers are drawn from the practising profession, and they do not, with a few exceptions, have prior qualifications in psychology or mental health.

Expressions of interest in teaching the workshop were called for, and consideration was given to the attributes of lecturers and their demonstrated levels of interest and enthusiasm.

The workshop was named *Resilience and Wellbeing for Lawyers* as this echoed students' comments expressed in focus groups that the material be introduced through positive concepts such as resilience and wellbeing rather than terms such as depression and anxiety.[38]

The College ran two pilot workshops in Sydney prior to the rollout.[39] The 40 participating students completed an evaluation at the end of the workshop. The evaluations were overwhelmingly positive as to the relevance of the material and the presentation of the workshop.[40] These results were most encouraging, and so the College proceeded to incorporate the workshop into the programme.

Initially the workshop was placed at the end of an onsite week and close to assessments; however it was evident that students were more focused on the assessments and less on the workshop. A timetable change resulted in the workshop being held early in the week, and lecturers reported that students appeared to be more receptive to the workshop. Timing of the workshop was regarded as an important factor.

Evaluations of the Resilience and Wellbeing for Lawyers' Workshop

The workshop was rolled out in the College PLT offerings in Sydney, Melbourne, Brisbane, Perth, Canberra and London in 2011; and evaluations were sought from students during the first six months of the roll-out.[41] A total of 1,216 students completed an evaluation of the workshop, with a response rate of nearly 77%.[42] In 2011 women comprised 60% and men 40% of College students, and 80% of students were 30 years of age or under. It is not possible to assert that the students evaluating the workshop were of a similar gender balance and age group to those in the broader student population for that year and, therefore, the lack of information on the gender and age of the respondents was a limitation of the evaluation's method.

First, students were asked to score the relevance of the materials presented in the workshop (Figure 7.1).[43] Over 83% of students indicated a score of 6 or higher on a scale of 0–10, where 0 indicated 'Not at all relevant' and 10 indicated 'Very relevant'.

Second, students were asked to score the presentation of the workshop (Figure 7.2). Over 93% of students indicated a score of 6 or higher on a scale of 0–10, where 0 indicated 'Not well presented' and 10 indicated 'Very well presented'.

From these responses, the vast majority of students perceived the workshop to be not only relevant but also well presented.

Students were also asked specific questions such as what aspects they liked or didn't like about the workshop, and what else they would like included in the workshop.

Finally, students were asked about their overall response to the workshop (Figure 7.3). The responses were grouped into positive, neutral and negative: 82% of comments were positive, 15% were neutral and 3% were negative. The overall response was extremely encouraging.

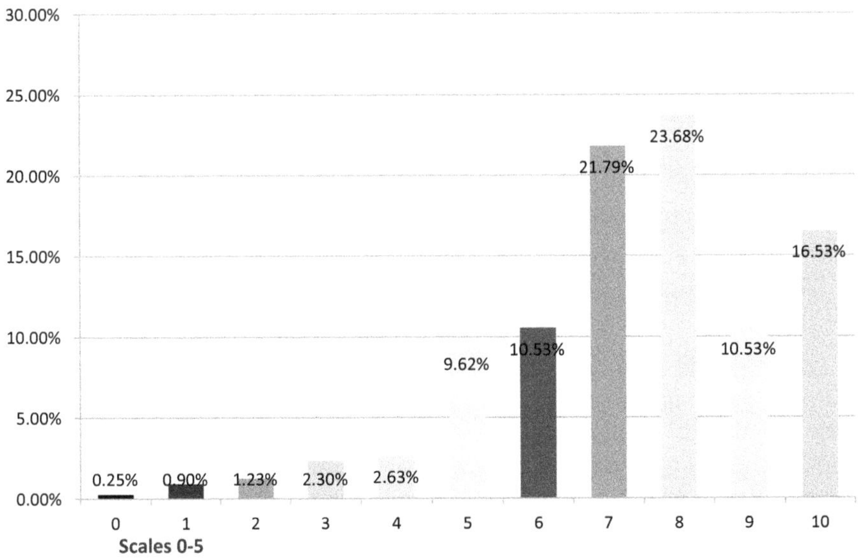

Figure 7.1 Student perceptions of the relevance of the workshop

Source: Responses to the Resilience and Wellbeing for Lawyers evaluation as at October 2011, College of Law.

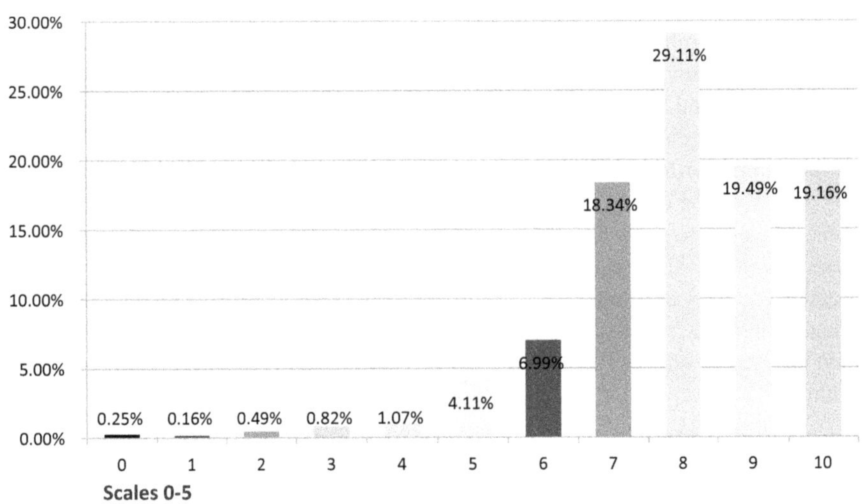

Figure 7.2 Student perceptions of how well the workshop was presented

Source: Responses to the Resilience and Wellbeing for Lawyers evaluation as at October 2011, College of Law.

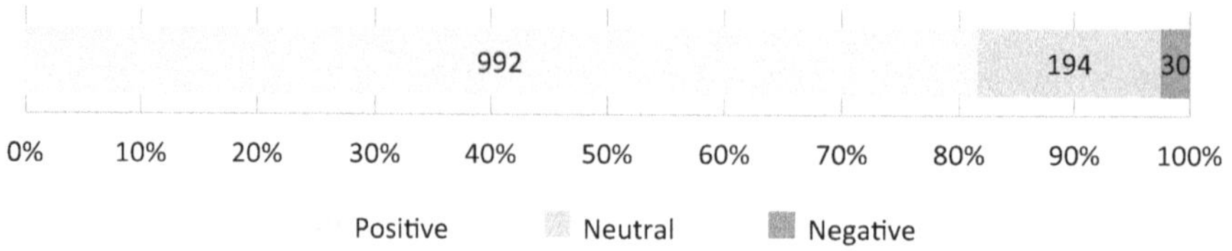

Figure 7.3 Students' overall response to the workshop

Source: Responses to the Resilience and Wellbeing for Lawyers evaluation as at October 2011, College of Law.

Lecturers had previously expressed concerns and fears about delivering material that might make them feel uncomfortable, being asked questions they may not feel competent to answer or needing to respond to difficult situations. The in-house training provided to lecturers addressed many of these issues. There is ongoing discussion among lecturers involved in delivery of the workshop, both informally and formally, about how it is working; whether any improvements can be made; and how lecturers can deal with difficult situations if they arise.

To assist lecturers during the workshop, there is a designated 'go to' person appointed when the workshop is delivered.[44] This person is available to provide support for a student who might become distressed, and allows the lecturer to continue with the workshop. The College has an arrangement with a group of psychologists so that a student who may be in crisis or suffering from a mental health problem can access help if they choose.[45]

The workshop has been taught for four years and the materials are reviewed for continuous improvement. Although the workshop provides an opportunity for discussion on mental health issues and enables students to acquire a better understanding of how they can build coping strategies and stay well, it may be timely for the College to do further research. There is certainly anecdotal evidence from students that they realized during or after the workshop that they may be suffering from a mental health problem, and the workshop was the trigger for them to seek help. Research might involve a longitudinal study which would follow graduates into practice and evaluate students at specific intervals, tracking the extent to which they retained and benefited from the information and training received. The results could then be used to inform changes to the workshop in terms of content, delivery and timing.

Research Into PLT Students and the Expansion of Resilience Programmes

The majority of research into law student wellbeing has focused on academic study. Until the recent research[46] into ANU's Professional Legal Education (PLE) programme, discussed later in this chapter, Australian research into the wellbeing of PLT students has been less prevalent for several reasons, including:

- the short duration of the course, usually 15–18 weeks on a full-time basis;
- the delivery of part of the course in off-campus mode, where there is seen to be less opportunity to interact with students;
- student circumstances, with most students working – some full time and some in a legal workplace;[47] and
- the lack of encouragement for academic research and writing in PLT.[48]

Prior to the awareness of mental health concerns, the importance of work/life balance referred to earlier in this chapter was a recognized factor in the profession. A 2008 survey of PLT graduates from UTS highlighted graduates' concern for their wellbeing.[49] Although the survey's objectives did not directly address health and wellbeing, respondents identified factors relating to work/life balance. Graduates were asked the following open-ended questions:

- What could PLT have done better to prepare you for practice?
- If you were entering practice now, what skills and/or knowledge would be most valuable?
- What would have better prepared you to deal with ethical dilemmas and/or challenges arising in practice?

Responses referred to needing more training and resources in personal wellbeing, including mental health; emotional intelligence; maintaining a work/life balance; self and priority management, including career goals; and how to deal with unethical behaviour and bullying.[50] These responses of mental health, work/life balance and bullying corresponded with recognized issues in the profession.[51]

As a result of the survey and the College's model resilience programme (*Resilience and Wellbeing for Lawyers*) presented at the 2010 APLEC Conference, a resilience unit was introduced in the PLT programme at UTS in the 2011 autumn semester. The unit's objectives were to:

- raise awareness among students of wellbeing as a significant element of legal practice; and
- provide a low risk environment for discussion by students around health and resilience.

The resilience unit, taught in the subject Legal and Professional Skills, was introduced as a one-week topic within a 12-week semester. Each topic is accompanied by a two-hour workshop attended by 20 students and a clinical practitioner. The unit was developed in consultation with the mental health educator who assisted the College. The initial workshop conducted by the educator was designed to provide practitioners with the resources and skills to facilitate the unit. Practitioners were asked to reflect on the unit design. Similar to the experience of the College, some practitioners expressed concern about teaching a topic that focused on health and emotional wellbeing with the possibility of exposing personal challenges for students and staff. This concern was addressed through a second workshop with the educator. In this workshop, a 'low-risk' approach to the unit was finalized. It was agreed that case studies were the most effective teaching method,[52] allowing for a general discussion of challenges and options for students and lawyers in dealing with issues. It was also agreed that practitioners should be encouraged to undertake the Mental Health First Aid Training provided by the University in order to resource them in recognizing the relevant signs of poor mental health and in the language and approaches relevant to mental health. The unit continues to be a component of the UTS programme and is reviewed and updated each semester. A recent addition to the unit is the work of the TJMF in the release of *Psychological Wellbeing: Best Practice Guidelines for the Legal Profession.*[53]

The workshop design is to establish a sustainable framework that enables students and the practitioner to feel safe and supported. The introductory groundwork is based on a general discussion of resilience and mental wellbeing. The aim of the discussion is to facilitate practitioner and student confidence in order to move to a tailored conversation around the issues and options for individuals and the profession in responding to mental health concerns and in building resilience for lawyers. Prior to the case studies, information and resources available to the profession and the community are given to students and discussed as a group. The aim of sharing information and resources is to establish an environment for collaboration. In order to facilitate a non-threatening environment for collaboration, the case studies are discussed from the role of students working through the issues and options with a friend or colleague facing personal and professional challenges in a legal workplace, including sole practitioner firms, mid-tier practices and large law firms.

The unit concludes with a reminder to students of the University's medical and counselling service. The important role of health professionals in working with PLT providers includes expertise in establishing a rigorous teaching programme and in providing counselling services to students and staff. Familiarity with accessing professional services provided by law societies, bar associations and some workplaces is also a valuable resource for students to have when entering practice.

Student feedback, through the University's end of semester student feedback surveys,[54] has been positive, and affirming of the unit's objectives:

> I think the most lasting thing for me was the three things to learn to say as a young lawyer: 1. No; 2. I don't know; 3. I need help.
>
> To be told by an experienced lawyer that it is OK to ask for help after reaching a huge stumbling block was a breath of fresh air.

> Approaches to dealing with difficult situations in work environments where I have had limited experience, especially the corporate environment. For example, how to deal with stressful situations where deadlines are not just mere assignments, but they actually matter to the firm.
>
> There should be the chance for students to sit in a group and think about the issues and how they can deal with them. There should also be an 'action plan' formulated in class which consolidates each of the ideas into one map as a guide to both recognizing and helping with mental health issues and resilience more generally.

Feedback is essential for reviewing and redrafting the unit; for example, the above suggestions prompted practitioners to be more explicit about the necessity for lawyers, as individuals, to create their own plan for developing or maintaining resilience and for responding, if relevant, to health concerns.

As noted by Tang and Ferguson, the delivery of PLT by a range of providers results in less consistency in pedagogy than the academic law courses offered by Australian universities.[55] The role of PLT as the vehicle in which final stage students or graduates transition from substantiative law study to legal practice depends on consistency in its objectives and outcomes. This collective task requires the sector to work with students to be work-ready and resilient entry-level lawyers with a sound sense of self-efficacy and a developing professional identity.[56] Indeed, Tang and Ferguson believe that it is 'incumbent' on PLT providers to 'ensure that they are not the cause of further distress'.[57]

In contrast to the research into students undertaking academic study, the study of the ANU Professional Legal Education (PLE) programme's students is particularly significant in that the preliminary results of a cohort of students in 2012 found that students' psychological distress was not dissimilar to the general population.[58] The research noted that the changes to the PLE programme's curriculum – including simulated practice, some online facilitation and mentors working with students' values – empowered students to transfer their experiential learning into their actual workplace.[59] The changes also had the effect of assisting students to respond to the uncertainties of practice.[60]

The research, particularly in Australia, concerning the mental health of lawyers and law students, together with the work of the TJMF, was a significant guiding factor in the resilience, wellbeing and self-management Competencies drafted in 2012 discussed later in the chapter.

2012 PLT Competencies: Recognition of Resilience, Wellbeing and Self-Management

In 2012 there was a review of the Competency Standards and a discussion paper was prepared by the APLEC Executive.[61] The discussion paper considered whether the Skills and Values categories should be changed.[62] The Executive, informed by the resilience literature, drafted Proposition 5:

> That the *Standards* should require PLT providers to make students aware of resources available to them relating to cultivating wellness, developing resilience and dealing with depression.

Of the 30 responses to the paper received from stakeholders throughout Australia there were 14 specific responses to Proposition 5.[63] These included responses from a number of large and medium law firms, law societies, PLT providers, government legal organizations and community legal centre associations. Commentary on the responses to Proposition 5 included:

> There was overall agreement and support for this proposition. Raising students' awareness of the resources available to them was considered to be the minimum requirement for PLT providers. The requirement simply to make students aware was viewed as insufficient and 'tokenistic'.[64]

Proposition 5 was accepted and included in the Uniform Admission Rules 2014. The Rules include the new Competency Standards and retain the same title which has now become familiar.[65] Schedule 2, the Competency Standards for Entry-Level Lawyers, took effect nationally on 1 January 2015. Under Schedule 2, a new requirement was added to Resilience and Well-being,[66] namely all PLT providers and Supervised Workplace Training providers are required to:

- make applicants aware of the importance of resilience and the demands of practice and the benefits of developing and maintaining personal wellbeing in their personal and professional lives;
- provide applicants with appropriate information and access to resources to help develop resilience and maintain wellbeing and information to identify and deal with mental health difficulties.

Item 5.16 in the Competency Standards – 'Work Management and Business Skills' – was amended and a new element of 'Self-Management' added which requires an entry-level lawyer to demonstrate an ability to manage work and personal issues consistent with principles of resilience and wellbeing.[67]

The above changes are welcomed as a positive step in legal education and professional training. It is vital that PLT providers give appropriate consideration as to how these changes are implemented.

Conclusion

This chapter has discussed the role of professional training in the education of law graduates and the contribution of this sector to the increasing awareness and response to concerns about lawyers' mental health. The value of the resilience, wellbeing and self-management competencies in PLT programmes is not simply the recognition that resources and information about personal health are essential components of professional training. More importantly, it is an acknowledgement that the well-designed work of law schools in establishing a pedagogical framework for self-management, reflective practice and the development of a healthy professional identity must be embedded in the realities of professional practice.

PLT providers are strategically placed to make a meaningful contribution to the wellbeing of the law student body and the profession. Building on the work of law schools, PLT can offer an environment where integrity, self-efficacy and advocacy for safe workplaces underpin the training of new lawyers. PLT, as the transitioning partner with law schools and the profession, must ensure that law students and lawyers do not bear the sole responsibility for their health.

Notes

* Judy Bourke, Senior Lecturer, The College of Law; Maxine Evers, Senior Lecturer, University of Technology, Sydney (UTS).

1 There are several descriptions and variations for practical training. The Law Admissions Consultative Committee (LACC) refers to 'Practical Legal Training' in its Competency Standards, at http://www1.lawcouncil.asn.au/LACC/images/pdfs/LACCCompetencyStandardsforEntryLevelLawyers-Jan2015.pdf.

2 PLT programmes are diverse in their delivery and include face-to-face and online teaching, a blend of both modes and part-time and full-time courses.

3 Other PLT providers have introduced resilience and wellbeing into their programmes. For example, the Australian National University's (ANU) programme is discussed by Stephen Tang and Anneka Ferguson, 'The Possibility of Wellbeing: Preliminary Results from Surveys of Australian Professional Legal Education Students (2014) 14(1) *QUT Law Review* 27.

4 Maxine Evers, Bronwyn Olliffe and Robyn Pettit, 'Looking to the Past to Plan for the Future: A Decade of Practical Legal Training' (2011) 45(1) *Law Teacher* 18, 22.

5 Either a stand-alone or a combined law degree.

6 Juris Doctor (JD).

7 The Priestley 11 knowledge areas were named after Justice Priestley, former New South Wales Court of Appeal judge and chair of the Committee, who determined the compulsory subjects for an Australian law degree. LACC, above n1, 25–33. See also Chapter 6 this volume.

8 LACC, above n1, 2.

9 See Geoffrey Monahan and Bronwyn Olliffe, 'Competency-Based Education and Training for Law Students in Australia' (2001) 3 *UTS Law Review* 181, 187.

10 APLEC was formed in the 1970s and represents the professional legal training courses in Australia and New Zealand.

11 For details of the pre-2000 history of PLT, see Monahan and Olliffe, above n9.

12 Skills consist of Lawyer's Skills, Problem Solving, Work Management and Business Skills and Trust and Office Accounting. See LACC, above n1, 35.

13 Practice areas consist of Civil Litigation Practice, Commercial and Corporate Practice, Property Law Practice; one of Administrative Law Practice or Family Law Practice; and one of Consumer Law Practice, Employment and Industrial Law Practice, Planning and Environmental Law Practice or Wills and Estates Practice. Ibid.

14 Values are covered in Ethics and Professional Responsibility. Ibid.

15 Tang and Ferguson, above n3, 29.
16 See Walter Bennett, *Lawyer's Myth: Reviving Ideals in the Legal Profession* (University of Chicago Press, 2002) and Molly Townes O'Brien, 'Facing Down the Gladiators: Addressing Law School's Hidden Adversarial Curriculum' (2011) 37(1) *Monash University Law Review* 43.
17 LACC, above n1, 17.
18 Ibid.
19 William M Sullivan et al, *Educating Lawyers: Preparation for the Profession of Law* (Jossey-Bass, 2007).
20 Sally Kift, Mark Israel and Rachael Field, *Learning and Teaching Academic Standards Project: Bachelor of Laws Learning and Teaching Academic Standards Statement December 2010*, Australian Learning and Teaching Council. Available at http://www.utas.edu.au/__data/assets/pdf_file/0007/456829/altc_standards_LAW.pdf.
21 The six TLOs are Knowledge, Ethics and Professional Responsibility, Thinking Skills, Research Skills, Communication and Collaboration and Self-Management. Ibid.
22 Ibid. 1.
23 Kift, Israel and Field, above n20, 23.
24 Norm Kelk et al, Courting the Blues: Attitudes towards Depression in Australian Law Students and Lawyers (Brain and Mind Research Institute, 2009). Available at http://www.cald.asn.au/docs/Law%20Report%20Website%20version%204%20May%2009.pdf.
25 Kift, Israel and Field, above n20, 23.
26 TJMF, http://www.tjmf.org.au/.
27 Associate Professor Dr Mamta Gautam MD FRCP (c), a leading Canadian psychiatrist specializing in professional health. TJMF lecture 2006 – 'Towards Managing Mental Wellness in the Legal Profession'.
28 Kelk et al, above n24, viii.
29 Ibid.
30 DAWG included Allens (formerly Allens Arthur Robinson), Ashurst (formerly Blake Dawson), Clayton Utz, Herbert Smith Freehills (formerly Freehills), and King & Wood Mallesons (formerly Mallesons).
31 The College provides practical legal training for law graduates as well as Masters of Law degrees in a number of Australian jurisdictions and Continuing Professional Development for the NSW legal profession.
32 A meeting held at the College on 5 November 2009 was attended by representatives of the NSW Law Society, NSW Bar Association, LawCover, LawCare, TJMF, BMRI, University of Sydney Law School, University of NSW Law School, NSW Young Lawyers and beyondblue, as well as a psychiatrist and a psychologist.
33 http://www.probonoaustralia.com.au/news/2010/03/depression-anxiety-working-group-launch#.
34 Kelk et al, above n24, iii.
35 LACC, above n1.
36 Susan Goldie – former mental health educator and lawyer.
37 https://www.mhfa.com.au/cms/.
38 Three student focus groups were facilitated by College lecturers with Human Resources (HR) professionals representing the DAWG law firms.
39 The first pilot workshop, of 2 hours' duration, was insufficient time to cover the material, and so the second pilot workshop was of 2.5 hours' duration.
40 The evaluations by pilot students were analysed by Bryan Brown, statistician for the College, who found that the responses were 'generally very positive' and that there was a 'broadly consistently positive view of the program, both in qualitative and quantitative measurement': Report on results of Student Evaluation of Resilience@law on 10 November 2010.

41 The student evaluation contained two quantitative questions and four qualitative questions.
42 This relatively high response rate may have been achieved because the evaluations were completed in class at the end of the workshop.
43 In the evaluations the words 'workshop' and 'programme' were sometimes used interchangeably.
44 The 'go to' person is a lecturer who has completed a Mental Health First Aid Course and also teaches the workshop.
45 The College, St Leonards, NSW campus has an arrangement with a group of psychologists located nearby. A similar arrangement is being set up at the other College campuses.
46 Tang and Ferguson, above n3.
47 Ibid., 47.
48 Ibid., 28.
49 Evers, Olliffe and Pettit, above n4.
50 Ibid., 40.
51 Law Societies have developed policies and guidelines in relation to workplace bullying, work/life balance and mental health.
52 Case studies are based on PLT practitioners' own experiences and experiences shared by practising lawyers.
53 TJMF, *Psychological Wellbeing: Best Practice Guidelines for the Legal Profession* (2014), http://www.tjmf.org.au/raise-the-standard/the-guidelines-at-a-glance.
54 Student feedback surveys administered by the University for the subject Legal and Professional Skills in autumn 2011.
55 Tang and Ferguson, above n3, 29.
56 The development of professional identity for a cohort of ANU entry-level lawyers is discussed by Vivien Holmes et al, 'Practising Professionalism: Observations from an Empirical Study of New Australian Lawyers' (2012) 15 *Legal Ethics* 29.
57 Tang and Ferguson, above n3, 29.
58 Ibid., 44.
59 Ibid., 47.
60 The uncertainties of legal practice are discussed by Stephen Tang and Tony Foley, 'The Practice of Law and the Intolerance of Certainty' (2014) 37 *UNSW Law Journal* 1198.
61 Review of the APLEC and LACC Competency Standards for Entry-Level Lawyers (2002) Discussion Paper prepared by the APLEC Executive, June 2012 v 6.
62 Ibid., 11.
63 Review of the APLEC and LACC Competency Standards for Entry-Level Lawyers (2002) Submissions Summary.
64 Ibid., 9.
65 LACC, Uniform Admission Rules. Available at http://www1.lawcouncil.asn.au/LACC/images/pdfs/Uniform_Admission_Rules_2014_-_June2014.pdf.
66 Ibid. The new requirement is 4.7 'Resilience and well-being'.
67 Ibid., 40.

8 Resilient Lawyers

Maximizing Well-Being in Legal Education and Practice

*Colin James**

Introduction

> You are not your body, or your mind
> *Deepak Chopra*

Resilience is used here as the capacity to endure by adapting to adversity. It is essential for everyone who aspires to thrive in the legal profession. However it is not useful to advocate to law students and lawyers that they simply need a 'thick skin' in order to 'bounce back' from stressful experiences. In this chapter I use resilience not as a trait or a practice, but as a personal quality that emerges from a dynamic relationship between the individual and his or her environment.[1] It is dynamic because I use both 'individual' as a constantly changing-with-experience person and 'environment' as the evolving yet wonderful complexity of human life, which includes the cultures of legal education and professional legal practice. Adopting this relationship approach to resilience is to understand it as an ecology, which I deconstruct for analysis into the domains of physical, cognitive, emotional and ethical fields of experience. The more we model, enable and motivate in ourselves, our students and colleagues the development of self-awareness through these domains, the more we will actually 'bounce forward' through challenges with purpose and a sense of acceptance that life in law necessarily involves difficult, even negative experiences that do not need to be a barrier to a good and happy life.

A useful theory for understanding resilience is to see it as a capacity that begins to develop in infancy as we attach to our primary caregiver, and experience everyday stress in moments of frustration, hunger, discomfort and separation. According to the quotidian theory, an individual's resilience derives not from their response to extreme adversity but from the experience of everyday stress regulation beginning in infancy.[2] Adults are more likely to have high physiological resilience if during infancy their mothers were able to recognize, understand and respond promptly to their child's behavioural signals.[3] The primary importance of childhood experiences in determining an adult's base-line capacity for resilience is supported by other studies which confirm that the strongest predictor of low resilience in adults is unresolved childhood trauma.[4]

Complementing this view is a significant body of research on attachment theory.[5] The original theory holds that the quality of attachment, whether secure, ambivalent or avoidant, between a child and their care-giver will significantly influence the person's capacity to relate to others in their adult life.[6] Later iterations of the theory hold that the quality of early attachment influences how a person relates to *themselves* in later life, including their self-concept, self-esteem, self-confidence and self-regulation as well as their communication skills.[7] In fact, attachment theory argues that early influences help shape not only our personality, but also contribute significantly to our life-long capacity for resilient behavioural responses to adverse situations.[8]

Attachment theory provides a useful starting point for understanding the complexities of individual resilience, but it offers no strategies for continued development without resorting to psychotherapy. Overstating the role of attachment in infancy risks implying an unavoidable pathology or fixed personality that does not allow for continued learning, adaptive change or development. Given what we now understand about the plasticity of the brain,[9] and the importance of adopting a growth mindset,[10] the effects of experiences as an infant should not be seen as immutable. Other evidence shows that adaptive opportunities can be generated through understanding resilience as a dynamic relationship involving the person in context, over their whole life.

The following sections examine this context specifically, with relevance to legal professionals who aspire to more than 'mere survival' in challenging circumstances. Concepts of peak performance and flow are not preserved solely for sport or artistic expression, and can be attained by legal professionals working in challenging circumstances who have integrated well with their environmental domains, including their own physical, cognitive, affective and ethical potential. However, just as the relational model of resilience does not see it solely as a personal capacity or trait, the obligation to act on our knowledge extends to institutions such as law schools, law firms and law societies as much as it does to the individual.

The Role of Physical Well-Being in Resilience

Overall physical well-being includes three primary interacting dimensions: sleep, diet and physical fitness. The first step then is to develop an attitude that acknowledges the priority of these domains. In law as in life, developing ideal habits becomes more sustainable if awareness is aligned with best practice and current knowledge. First is the importance of sleep. Many law students and lawyers believe they can function well on little sleep, and it is this fallacy we now address.

Although sleep has an important role in physical and mental performance, as well as in repair and restoration, it is not a passive state. There are at least two processes that manage our sleep: one is 'sleep pressure' which builds up at night and is related to the amount of time we have been awake. The other is the 'circadian clock', which is related to the habitual timing or cycle of when we are asleep and awake.[11] There are also two main types of sleep: REM (rapid eye movement) associated most with dreaming and bodily paralysis; and 'deep' non-REM sleep, which occurs several times each night in approximately 90-minute cycles. A growing body of research supports the synaptic homeostasis hypothesis, which proposes that sleep is the price we pay for brain plasticity.[12] In other words, how well we learn, respond and adapt to experience measured by rates of change and the quality of our neural connections is a function, inter alia, of the amount of sleep we get, specifically the non-REM. Also, it is during this 'slow-wave' sleep that the body actually regenerates tissue and builds bone and muscle, and strengthens the immune system.[13]

Sleep deprivation is widespread in society, and given the propensity of lawyers to overwork, it is likely common among law students and lawyers.[14] Adults need around 8 hours sleep per night and adolescents need about 9 hours.[15] The effects of sleep deprivation include negative impacts on memory, cognitive function, cardio-vascular function, and mood and performance measures,[16] as well as increased risk of cardiovascular disease and type-2 diabetes.[17] Sleep deprivation also interferes with the dreaming function which occurs in REM stages, and increasing evidence links dreaming with the modulation of negative affect.[18] Less controversial are findings that sleep has significant benefits for bodily processes beyond the brain, including reducing cellular stress and enhancing organ-specific molecular functions.[19] Consequently, regardless of how well they rationalize it and present an appearance of normality, people who don't sleep well are likely to be underperforming and compromising their mental and physical potential. Strategies for improving sleep habits are diverse, including avoiding heavy meals and alcohol before sleep; reducing caffeine and other stimulants; ensuring a sleep environment that is dark, quiet, cool and comfortable; and exercising every day.[20]

Alongside sleep hygiene, our eating habits contribute significantly to our personal resilience in responding to significant stresses and everyday challenges that confront us as legal professionals. A 'resilient diet' is one that not only provides sufficient mental and physical energy but also enables adequate response and recovery from trauma, sustaining high-level cognitive performance with sufficient endurance and neurological adaption to ensure we are able to learn from experience. Such a daunting list of functions is achieved by a relatively uncomplicated diet that includes a diversity of foods from all the main groups to ensure intake of sufficient protein, fats, carbohydrates, vitamins, minerals and water. Current research offers little support for the value of dietary supplements for people who have a healthy diet. However there is a growing body of evidence for the dangerous effects of sugar (sucrose and fructose), commonly present in processed foods, and its association with type-2 diabetes and some forms of cancer.[21] There is good empirical evidence supporting the high consumption of vegetables and fruit, and low consumption of fat.[22] While the low-fat diet which was popular for several decades has been exposed as myth,[23] there is consensus about no safe level of 'trans fats', which have been banned in many countries.[24] No empirical evidence yet examines fat and sugar consumption of legal practitioners. There is anecdotal evidence that distressed lawyers compensate with unhealthy diets, in addition to the well-known propensity of lawyers to overindulge in alcohol and other drugs.[25] Individual lawyers need to be aware of what and how they consume, keeping a mindful attitude to quality and sufficiency and a knowledgeable awareness of their needs in the context of their lifestyle.

Physical fitness is the final component in the triad construct of physical well-being, and the research on the benefits of fitness offers good support for anyone wanting to develop their resilience in other areas of life. A sedentary life on the other hand, common among desk-bound lawyers, involves increased risk of cardiovascular disease.[26] A fitness regime would not only avoid hormonal damage but actually lead to improved cognitive performance. Specifically, executive function can be improved measurably in both children and adults through a programme of physical activity alone.[27] Executive function is the umbrella term that refers to how we apply knowledge from past experience to inform present situations, and includes management of working memory, reasoning, problem solving, planning, decision-making and task performance. As lawyers we draw on these capacities regularly in our professional life, as they enable us to cope with complex and challenging situations.

Improved cognitive function will only result from physical fitness if our exercise practice includes aerobic activities and occurs frequently.[28] Studies suggest that occasional exercise would be less beneficial because the neural system will be occupied in facilitating the activity.[29] However, if we can develop a habit of exercise, the likely benefits include not only improved executive function but also enhanced creativity and mental flexibility required for problem solving,[30] as well as a range of mental competencies required for professional and academic performance.[31] Building physical resilience through regular fitness activities incorporated into our lifestyle can establish a foundation for the next step in developing our cognitive resilience.

The Role of Cognitive Well-Being in Resilience

Cognitive resilience refers to how effectively we engage our thinking for the long term, including our use of reflection, analysis, memory, planning and decision-making in responding to problems, failures or difficulties in achieving our goals. It can be developed as an individual capacity and it can be promoted as a strategy of organizations and other complex adaptive systems to enhance resilient behaviours of professionals, management and staff.[32] We tend to associate cognitive performance with rational decision-making; however we often make irrational decisions due to a myriad of biases and justify them later with 'invented' reasons.[33] Overcoming our biases begins with self-awareness, and from there we can learn to improve our cognitive performance as lawyers by practising simple strategies such as manually listing the pros and cons for each option; getting independent advice and confirmation of facts; generating counter-arguments for each option; and adopting an 'objective' or outside perspective.[34] In addition, structured reflection is an under-used but powerful practice in law firms and is linked with the development of cognitive resilience.[35] Law schools however have been using reflection effectively to enhance cognitive performance, to promote well-being and to help develop professional attitude.[36]

Arguably, western cultures have a cognitive bias, leading us to privilege cognitive solutions to problems at the expense of other approaches. Cognitive theories have dominated mental health professions for a number of decades, with the popularity of cognitive behaviour therapy (CBT) as a cheap and effective response to mental health issues, although recent critiques have emerged.[37] An alternative model of acceptance and commitment therapy (ACT), which helps people better align their actions with their thoughts and values, has potential to promote resilient cognitions through an optimistic and growth mindset.[38] There is also growing interest in ways to integrate First Nation perspectives and cultural content into professional training.[39] Research has confirmed the value of enhancing people's cognitive style and increasing the number of positive life events as a strategy for improving resilience against depression.[40]

Over-reliance on cognitive approaches to decisions, without mindfulness, emotional awareness or other moderators, is prone to several weaknesses through biases such as anchoring, overconfidence, self-serving bias, status quo bias and framing bias.[41] Lawyers may be particularly prone to some biases, such as overconfidence, which may be facilitated by competitive workplace environments and client expectations.[42] Various illusions and fallacies may compromise our decisions and judgements, such as the *affect heuristic*, which involves making gut-level decisions based on emotions rather than knowledge or good analysis of a situation.[43] 'Representativeness' is another cognitive bias risk relevant to lawyers, and involves inductively presuming a cause is likely to be similar in size and nature to its effect.[44]

An effective strategy for improving cognitive resilience through minimizing biased cognition is mindfulness, a practice more often associated with its power to moderate anxiety.[45] Mindfulness is the cognitive practice of intentionally paying attention to the present moment, noticing thoughts, feelings, bodily sensations and surrounding environment, without judgement.[46] Often associated with meditation, which is a practice that can enhance mindfulness, mindfulness promotes resilience by mediating our conscious awareness and moderating distractions that take us from thinking about the task at hand. Resilience develops with repeated practice of mindfulness, since we tend to learn from what works and avoid what doesn't work towards achieving desired ends. One of the benefits of mindfulness practice is improved self-awareness, since we are more able to see our own capacities, habits, strengths and weaknesses with less of the hindering biases discussed above. However, since much of our thinking is guided by and integrated with our emotions, our emotional intelligence needs to be examined for its contribution to resilience in the practice of law.

The Role of Emotional Well-Being in Resilience

Emotional intelligence is a construct that can be understood as the combined *ability* to identify emotions; to use emotions to facilitate and influence our thoughts;

to understand emotions in ourselves and others; and to manage the integration of emotions into our thinking.[47] Our emotions can be specific and temporary, while our moods are often longer lasting and less intense. Since both moods and emotions impact our physiology, cognitive processes and behaviour, we can improve our resilience to the extent that we can develop our emotional intelligence.

Our emotional well-being is the most important *type* of resilience because it is emotions that connect our values to our behaviour. It may be counter-intuitive, but for many people how we feel about something informs our attitudes more than what we think. Our emotions drive our decisions about how to act on our knowledge and beliefs, our hopes and fears. In fact, all conscious decisions are made with emotional input, no matter how 'rational' we think we are.[48] The effects of emotion on the decisions we make in work and life can be either good or bad, although the process is complex, so it would help to improve our emotional intelligence in understanding our emotions and managing their effects on our thinking and decision-making habits. Empirical research has found significant correlations between high emotional intelligence and less stress, better general health and well-being, and leadership capacity.[49] Other studies have confirmed the important role that emotional intelligence plays in using adaptive coping strategies and reducing work-related stress.[50]

The broaden-and-build theory of positive emotions relies on an evolutionary view of negative emotions, which narrow attention to cope with a threat, and positive emotions which lead to open-minded appreciation of discovery, new skills and alliances.[51] Significant empirical studies have confirmed associations between flourishing mental health and a higher positivity ratio, which is the proportion of positive emotions to negative emotions over time.[52] The explanation is associated with the construct of ego resilience, which is the capacity of an individual to adapt to changing environments.[53] A controversial finding is that due to the negativity bias, common experiences of negative affect are about three times more powerful than common positive experiences in contributing to overall well-being.[54] We can promote resilient well-being therefore by enabling a positivity ratio greater than three positive experiences for every one negative experience.

Another theory proposes that emotions have two forms: *affect*, which is an automatic and largely unconscious response to stimuli; and *emotion*, which is a conscious, strong, specific and subjective feeling which may include a physical arousal.[55] The evidence is that emotion, as such, often leads to 'bad' decisions, such as those made when we are distraught or euphoric, and that emotional distress actually impairs cognitive function.[56] However, a good decision is often inspired by anticipated emotion, which is how we think we will feel if we take a particular course of action.[57] So again the more self-aware we are, particularly of our emotional propensities, the more likely our cognitive choices will align with our values and guide our behaviour towards outcomes we want to achieve. Resilience develops here through the experience of failures in a growth mindset: as we learn more about ourselves we are better able to anticipate how we will feel if we achieve certain outcomes. If we don't feel that way, contrary to expectations, we can refine our anticipation to more accurately guide the decisions we make in future.

The Role of Ethical Standards in Resilience

Ethical resilience is the capacity of lawyers to endure the challenges and resist the opportunities to act unprofessionally in legal practice. We can develop ethical resilience by engaging both cognitive and emotional capacities in the many challenging decisions of our day-to-day legal practice. Historically in common law jurisdictions the lawyer–client relationship was one of 'extreme partisanship with moral non-accountability'.[58] In recent decades however, legal ethics has become an important focus in legal education, especially following a number of cases of lawyers displaying unethical behaviour at the most senior levels.[59] Legal educators can maximize the development of ethical resilience in their law students by ensuring they are aware of the priority of their professional reputation, and the risks of plagiarism, collusion or other forms of cheating in law school, which can undermine students' self-esteem and developing professional identity.[60] University rules of academic integrity and Solicitors' Rules provide a guide for behaviour and a reference point for difficult cases; however ethical resilience in law involves an attitude beyond rule compliance.[61]

In an important sense, legal practice is applied ethics. Subject to cultural and historical variations, most developed societies have, or at least aspire to, a legal system based on ethical principles of justice, equality, due process and the rule of law. Honesty is crucial for trust, and in legal practice trust is at the heart of the lawyer–client relationship. So despite the well-publicized rare examples to the contrary, most lawyers value honesty as a basis for their professional integrity. If a lawyer is found to have behaved dishonestly, they may well be castigated as having a flawed character. Some researchers suggest authorities tend to prosecute less experienced lawyers for dishonesty, rather than higher ranked lawyers and prestigious firms, and ignore the role that stress can play in dishonest practices.[62] Time-billing, for example, has been criticized for not only driving inefficiency in legal practice but also contributing measurably to poor psychological outcomes for the lawyer.[63]

In many cases dishonesty is not only a product of stress in legal practice, but also an agent that causes significant psychological harm. Subject to personality differences, a dishonest act can impact inwardly through the experience of shame and feelings of guilt.[64] These feelings may be subconscious, but can still impact on the lawyer's mental health status in several ways, including on their performance as a lawyer, relationships with clients and as a team member in a firm.[65] In some cases the dishonesty is institutionalized into the practice, so young lawyers feel they have little choice but to comply with unethical practices, which they then try to rationalize, potentially leading to 'ethical blindness'.[66] Studies have shown that the inner conflict involved in the process of rationalizing unethical behaviour draws heavily on a person's capacity for self-regulation, leading to 'ego depletion' and lowered threshold for subsequent breaches.[67] The more law students and legal practitioners aspire to rigorous ethical standards, resisting contrary expectations and other potential contaminants of their professional identity, the stronger will be their ethical resilience that will help protect their well-being in the future.

Integration

Analysis of the four constructs of resilience – physical, cognitive, emotional and ethical – enables us to reflect on our own habits and identify those likely to protect and develop, or to hinder, our unique professional identity as a lawyer. None of the constructs will sustain alone. They are relational and interconnected, so that each depends on an adequacy in the other three to inform the attitudes and behaviours most likely to ensure we not only endure but are able to thrive as students and practitioners in our areas of law. Through reflection, students can understand how their cognitive performance responds to their capacity to manage their emotions, and monitor their diet, sleeping habits and fitness levels.

Contrary to the adage, the older we get the more we *can* learn 'new tricks' as we develop in self-awareness, practising mindfulness, and relaxing the hindrances and occasionally imprudent aspirations of youth. As young lawyers we can thrive before our dotage if we learn from the experience of others as well as our own, becoming more mindful each day, noticing how we integrate and engage our body, thoughts, emotions and decisions in ways congruent with our values. A personal, virtuous and flourishing legal practice is possible if we relate well to significant others, work colleagues and clients, and most importantly to ourselves.

Notes

* Dr Colin James is a solicitor and a senior lecturer with the ANU. E: Colin.James@anu.edu.au.

1 Richard M. Lerner et al, 'Resilience Across the Life Span' in *Annual Review of Gerontology and Geriatrics* (Springer, 2012) Ch.14.

2 Jennifer A. DiCorcia and Ed Tronick, 'Quotidian resilience: Exploring Mechanisms that Drive Resilience from a Perspective of Everdyay Stress and Coping' (2011) 35 *Neuroscience and Biobehavioral Reviews* 1593.

3 E.M. Leerkes, A.N. Blankson and M. O'Brien, 'Differential Effects of Maternal Sensitivity to Infant Distress and Nondistress on Social-Emotional Functioning' (2009) 80 *Child Development* 762.

4 Daphne Simeon et al, 'Factors Associated with Resilience in Healthy Adults' (2007) 32 *Psychoneuroendocrinology* 114.

5 Nicola Atwool, 'Attachment and Resilience: Implications for Children in Care' (2006) 12(4) *Child Care in Practice* 315.

6 Mary D.S. Ainsworth et al, *Patterns of Attachment: A Psychological Study of the Strange Situation* (Erlbaum, 1978). John Bowlby, *Attachment and Loss* (Hogarth, 1969).

7 J.W. Santrock, *Life-Span Development* (McGraw-Hill, 2008).

8 Daniel J. Siegel, *Mindsight: The New Science of Personal Transformation* (Bantam, 2010).

9 Norman Doidge, *The Brain that Changes Itself: Stories of Personal Triumph from the Frontiers of Brain Science* (Viking, 2007).

10 Carol S. Dweck, *Mindset: The New Psychology of Success* (Ballantine, 2007).

11 Daniel J. Buysse et al, 'Can an Improvement in Sleep Positively Impact on Health?' (2010) 14(6) *Sleep Medicine Reviews* 405.

12 Giulio Tononi and Chiara Cirelli, 'Sleep and the Price of Plasticity: From Synaptic and Cellular Homeostasis to Memory Consolidation and Integration ' (2014) 81(1) *Neuron* 12.

13 Vilma Aho et al, 'Partial Sleep Restriction Activates Immune Response-Related Gene Expression Pathways: Experimental and Epidemiological Studies in Humans' (2013) 8(10) *PLOS ONE* 1.
14 Bronwyn Fryer, 'Sleep Deficit: The Performance Killer. A Conversation with Charles A. Czeisler' (2006) 84(10) *Harvard Business Review* 53.
15 National Sleep Foundation, *The Sleep Disorders* (2014), http://www.sleepfoundation.org/article/how-sleep-works/how-much-sleep-do-we-really-need.
16 There is an enormous amount of research confirming the range of deficits caused by sleep deprivation; for example, Julia Dewald-Kaufmann et al, 'Why Sleep Matters: Differences in Daytime Functioning between Adolesecents with Low and High Chronic Sleep Reduction and Short and Long Sleep Durations' (2013) 13(1a) *Journal of Cognitive and Behavioral Psychotherapies* 171.
17 Aho et al, above n13.
18 Rosalind Cartwright, *The Twenty-Four Hour Mind: The Role of Sleep and Dreaming in Our Emotional Lives* (Oxford University Press, 2010).
19 Ron C. Anafi et al, 'Sleep Is Not Just for the Brain: Transcriptioinal Responses to Sleep in Peripheral Tissues' (2013) 14 *BMC Genomics* 362.
20 Running on Empty: Fatigue and Healthcare Professionals: The Consequences of Inadequate Sleep. NIOSH: Workplace Safety and Health, 2 August 2012.
21 Q. Yang et al, 'Added Sugar Intake and Cardiovascular Diseases Mortality among US Adults' (2014), published online 3 February 2014. doi:10.1001/jamainternmed.2013.13563 *JAMA Internal Medicine*. Maki Inoue-Choi et al, 'Sugar-Sweetened Beverage Intake and the Risk of Type I and Type II Endometrial Cancer among Postmenopausal Women' (2013) 22(12) *Cancer Epidemiology, Biomarkers and Prevention* 2383.
22 David G. Blanchflower, Andrew J. Oswald and Sarah Stewart-Brown, 'Is Psychological Well-Being Linked to the Consumption of Fruit and Vegetables' (2013) 114 *Social Indicators Research* 785.
23 Peter Lloyd, 'Scientific Links between Cholesterol and Heart Disease Called into Question' (2013) *ABC PM*, 24 October 2013, http://www.abc.net.au/pm/content/2013/s3876403.htm. Walter Willett and Amy Myrdal Miller, 'Ask the Experts: Healthy Fats' (2012) *Harvard School of Public Health*, http://www.hsph.harvard.edu/nutritionsource/2012/06/21/ask-the-expert-healthy-fats/.
24 Rachel H. Foster and Nick Wilson, 'Review of the Evidence for the Potential Impact and Feasibility of Substituting Saturated Fat in the New Zealand Diet' (2013) 37(4) *Australian and New Zealand Journal of Public Health* 329. Heart Foundation of Australia (2009), 'Q&A: Dietary Fats, Dietary Cholesterol and Heart Health', http://www.heartfoundation.org.au/SiteCollectionDocuments/Dietary-Fats-Dietary-Cholesterol-and-Heart-Health.pdf.
25 The Legal Profession Assistance Conference, *Drug and Alcohol Addiction and Abuse in the Legal Profession*, http://www.benchmarkinstitute.org/t_by_t/mcle/sa.pdf [accessed 9 March 2014].
26 Samia Mora et al, 'Physical Activity and Reduced Risk of Cardiovascular Events: Potential Meidating Mechanisms' (2007) 116 *Circulation* 2110. Rebecca Seguin et al, 'Sedentary Behavior and Mortality in Older Women: The Women's Health Initiative' (204) 46(2) *American Journal of Preventative Medicine* 122.
27 Jennifer L. Etnier and Yu-Kai Chang, 'The Effect of Physical Activity on Executive Function: A Brief Commentary on Definitions, Measurement Issues, and the Current State of the LIterature' (2009) 31(4) *Journal of Sport and Exercise Psychology* 469.
28 Patrick J. Smith et al, 'Aerobic Exercise and Neurocognitive Performance: A Meta-Analytic Review of Randomized Controlled Trials' (2010) 72 *Psychosomatic Medicine* 239.

29 Lorenza S. Colzato et al, 'The Impact of Physical Exercise on Convergent and Divergent Thinking' (2013) 7(924) *Frontiers in Human Neuroscience* 1.
30 D.M. Blanchette et al, 'Aerobic Exercise and Creative Potential: Immediate and Residual Effects' (2005) 17 *Creative Research Journal* 257.
31 J.N. Booth et al, 'Associations between Objectively Measured Physical Activity and Academic Attainment in Adolescents from a UK Cohort' (2014) 48 *British Journal of Sports Medicine* 265. Terry McMorris et al, 'Acute, Intermediate Intensity Exercise, and Speed and Accuracy in Working Memory Tasks: A Meta-Analytical Comparison of Effects' (2011) 102 *Physiology and Behavior* 421.
32 Fabrizio Bracco, Rita Gianatti and Luciano Pisano, 'Cognitive Resilience in Emergency Room Operations: A Theoretical Framework' in Eric Rigaud, Erik Hollnagel and François Pieri (eds), *Proceedings of the Third Resilience Engineering Symposium* (Mines Paris, 2008).
33 Dan Ariely, *The Upside of Irrationality: The Unexected Benefits of Defying Logic at Work and Home* (Harper, 2010).
34 Jennifer K. Robbennolt and Jean R. Sternlight, *Psychology for Lawyers: Understanding the Human Factors in Negotiation, Litigation, and Decision Making* (American Bar Association, 2012), Ch.4.
35 Silvia Jordan, Martin Messner and Albrecht Becker, 'Reflection and Mindfulness in Organizations: Rationales and Possibilities for Integration' (2009) 40(4) *Management Learning* 465.
36 Kelley Burton and Judith McNamara, 'Assessing Reflection Skills in Law Using Criterion-Referenced Assessment' (2009) 19(1–2) *Legal Education Review* 171. Mary Anne Kenny, Irene Styles and Archie Zariski, 'Looking at You Looking at Me Looking at You: Learning through Reflection in a Law School Clinic' (2004) 11(1) *E Law: Murdoch University Electronic Journal of Law*.
37 David Pilgrim, 'The Hegemony of Cognitive-Behaviour Therapy in Modern Mental Health Care' (2011) 20(2) *Health Sociology Review* 120. A. Grant, 'A Critique of the Representation of Human Suffering in the Cognitive Behavioural Therapy Literature with Implications for Mental Health Nursing Practice' (2011) 18 *Journal of Psychiatric and Mental Health Nursing* 35.
38 M. Kotze and R. Kleynhans, 'Psychological Resource Capacities (Hope, Optimism and Resilience) as Predictors of Burnout in First-Year Students at a Higher Education Institution' (2013) 19(2) *International Journal of Learning in Higher Education* 31. See also Dweck, above n10 and K.L. Polk and B. Schoendorff (eds), *The ACT Matrix: A New Approach to Building Psychological Flexibility Across Settings and Populations* (New Harbinger, 2014).
39 Pat Dudgeon et al (2014), 'Curricular Approaches to Increasing Cultural Competence and Indigenous Participation in Psychology Education and Training', Project of the Office of Teaching and Learning, Australian Government, http://www.olt.gov.au/project-curricular-approaches-increasing-cultural-competence-and-indigenous-participation-psychology.
40 Gerald J. Haeffel and Ivan Vargas, 'Resilience to Depressive Symptoms: The Buffering Effects of Enhancing Cognitive Style and Positive Life Events' (2011) 42 *Journal of Behavior Therapy and Experimental Psychiatry* 13.
41 Andrea Caputo, 'A Literature Review of Cognitve Biases in Negotiation Processes' (2012) 24(4) *International Journal of Conflict Management Learning* 374.
42 Spencer Rand, 'Teaching Law Students to Practice Social Justice: An Interdisciplinary Search for Help through Social Work's Empowerment Approach' (2006) 13 *Clinical Law Review* 1.

43 Melissa L. Finucane et al, 'The Affect Heuristic in Judgments of Risks and Benefits' (2000) 13(1) *Journal of Behavioral Decision Making* 1. See other references in Robbennolt and Sternlight, above n34, Chs.4 and 5.
44 Thomas Gilovich and Kenneth Savitsky, 'Like Goes with Like: The Role of Representativeness in Erroneous and Pseudo-Scientific Beliefs' in Thomas Gillovich, Dale Griffin and Daniel Kahneman (eds), *Heuristics and Biases: The Psychology of Intuitive Judgment* (Cambridge University Press, 2002).
45 Yi-Yuan Tang, Michael I. Posner and Mary K. Rothbart, 'Meditation Improves Self-Regulation over the Life Span' (2013) 1307(1) *Annals of New York Academy of Science* 104.
46 Jon Kabat-Zinn, *Wherever You Go, There You Are* (Hyperion, 1994).
47 David R. Caruso and Peter Salovey, *The Emotionally Intelligent Manager: How to Develop and Use the Four Key Emotional Skills of Leadership* (Jossey-Bass, 2004).
48 Antonio R. Damasio, *Descartes' Error: Emotion, Reason and the Human Brain* (Putnam, 1996). Jonah Lehrer, *The Decisive Moment: How the Brain Makes Up Its Mind* (Text Publishing, 2009).
49 Mark Slaski and Susan Cartwright, 'Emotional Intelligence Training and Its Implications for Stress, Health and Performance' (2003) 19 *Stress and Health* 233. I. Gardner and C. Stough, 'Examining the Relationship between Leadership and Emotional Intelligence in Senior Level Managers' (2002) 23 *Leadership and Organizational Development Journal* 68.
50 B. Montes-Berges and J.M. Augusto, 'Exploring the Relationship between Perceived Emotional Intelligence, Coping, Social Support and Mental Health in Nursing Students' (2007) 14(2) *Journal of Psychiatric and Mental Health Nursing* 163.
51 M.A. Cohn et al, 'Happiness Unpacked: Positive Emotions Increase Life Satisfaction by Building Resilience' (2009) 9 *Emotion* 361.
52 B.L. Fredrickson, 'Positive Emotions Broaden and Build' in E. Ashby Plant and P.G. Devine (eds), *Advances on Experimental Social Psychology* (Academic Press, 2013) vol 47, 1.
53 Tera D. Letzringa, Jack Blockb and David C. Fundera, 'Ego-Control and Ego-Resiliency: Generalization of Self-Report Scales Based on Personality Descriptions from Acquaintances, Clinicians, and the Self' (2005) 39(4) *Journal of Research in Personality* 395.
54 Fredrickson has accepted the critique of the original proposition by her and Losada that the threshold positivity ratio is 3:1. B. L. Fredrickson, 'Updated Thinking on Positivity Ratios' (2013) 68(9) *American Psychologist* 814.
55 R.F. Baumeister et al, 'How Emotion Shapes Behavior: Feedback, Anticipation, and Reflection, Rather than Direct Causation' (2007) 11(2) *Personality and Social Psychology Review* 167.
56 Hockey G. Robert J. et al, 'Effects of Negative Mood States on Risk in Everyday Decision Making' (2000) 14(6) *Cognition and Emotion* 823.
57 Kathleen D. Vohs, Roy F. Baumeister and George Loewenstein, *Do Emotions Help or Hurt Decision Making? A Hedgefoxian Perspective* (Russell Sage Foundation, 2007) Ch.1.
58 David Luban, 'Twenty Theses on Adversarial Ethics' in Helen Stacy and Michael Lavarch (eds), *Beyond the Adversarial System* (Federation Press, 1999).
59 Deborah L. Rhode and Paul D. Paton, 'Lawyers, Ethics and Enron' (2002–2003) 8(1) *Stanford Journal of Law, Business and Finance* 625. Edwina Dunn, 'James Hardie: No Soul to Be Damned and No Body to Be Kicked' (2005) 27(2) *Sydney Law Review* 339. William Birnbauer, 'I Helped Tobacco Firm Destroy Documents: Lawyer', *The Age*, 26 September 2004 http://www.theage.com.au/articles/2004/09/25/1095961911370.html.

60 Colin James and Saadia Mahmud, 'Promoting Academic Integrity in Legal Education: "Unanswered Questions" on Disclosure' (2014) 10(2) *International Journal for Educational Integrity* 3.
61 See Rachael Field, 'National Wellness for Law Forum: Keynote Address', Australian National University, Canberra, 5 February 2015.
62 Kath Hall, 'Tough Love: Professional Regulation of Lawyer Dishonesty' (2013) ANU College of Law Research Paper No. 13–11, http://ssrn.com/abstract=2307325.
63 Adele J. Bergin and Nerina L. Jimmieson, 'Australian Lawyer Well-Being: Workplace Demands, Resources and the Impact of Time-Billing Targets' (2013) *Psychiatry, Psychology and Law* 427. 'CJ Makes Case against Time Sheets' *Lawyers Weekly*, 17 February 2011, http://www.lawyersweekly.com.au/news/cj-makes-case-against-timesheets.
64 Sangmoon Kim, Ryan Thibodeau and Randall S. Jorgensen, 'Shame, Guilt, and Depressive Symptoms: A Meta-Analytic Review' (2011) 137(1) *Psychological Bulletin* 68.
65 Trevor Bentley, 'Shame in Organisations' (2011) 16(1) *Gestalt Review* 88.
66 Andrew M. Perlman, 'Unethical Obedience by Subordinate Attorneys: Lessons From Social Psychology' (2007) 36 *Hofstra Law Review* 451. Kath Hall and Vivien Holmes, 'The Power of Rationalization to Influence Lawyers' Descisions to Act Unethically' (2008) 11(2) *Legal Ethics* 137.
67 Roy F. Baumeister and Kathleen D. Vohs, 'Self-Regulation, Ego Depletion and Motivation' (2007) 1(1) *Social and Personality Psychology Compass* 115.

9 Using Peer Assisted Learning to Develop Resilient and Resourceful Learners

Penelope Watson[*]

Introduction

It has been said that 'achieving happiness is one of the major goals, if not the ultimate goal, of human beings'.[1] Some even regard it as an 'inalienable right'.[2] Yet for many a sense of wellbeing is elusive. Australian youth (18–24 years old) have a higher prevalence of mental illness than any other age group,[3] and statistics are burgeoning.[4] Suicide is the leading cause of death in Australia for people aged 15–24.[5] The figures on psychological distress for university students generally are high[6] as compared with their age-matched peers, with law students faring worst of all. Ground-breaking Australian work by the Brain and Mind Research Institute (BMRI) confirmed international findings concerning the alarming levels of distress in law.[7] The study's findings demonstrated a 'much higher level than expected of reported psychological distress and risk of depression on all measures used'.[8] Since the release of the BMRI Report, other significant studies have been completed, and a solid body of Australian literature is emerging[9] in addition to the copious USA literature.[10] Much of the literature attempts to isolate causes, proposing reforms to legal education on multiple levels. These things are beyond the scope of the present chapter, which focuses on the learner and suggests one means to promote development of characteristics that enhance wellbeing.

This chapter discusses how a student-run peer-assisted learning programme, designed in accordance with principles from positive psychology and self-determination theory, can help students help themselves to become more resilient and resourceful learners and individuals. The following part briefly outlines the concepts of wellbeing or happiness, resilience and resourcefulness, and how they interact and apply to individuals in education. The next part then discusses the LAWPAL model of peer-assisted learning. Peer tutoring is well known to improve academic outcomes,[11] and the LAWPAL model is specifically designed to challenge and extend students by actively fostering autonomy, resourcefulness, competence and relatedness. It encourages and enables learners to acquire and embed transferable and sustainable attitudes, skills and values. The focus on student leadership, cognitive and discipline-specific skills, collaboration and self-help and academic enhancement avoids the criticisms raised by disaffected commentators concerning 'therapy' in education.[12]

Wellbeing and Happiness

Wellbeing or 'happiness' is subjective, and notoriously difficult to define,[13] but is usually conceptualized as consisting of a cognitive component (individual's overall satisfaction with life judged against their own criteria such as experiences, accomplishments, relationships) and an affective component (presence of positive affect/absence of negative affect).[14] It is a dynamic concept that includes social, psychological and subjective dimensions as well as health-related behaviours. Self-reports of wellbeing have consistently been shown to correspond with other measures, such as witness reports and magnetic resonance imaging.[15] 'Happiness' can be understood as hedonistic (maximizing pleasure, minimizing pain) or eudaimonic (identifying one's virtues, cultivating them and living in accordance with them).[16] Eudaimonia emphasizes the challenges that individuals encounter as they strive to function to their full potential and realize their unique talents.[17] It is in this latter Aristotelian sense of achieving fulfilment that happiness is used here.[18] This concept of happiness corresponds closely to Seligman's positive psychology notion of wellbeing as 'flourishing', the elements of which are positive emotion, engagement, relationships, meaning and accomplishment.[19] This aligns with early work by Ryff,[20] who identified aspects that constitute wellbeing as: autonomy; environmental mastery; positive relationships with others; purpose in life; and realization of potential and self-acceptance. More recent research has placed different emphases on what wellbeing is: ability to fulfil goals,[21] happiness[22] and life satisfaction.[23] Sheldon et al. argue that wellbeing requires social connectedness, a sense of competence, autonomy and self-esteem.[24]

The BMRI study measured 'reported psychological distress and risk of depression'. It is at this point (distress and risk) that universities and law schools need to take action, addressing distress early before it becomes clinically significant.[25] Many researchers agree that wellbeing is partly determined by genetics (50 per cent) and external factors such as demographics and circumstances (10 per cent), but a surprisingly large component is malleable. Around 40 per cent of the variance in an individual's happiness or wellbeing is governed by intentional activity,[26] and this provides the window for action.

Lykken posits individual 'happiness set points' which are the stable and highly heritable (genetic) component of wellbeing.[27] He argues that over time individuals tend to return to their original happiness levels or set points, but that this can be altered by their decisions and environmental fit. He suggests that 'the true formula is not Nature *versus* Nurture, but rather, Nature *via* Nurture'.[28] Lykken argues that human strengths such as self-awareness, future orientation, aesthetic appreciation and curiosity interact with genes to influence the experiences and environments that are sought, and these experiences can push individuals beyond their set points.

Lyubomirsky et al. consider that intentional behaviour, cognitive or volitional activity, potentially offers the best route for achieving sustainable increases in wellbeing. Intentional activity is understood as discrete actions or practices that individuals must choose to engage in and that require some effort to enact.[29] Their subsequent meta-analysis of positive psychology interventions identified clear evidence that wellbeing can be intentionally increased,[30] and methods for self-generating positive emotions including skills, can be learned.[31] Positive emotions are both predictive and causative of desirable short- and long-term mental and physical health outcomes, successful coping, closer relationships[32] and other benefits such as increased productivity and better workplace performance.[33]

Resilience and Resourcefulness

Mental health is a very complex field in which law teachers are not experts, so we need to proceed with caution. The approach adopted in the design and implementation of the LAWPAL programme discussed here is that of beneficence, which is understood broadly in ethical theory to include effectively all forms of action intended to benefit or promote the good of other persons. As a principle or rule it encapsulates a normative statement of a moral obligation to act for the others' benefit, helping them to further their important and legitimate interests, often by preventing or removing possible harms.[34]

As law teachers we can use our educational expertise, guided by an understanding of the literature and evidence on wellbeing, to design and implement programmes that provide opportunities for students to acquire and practise strategies and attitudes that strengthen and sustain them as learners and as individuals. There is clearly an ethical and moral imperative,[35] but it goes beyond this. In view of what we know about the hazards legal education poses to wellbeing and the foreseeability of harm for a significant number, there is certainly a legal duty to warn; and it is strongly arguable that the 'reasonable law school' would be expected to interpret its duty more expansively and actively. The LAWPAL programme is one such active intervention, providing opportunities for students to engage in activities that both improve academic outcomes and promote resilience and resourcefulness. The concepts of resilience and resourcefulness are explored briefly below.

Resilience

The concept of resilience originated in the natural and physical sciences. The term is used to describe the relationship between the system under observation and externally induced disruption, stress, disturbance or crisis.[36] In physics, mathematics or engineering it refers to the capacity of a system or material to recover its shape following displacement or disturbance,[37] whereas in ecology it emphasizes the capacity of an ecosystem to absorb shocks and maintain functioning,[38] transforming itself through the emergence of new structures and behaviours. The psychology literature is extensive, and includes educational applications focusing on resilience in individuals,[39] defined as 'the capacity for successful adaptation and functioning despite high risk, stress or trauma'.[40] This definition aligns with the ecological concept, which is most suited to educational contexts because of its emphasis on transformation and adaptation, or learning. The antonym is vulnerability.[41]

Drawing on a wide-ranging review of the psychobiological mechanisms of resilience, Haglund et al. identified six key attitudinal and behavioural factors that can help maintain wellbeing under stress.[42] They are: positive attitude (optimism, sense of humour); active coping; cognitive flexibility; moral compass; physical exercise;

and social support and role models. These are consistent with the six dimensions identified in Ryff's Wellbeing scale, discussed above.[43] Similarly, Lykken[44] focuses on the role of mental energy; active versus passive leisure activities; meaningful goals; intrinsically motivating activities; and the importance of avidly seeking experiences that challenge personal resources and cause an individual to be fully absorbed and devoid of self-consciousness, as a means of enhancing wellbeing.

Resourcefulness

Standard dictionary definitions of resourceful/resourcefulness – such as 'able to act effectively or imaginatively, especially in difficult situations'[45] or 'able to deal well with new or difficult situations and to find solutions to problems'[46] – capture much of the essence of resilience, conceptualizing it as a psychological quality or property of the individual that underpins action. This chapter argues that the concept can be usefully extended in the educational setting to capture ideas such as the following:

> Resourceful, knowledgeable learners . . . bring considerable prior knowledge to new learning; they activate that prior knowledge to identify, organize, prioritize and assimilate new information. They recognize the tools and resources that would help them find, structure, and remember new information; and they know how to transform new information into meaningful and useable knowledge.[47]

A resourceful learner is conceptualized here as one who makes use of strategies, knowledge and a positive or independent (autonomous) attitude. Such a learner is able to identify when resources are needed; knows where and how to locate them; and possesses sufficient sense of self-efficacy to employ proactive rather than reactive strategies, accessing resources as needed. Yeager and Dweck demonstrate the importance of the psychology underlying students' responses, principally their implicit or unconsciously held beliefs.[48] Their studies on students' beliefs about intelligence demonstrated that believing intelligence is fixed compromises resilience in academic settings, even among high-achieving students. Interventions that may otherwise be sound will not be effective unless students possess what Dweck refers to as 'growth mind-sets' (as opposed to fixed mindsets) – that is, a belief that change and improvement are possible, and outcomes are not predetermined.[49] The following discussion of LAWPAL demonstrates how the programme's design and implementation promote resilience and resourcefulness in both learners and (student) leaders.

A Student-Designed and Student-Led Peer-Assisted Learning Programme

This section briefly describes a student/staff collaboration to design and implement a structured peer tutoring and informal mentoring programme, called LAWPAL at Macquarie University, Sydney.[50] The programme began as a student response to the BMRI wellbeing research. A modest two-week trial in one subject progressed into a larger funded pilot study across three units for a semester.[51] The programme expanded rapidly, encompassing almost the entire core curriculum, from first to fifth years. Over 4,000 voluntary student visits (attendances) were recorded in the first 12 months. In just under two years, it had become the largest PAL programme in any Australian law school, operating 22 sessions (classes) per week over 10 weeks, every semester. The initial team of six student leaders and two student coordinators had expanded to over 60 students – all volunteers recruited for their academic excellence, outstanding interpersonal skills and demonstrated evidence of altruism. The programme was unique in its emphasis on shared leadership, responsibility and decision-making; that is, total partnership, between one staff member and a team of students.[52]

Particular care was taken in the design to address wellbeing as an aspect of human sustainability and social capital.[53] LAWPAL was built on the three pillars of autonomy, competence and relatedness, identified in self-determination theory (SDT) as innate psychological needs necessary for growth, integrity and wellbeing.[54] Sheldon and Krieger's study of American law students confirms the positive outcomes stemming from increased autonomy.[55] Leaders and learners (session attendees) are actively encouraged and guided to become more autonomous in their learning, more competent at learning and more adept at applying their skills to particular content. Learning activities are deliberately designed to be fun, engaging and purposeful – all qualities known to enhance life satisfaction.[56] Teamwork is a key feature for PAL leaders, who work in pairs in the classroom, co-operate in a larger subject team and form part of the entire LAWPAL community. In so doing they support one another and model, as well as develop, the skills of collaboration and co-operation (relatedness). Group work is just as important for learners, who typically interact in sessions in guided group activities such as problem solving, quizzes, interviews, games or role plays. The introduction of Threshold Learning Outcomes (TLOs) for law schools has emphasized the importance and centrality of attributes such as these.

'Instruction' in the didactic sense is forbidden and leaders are rigorously trained as facilitators, using an instruction manual written and developed by the student team. Learners are guided towards finding answers themselves and/or in collaboration with others, enhancing resourcefulness and self-reliance. Leaders exhibit high levels of autonomy – for example, as regards session planning and development of learning activities – and are encouraged and expected to be creative and innovative. They are supported throughout by regular peer and staff observation and feedback; rigorous training that includes learning theory and detailed pedagogy along with practical instruction and practice; guided reflection; class discussion and sharing of problems; and celebration of successes. The programme enables students in leadership roles to achieve a cultural shift in self-concept, to embrace a vision of themselves as teachers and learners concurrently. It also enables those in learner roles to visualize themselves transitioning into future leaders, since some students will occupy the roles of leader (of an early year subject) and learner (in a later year subject) concurrently. This promotes Dweck's 'growth mind-set', discussed above. All leadership, policy making and day-to-day activities of the programme, with two exceptions, were staff–student collaborations.[57] This shared leadership and collaboration are amongst the programme's greatest strengths.

Over time, learning communities or communities of practice evolved,[58] defined as 'groups of people who share a concern or a passion for something they do and learn how to do it better as they interact regularly'.[59] This enabled students to experience the attendant social and affective benefits that drive engagement and learning. Developing connectedness around shared learning, values and practices meant students became more engaged with one another, with the discipline and with the law school. Anecdotal evidence confirms the affective and community-building gains, and external evaluation of the two year pilot was extremely positive.[60] The success indicators for evaluation are shown in Table 9.1.

The external evaluator's assessment of the programme included the following comments:

> The Law PAL program's design and conduct attests to the effectiveness of the collaboration between staff and students, the shared commitment to the multiple mutual benefits, and the clarity of roles and responsibilities. This uniquely shared stewardship is a great strength of the program – students are empowered by the obligations entrusted to them, the academic oversight of

Table 9.1 Extrapolated success indicators for evaluating the LAWPAL programme[61]

Indicator	Category
Programme participants are representative of target group diversity Student participation is well supported The experience of participating in the programme is positive Intended learning outcomes for participants are achieved	**Student engagement and experience**
Quality assurance and improvement processes are effective Evidence-based evaluation processes are in place to assess effectiveness and impact	**Quality assurance and improvement**
Outcomes from the project are disseminated for scholarly critique Peer reviews of scholarly outputs are positive	**Dissemination and scholarship**
Programme is endorsed by key stakeholder groups Programme is embedded in plans, policies and practices within local context Programme is scalable to accommodate variations in demand Programme is viable within projected resources envelope Programme is adopted in (or adapted to) other contexts	**Sustainability and transferability**
Improvement is discernible in student wellbeing and belonging in an inclusive community Supportive learning community network is self-sustaining over the long term Programme's reach extends beyond university contexts	**Impact**

> the program ensures the institution's duty of care obligations are met along with the assurance of academic standards, and the inter-relationships between students and staff, and between learning and teaching, offer palpable evidence of the dynamic learning community which is being fostered by the program . . .

It concluded:

> All in all, the Macquarie Law PAL program is an exemplary initiative . . . The program has excellent potential to be sustained as part of the bedrock of the learning and teaching infrastructure . . .[62]

Conclusion

The benefits of peer tutoring are well documented,[63] with clear evidence in the literature that the tutor/leader benefits as much as or more than the person being tutored. The small session (class) sizes, peer leaders, absence of assessment, voluntary attendance, informal friendly and welcoming atmosphere, and emphasis on group work and collaborative activity all encourage students to attend and participate – even those who might normally be more withdrawn. It also allows learners to obtain individual attention, build networks, take advantage of informal mentoring opportunities and provide mutual support. By building a programme around academic competence, LAWPAL was able to consistently expose students to its practices, values and ethos from first year onwards, right through the curriculum. We were able to consistently attract large numbers, both to fill leadership places and attend sessions; and participant feedback was overwhelmingly positive on all our success indicators and measures of wellbeing.

Notes

* Senior lecturer, Macquarie Law School, Sydney, Australia.
1 RJ Larsen and M Eid, 'Ed Diener and the Science of SWB' in M Eid and RJ Larsen (eds) *The Science of Subjective Wellbeing* (Guilford Press, 2008) 1.
2 The Declaration of Independence, para 2 (US, 1776).
3 Blackdog Institute, 'Facts and Figures about Mental Health and Mood Disorders'. (updated October 2012).<http://www.blackdoginstitute.org.au/docs/Factsandfiguresaboutmentalhealthandmooddisorders.pdf>.
4 Beyondblue estimates that mental health problems are costing employers $10.9 billion a year. One of the strategies advocated is resilience training. Kathryn Powley, 'Mental Health Costs Boss $10.9b a Year' *Herald Sun*, 20 May 2014, News, 06.
5 Australian Bureau of Statistics (2012). ABS 3303.0 Causes of Death, Australia, 2010; cited in Blackdog, above n3.
6 Catherine M Leahy et al, 'Distress Levels and Self-Reported Treatment Rates for Medicine, Law, Psychology and Mechanical Engineering Tertiary Students: Cross-Sectional Study' (2010) 44 *Australian and New Zealand Journal of Psychiatry* 608. This Australian study found that 48% of the students overall were psychologically distressed. Grouped by discipline, the figures were: law (58%); mechanical engineering (52%); medicine (44%); and psychology (40%). But note Wendy Larcombe et al,

'Does an Improved Experience of Law School Protect Students against Depression, Anxiety, and Stress? An Empirical Study of Wellbeing and the Law School Experience of LLB and JD Students' (2013) 35 *Sydney Law Review* 407, which found that although Juris Doctor (graduate entry law) cohorts of students at Melbourne University reported significantly higher levels of satisfaction with studying law as compared with their LLB undergraduate counterparts, there were 'no statistically significant differences in the levels of depression, anxiety, and stress', suggesting that 'overall course satisfaction does not have a direct effect on students' levels of psychological distress'.

7 Norm Kelk et al, *Courting the Blues: Attitudes Towards Depression in Australian Law Students and Lawyers* (Brain and Mind Research Institute, 2009) <http://www.cald.asn.au/docs/Law%20Report%20Website%20version%204%20May%2009.pdf>: 35.2% of law students, 17.8% of medical students and only 13.3% of their age-matched peers experienced high to very high psychological distress (BMRI, 12).

8 BMRI, above n7, 37.

9 Massimiliano Tani and Prue Vines, 'Law Students' Attitudes to Education: Pointers to Depression in the Legal Academy and the Profession?' (2009) 19 *Legal Education Review* 3; Colin James, 'Lawyer Dissatisfaction, Emotional Intelligence and Clinical Legal Education' (2008) 18 *Legal Education Review* 123; Kath Hall, 'Where to Start: The Importance of Psychological Wellbeing in Australian Law Schools' (2009) 9(1) *QUT Law and Justice Journal* 1; Molly Townes O'Brien, Stephen Tang and Kath Hall, 'Changing our Thinking: Empirical Research on Law Student Wellbeing, Thinking Styles and the Law Curriculum' (2011) 21 *Legal Education Review* 149; Molly Townes O'Brien, 'Walking the Walk: Using Student-Faculty Dialogue to Change an Adversarial Curriculum' (2011) 4 *Journal of the Australasian Law Teachers Association* 129; Larcombe et al., above n6; James Duffy, Rachael Field and Melinda Shirley, 'Engaging Law Students to Promote Psychological Health' (2011) 36(4) *Alternative Law Journal* 250; Molly Townes O'Brien, 'Connecting Law Student Wellbeing to Social Justice, Problem-Solving and Human Emotions' (2014) 14(1) *QUT Law Review* 52; Kate Galloway et al, 'Approaches to Student Support in the First Year of Law School' (2011) 21(2) *Legal Education Review* 235; Rachael Field and Sally Kift, 'Addressing the High Levels of Psychological Distress in Law Students through Intentional Assessment and Feedback Design in the First Year Law Curriculum' (2010) 1 *International Journal of the First Year in Higher Education* 65 <https://www.fyhe.com.au/journal/index.php/intjfyhe/article/view/20>. Council of Australian Law Deans, 'Promoting Law Student Well-Being: Good Practice Guidelines for Law Schools' (2013); Australian Law Students Association, *Depression in Australian Law Schools: A Handbook for Law Students and Law Student Societies* (2009).

10 Kennon M Sheldon and Lawrence S Krieger, 'Does Legal Education Have Undermining Effects on Law Students? Evaluating Changes in Motivation, Values and Well-Being' (2004) 22 *Behavioural Science and Law* 261; G Andrew H Benjamin et al, 'The Role of Legal Education in Producing Psychological Distress Among Law Students and Lawyers' (1986) 2 *American Bar Foundation Research Journal* 225; Ann L Iijima, 'Lessons Learned: Legal Education and Law Student Dysfunction' (1998) 48 *Journal of Legal Education* 524; Lauren Carasik, 'Renaissance or Retrenchment: Legal Education at a Crossroads' (2011) 44 *Indiana Law Review* 735; Jennifer Jolly-Ryan, 'Promoting Mental Health in Law School: What Law Schools Can Do for Law Students to Help them Become Happy, Mentally Healthy Lawyers' (2009) 48 *University of Louisville Law Review* 95.

11 Keith Topping and Stewart Ehly (eds), *Peer Assisted Learning* (Erlbaum, 1998); Keith Topping, 'The Effectiveness of Peer Tutoring in Further and Higher Education: A Typology and Review of the Literature' (1996) 32(3) *Higher Education* 321; Sinclair Goodlad and B Hirst, *Peer Tutoring: A Guide to Learning by Teaching* (Nichols, 1989); David Boud, Ruth Cohen and Jane Sampson, *Peer Learning in Higher Education* (Routledge, 2001); Paula Green, 'A Literature Review of Peer Assisted Learning (PAL)' (2011)

<http://www.bradford.ac.uk/management/media/management/els/A-Literature-Review-of-Peer-Assisted-Learning.pdf>; Sinclair Goodlad, *Mentoring and Tutoring by Students* (Kogan Page, 1998); Audrey Gartner and Frank Riessman, 'Peer-Tutoring: Toward a New Model' (ERIC Clearinghouse on Teaching and Teacher Education, 1993) <http://www.ericdigests.org/1994/peer.htm>; Stuart Capstick, 'Benefits and Shortcomings of Peer Assisted Learning (PAL) in Higher Education: An Appraisal by Students' (2004) <http://pal.bournemouth.ac.uk/documents/Bnfts%20%26%20 Shrtcmngs%20%20of%20PAL3.pdf>. Stuart Capstick, H Fleming and J Hurne (2004) 'Implementing Peer Assisted Learning in Higher Education: The Experience of a New University and a Model for the Achievement of a Mainstream Programme' <http://pal.bournemouth.ac.uk/documents/implmntng%20pal%20article61.pdf>; 'Peer Assisted Learning Project (Bournemouth University): Evaluation Report', 2004.

12 Kathryn Ecclestone and Dennis Hayes, *The Dangerous Rise of Therapy in Education* (Routledge, 2008): e.g. the new therapeutic ethos in Britain 'reveals a decline in what we think children and young people are capable of, refracted through the prism of what policy makers and the emotional well-being industry think they need . . . [T]he collapse in belief in human potential is palpable', 143; Paul Smeyers, Richard Smith and Paul Standish, *The Therapy of Education: Philosophy, Happiness and Personal Growth* (Palgrave Macmillan, 2007); Kristján Kristjánsson, *Aristotle, Emotions and Education* (Ashgate, 2007); Avi Mintz, 'Has Therapy Intruded into Education?' (2009) 43(4) *Journal of Philosophy of Education* 633.

13 Rachel Dodge et al, 'The Challenge of Defining Wellbeing' (2012) 2(3) *International Journal of Wellbeing* 222; Carol D Ryff, 'Happiness is Everything, or is It? Explorations on the Meaning of Psychological Well-Being' (1989) 57(6) *Journal of Personality and Social Psychology* 1069.

14 Vivien L Giannopoulos and Dianne A Vella-Brodrick, 'Effects of Positive Interventions and Orientations to Happiness on Subjective Well-Being' (2011) 6(2) *Journal of Positive Psychology* 95; E Diener and E Suh, 'Measuring Quality of Life: Economic, Social and Subjective Indicators' (1997) 40(1–2) *Social Indicators Research* 189.

15 *Contributions of the Ed Diener Laboratory to the Scientific Understanding of Well-Being* <http://www.psych.uiuc.edu/~ediener/contributions_of_lab.htm>.

16 Ryff, above n13; Carol D Ryff and B Singer, 'The Contours of Positive Human Health' (1998) 9 *Psychological Inquiry* 1; Carol D Ryff and B Singer, 'Know Thyself and Become What You Are: An Eudaimonic Approach to Psychological Wellbeing' (2008) 9 *Journal of Happiness Studies* 13.

17 CLM Keyes et al, 'Evaluation of the Mental Health Continuum- Short Form (MHC-SF) in Setswana-Speaking South Africans' 15 *Clinical Psychology and Psychotherapy* 181.

18 Aristotle, *Nicomachean Ethics*, translated by H Rackham (Cornell University Press, 1947), asserts that the highest good for humans or the highest of all goals achievable by human action is eudaimonia, usually translated from the Greek as happiness or wellbeing. Similar views were espoused by Socrates and Plato; see Darrin M McMahon, *Happiness: A History* (Atlantic Monthly Press, 2006) 24–40. The terms wellbeing and eudaimonic happiness are considered interchangeable for the purposes of this chapter, although they are not so regarded in the psychology literature for experimental purposes.

19 Martin Seligman, *Flourish: A Visionary New Understanding of Happiness and Well-Being – and How to Achieve Them* (Nicholas Brealey, 2011). In this work Seligman differentiates happiness (more limited) from wellbeing.

20 Ryff, above n13 (Ryff Scales of Psychological Well-Being).

21 *Final Project Report,* Foresight Mental Capital and Wellbeing Project (Government Office for Science, London, 2008).

22 E Pollard and P Lee, 'Child Well-Being: A Systematic Review of the Literature' (2003) 61(1) *Social Indicators Research* 9.

23 Diener and Suh, above n14, 189; Martin Seligman, *Authentic Happiness: Using the New Positive Psychology to Realize Your Potential for Lasting Fulfillment* (Nicholas Brealey, 2002). See also Ed Diener et al, 'Subjective Well-Being: Three Decades of Progress' (1999) 125(2) *Psychological Bulletin* 276.

24 Kennon M Sheldon et al, 'What Is Satisfying about Satisfying Events? Testing 10 Candidate Psychological Needs' (2001) 80 *Journal of Personality and Social Psychology* 325.

25 Interventions for depression are generally different to those for anxiety and stress. Larcombe et al, above n6, 415.

26 Sonia Lyubomirsky, Kennon M Sheldon and David Schkade, 'Pursuing Happiness: The Architecture of Sustainable Change' (2005) 9 *Review of General Psychology* 111, 116; Dr Claire Rees, Curtin University School of Psychology, quoted in Marnie McKimmie, 'You Can't Put a Price on Happiness' *The West Australian* 1 April 2011. Arguing that the figure is closer to 20%, see Davis Lykken and Auke Tellegen, 'Happiness Is a Stochastic Phenomenon' (1996) 7 *Psychological Science* 186 (estimated that the heritability of the stable component of subjective wellbeing approaches 80%, based on a longitudinal study of identical twins raised apart; but see additional research on twins by Lykken and colleagues that concludes that 40–50% of variance in happiness in individuals can be attributed to genetics); David Lykken, *Happiness: The Nature and Nurture of Joy and Contentment* (St Martin's, 2000).

27 Lykken, above n26.

28 Ibid., 60.

29 Lyubomirsky, Sheldon and Schkade, above n26 111.

30 NL Sin and Sonia Lyubomirsky, 'Enhancing Well-Being and Alleviating Depressive Symptoms with Positive Psychology Interventions: A Practice-Friendly Meta-Analysis' (2009) 65 *Journal of Clinical Psychology: In Session* 467.

31 RA Emmons and E McCullough, 'Counting Blessings vs Burdens: An Experimental Investigation of Gratitude and Subjective Well-Being in Daily Life' (2003) 84 *Journal of Personality and Social Psychology* 377; Kennon M Sheldon and Sonia Lyubomirsky, 'How to Increase and Sustain Positive Emotion: The Effects of Expressing Gratitude and Visualizing Best Possible Selves' (2006) 1 *Journal of Positive Psychology* 73; Martin Seligman et al, 'Positive Psychology Progress: Empirical Validation of Interventions' (2005) 60 *American Psychologist* 410.

32 Michael A Cohn and Barbara L Fredrickson, 'In Search of Durable Positive Psychology Interventions: Predictors and Consequences of Long-Term Positive Behavior Change' (2010) 5(5) *Journal of Positive Psychology* 355, 355.

33 Sonja Lyubomirsky, Laura A King and Ed Diener, 'The Benefits of Frequent Positive Affect: Does Happiness Lead to Success?' (2005) 131 *Psychological Bulletin* 803, 846.

34 'The Principles of Beneficence in Applied Ethics', *Stanford Encyclopedia of Philosophy* (first published 2 Jan 2008; substantive revision 3 Oct 2013) <http://plato.stanford.edu/entries/principle-beneficence/>.

35 Penelope Watson and Rachael Field, 'Promoting Student Well-Being and Resilience at Law School', in Sally Kift et al (eds), *Excellence and Innovation in Legal Education* (LexisNexis, 2011).

36 FH Norris et al, 'Community Resilience as a Metaphor, Theory, Set of Capacities, and Strategy for Disaster Readiness (2008) 41 *American Journal of Community Psychology* 127, cited in Danny MacKinnon and Kate Driscoll Derickson, 'From Resilience to Resourcefulness: A Critique of Resilience Policy and Activism' (2012) 37(2) *Progress in Human Geography* 253, 255.

37 Ibid.

38 C Folke, 'Resilience: The Emergence of a Perspective for Social-Ecological Systems Analysis' (2006) 16 *Global Environmental Change* 253, cited in MacKinnon and Derickson, ibid., 255.

39 For example, Stephen Sterling, 'Learning for Resilience or the Resilient Learner? Towards a Necessary Reconciliation in a Paradigm of Sustainable Education' (2010) 16(5) *Environmental Education Research* 511.
40 B Egeland, E Carlson and L Stroufe, 'Resilience as Process' (1993) 5 *Development and Psychopathology* 517, cited in MacKinnon and Derickson, above n36.
41 Sterling, above n39.
42 ME Haglund et al, 'Psychobiological Mechanisms of Resilience: Relevance to Prevention and Treatment of Stress-Related Psychopathology' (2007) 19 *Development and Psychopathology* 889.
43 Ryff's scale was one of the measures used in Larcombe et al, above n6.
44 Lykken, above n26.
45 <http://www.thefreedictionary.com/resourcefulness>.
46 <http://www.merriam-webster.com/dictionary/resourceful>.
47 'What are Expert Learners?' (2010) *Universal Design for Learning Guidelines* version 1.0 <http://udlguidelines.wordpress.com/introduction/what-are-expert-learners/>.
48 David S Yeager and Carol Dweck, 'Mindsets that Promote Resilience: When Students Believe that Personal Characteristics Can Be Developed' (2012) 47(4) *Educational Psychologist* 302. See also K Olsen and Carol Dweck, 'A Blueprint for Social Cognitive Development' (2008) 3 *Perspectives on Psychological Science* 193.
49 Carol S Dweck, 'Mind-Sets and Equitable Education' (2010) 10(5) *Principal Leadership* 26, citing the following research demonstrating that mind-sets have a direct influence on grades and that growth mind-sets raise grades and achievement test scores significantly: L Blackwell, K Trzesniewski and CS Dweck, 'Implicit Theories of Intelligence Predict Achievement Across an Adolescent Transition: A Longitudinal Study and Intervention' (2007) 78 *Child Development* 246; C Good, J Aronson and M Inzlicht, 'Improving Adolescents' Standardized Test Performance: An Intervention to Reduce the Effects of Stereotype Threat' (2003) 24 *Applied Developmental Psychology* 645.
50 Based on the Supplemental Instruction (SI) or Peer-Assisted Study Sessions (PASS) model of peer tutoring, developed at the University of Missouri, Kansas, and licensed to the University of Wollongong; known at Macquarie Law School as LAWPAL (Law Peer-Assisted Learning). The name PAL was adopted in preference to the more common PASS to emphasize the social connectedness aspect as well as to avoid remedial connotations.
51 Macquarie University Learning and Teaching Fellowship (2010–2011).
52 A second academic was recruited later to share the load of convening the Leading Peer Learning elective subject, the only elective in the law school to be offered every semester every year.
53 Dexter Dunphy, Andrew Griffiths and Suzanne Benn, *Organizational Change for Corporate Sustainability* (Routledge, 2003) 54.
54 Richard M Ryan and Edward L Deci, 'Self-Determination Theory and the Facilitation of Intrinsic Motivation, Social Development and Well-Being' (2000) 55 *American Psychologist* 68; Edward L Deci et al, 'Motivation and Education: The Self-Determination Perspective' (1991) 26 *Educational Psychologist* 325; Edward L Deci and Richard M Ryan, 'The "What" and "Why" of Goal Pursuits: Human Needs and the Self-Determination of Behaviour' (2000) 11 *Psychological Inquiry* 227; Kennon M Sheldon and Lawrence S Krieger, 'Understanding the Negative Effects of Legal Education on Law Students: A Longitudinal Test of Self-Determination Theory' (2007) 33(6) *Personality and Social Psychology Bulletin* 883, 884.
55 Sheldon and Krieger, above n54, 884: 'autonomy support predicted . . . higher subjective well-being . . . better graded performance . . . and more self-determined motivation to pursue the upcoming legal career'.
56 Todd Peterson and Elizabeth Peterson, 'Stemming the Tide of Law Student Depression: What Law Schools Need to Learn from the Science of Positive Psychology' (2009) 9 *Yale Journal of Health, Policy, Law and Ethics* 357, 391. Seligman, above n19.

57 These were (i) designing and teaching an elective known as Leading Peer Learning (staff member), important for resourcing, quality control and maintenance of standards; and (ii) an offshoot of LAWPAL known as LawSmart (student co-ordinator in conjunction with university psychologists). This offered workshops specially designed for law students on topics such as time management, work–life balance, healthy lifestyle and positive thinking.

58 Jean Lave and Etienne Wenger, *Situated Learning: Legitimate Peripheral Participation* (Cambridge University Press, 1991); Etienne Wenger, 'Communities of Practice: Learning as a Social System' *Systems Thinker* (1998) <http://www.co-i-l.com/coil/knowledge-garden/cop/lss.shtml>; Etienne Wenger, 'Communities of Practice: A Brief Introduction' (c 2007) <http://www.ewenger.com/theory/>; Etienne Wenger, Richard McDermott and William Snyder, *Cultivating Communities of Practice: A Guide to Managing Knowledge* (Harvard Business School Press, 2002).

59 Wenger, 2007, above n58.

60 Carolyn Webb, cwebbconsulting, External Evaluation of the Law Peer-Assisted Learning (PAL) Project: A Macquarie University Learning and Teaching fellowship 2010, awarded to Penelope Watson, Director (L&T), Macquarie Law School (2011).

61 Ibid., 1.

62 Ibid., 3, 4.

63 See above n11.

10 On Being, Not Just Thinking Like, a Lawyer

Connections Between Uncertainty, Ignorance and Wellbeing

Tony Foley and Stephen Tang[*]

Introduction

The process of becoming a lawyer – through law school, in professional legal education and in the workplace – is not an easy endeavour. It is a long and sometimes personally challenging journey which requires grasping a vast array of knowledge and information and encountering a multitude of complex, unpredictable and confronting situations.

Faced with such deep complexity, it is understandable that budding lawyers, as well as their teachers or supervisors who are tasked with teaching and preparing them, latch onto principles and identities that have been created as a way to cope with and make sense of this unfamiliar and unknown terrain. In the world of legal education and training, the predominant coping strategy is learning the habits of 'thinking like a lawyer'.

This chapter argues that the 'thinking like a lawyer' strategy tends to inflate the importance of certainty, knowledge and an answer-driven worldview at the expense of understanding and managing the many unknowns of the law and legal practice. It can be an unhelpful and inadequate coping strategy for the complexities of study and practice. There is a missing piece to the puzzle – the importance of uncertainty, lack of knowledge and a questioning perspective – which is just as much the core of legal practice. We contend that the neglect of the scope of ignorance and uncertainty in legal practice leaves out this obverse side and so sets up blind spots and false expectations about the nature of legal practice. These gaps between expectation and reality exist to the detriment of the psychological wellbeing, as well as the personal and professional potential of lawyers.

We have argued elsewhere that one way to challenge the dominance of certainty-seeking narratives is to reframe the practice of law as an activity that necessitates an 'intolerance of certainty'.[1] The idea we float in this chapter is to allow this unacknowledged side of practice to be given recognition within the scope of 'thinking like a lawyer' so as to recognize ignorance and uncertainty as further essential resources for wellbeing and professionalism, rather than sources of apprehension and fear. Learning to manage, embrace and value uncertainty and ignorance are skills which can and should be taught and modelled in legal education and training. This chapter argues for such an enlargement of the 'thinking like a lawyer' strategy. It first outlines the proposition that the strategy which begins a legal education needs to be expanded to include an appreciation and familiarity with uncertainty.

'Thinking Like a Lawyer': Light and Shade

The 'thinking like a lawyer' strategy is meant to equip law students and emerging lawyers with the resources necessary to make sense of the foreign and sometimes mystic language that cloaks the law.[2] As the Carnegie Report on US legal education observed, law schools do a very good job in teaching their students to master a high-order intellectual process which emphasizes the priority of analytic thinking, 'in which students learn to categorize and discuss persons and events in highly generalized terms'.[3] Judith Wegner has observed that this aspect of legal education is like 'learning a new narrative . . . like [entering] Middle Earth'.[4] While 'thinking like a lawyer' can be seen as a set of technical skills (e.g., conducting legal research, legal writing, advocacy skills),[5] it is also a way of being and a way of looking at a world. Thinking *like a lawyer*, by definition, means thinking *unlike* an 'ordinary person'. Learning to acquire this artificial behaviour is a threshold identity for law students. It has as its core an assumption that the complexity of human experience, and the complexity of the law, can be repackaged and made to make different sense by applying the skills of rational argumentation, rule construction and adherence to precedent to create an alternative reality.[6]

We do not contest that this conception of 'thinking like a lawyer' can be a good thing.[7] It is undoubtedly effective as a strategy to fill gaps in knowledge and as a toolbox of solutions through which to generate answers to unfamiliar problems. For students, it can also provide a sense of satisfaction and empowerment. The mastery of legal skills and techniques can be applied to the law-saturated nature of society and everyday life. This may partially explain the rapid changes in thinking styles and attitudes that take place upon mere exposure to the law school environment. Mertz found in her conversation analysis of the US law school classroom that the reconceptualization is reinforced by a tightly controlled classroom discourse where certain communication behaviour is approved (technical textual analysis) while other generally commonplace behaviour is disapproved (narrative storytelling and explicit considerations of social context or underlying morality).[8] However, it is the pressures associated with these changes which are also associated with the high levels of psychological distress in law students, as well as a sense of elitism, competitiveness and social isolation.[9]

Thus the very reason for the success of this strategy contains a shadow side: it inadvertently or intentionally creates a sort of tunnel vision in which certain aspects of the law and practice are elevated at the expense of other core aspects which remain undiscovered or actively hidden.[10] Specifically, the strategy provides no aid to navigate the pervasive nature of ignorance and uncertainty in legal practice. 'Thinking like a lawyer' is perhaps less of an *additive* set of skills (akin to, for example, a pair of 'X-ray glasses' which gives the wearer enhanced abilities not present in most people) and more a *subtractive* set of skills, to continue the analogy, more like wearing a pair of sunglasses. The strategy is most successful when it operates to exclude and filter information in a particular kind of way.

The main filter is achieved by reducing or distilling the complexity of law into concrete and often mechanical rules in order to use it as 'tests' for both matters of substance and procedure, and in distilling the reality and complexity of human affairs into neat 'facts' to which the tests can be applied. This sustains a subtle but insidious form of legal formalism.[11]

The concern is that while the subtractive method of 'thinking like a lawyer' is useful to make sense of the impermeable complexity of the law, its unfriendly stance towards intrinsic human needs and virtues because it is necessarily linear and 'rational' is antagonistic to both wellbeing and professionalism. The world-view generated by learning to think 'legally' creates the expectancy that problems are soluble by the mere application of legal reasoning, and that human need and its complexity can be filtered out. The reality of legal practice, however, often means that technical legal reasoning is only one part of the ever-changing nature of being a professional, given the unpredictability of legal rules, norms and the unpredictability of humans to whom they are applied. 'Thinking like a lawyer' can have the effect of relegating the person, the *being* of a lawyer, to the dim shadows. Ignoring this psychological and interpersonal space in which complexity and uncertainty can be held, managed and transformed comes at the expense of personal wellness and effective professional practice.

We therefore posit that to be an effective lawyer, what is needed – and what healthy and professional lawyers will learn for themselves through a protracted process of trial and error – is a more helpful way of facing, not avoiding, the complexity of law.[12] This set of skills is predicated on the development of professional judgement in the face of unknowns and unknowables for which the narrow conception of 'thinking like a lawyer' proves inadequate. In our view, a better response is to expand the 'thinking like a lawyer' strategy at the outset of legal education to include these abilities to identify, manage and embrace the ignorance and uncertainty for which knowledge-based analytical skills alone are ineffective. In other words, students do need to learn to 'think like a lawyer' in the traditional sense which includes rule-based reasoning (deductive reasoning), synthesis (inductive reasoning), analogical reasoning, distinguishing cases and policy-based reasoning.[13] But at the same time they also need to embrace the ignorance and uncertainty which, if itself ignored, otherwise sustains a potentially blinkered way of thinking and being.

Ignorance and Uncertainty

Before exploring the connections between wellbeing, being and thinking like a lawyer and the uncertainties and unknowns of legal practice, we must first set out some working definitions of 'ignorance' and 'uncertainty'. *Ignorance* is everything we don't know.[14] It is the inevitable and normal result of having finite knowledge in an unconstrained and ever-changing world. We are infinitely more ignorant than we are knowledgeable. We therefore do not use 'ignorance' pejoratively but humbly.[15] To be ignorant is not to be against knowledge: ignorance and knowledge are different sides of the same coin.[16] The more we know, the more we realize we don't know. What we know we don't know often drives us to discover and learn – on the condition that we know that we don't know everything. As such, simply identifying and modelling ignorance goes some way to dispel some of the unhelpful hierarchies and power structures which restrict the learning opportunities of law students and new lawyers. However, to be *meta-ignorant*[17] – to be unaware of one's own ignorance or to be overconfident or arrogant in one's limited knowledge – is a significant blind spot, and one that has serious consequences for lawyers fuelled by years of the certainty-view of training to 'think like a lawyer'.

By contrast, *uncertainty* is our subjective state of response to objective ignorance. Because of the sheer extent of what we do not know, we have boundaries on our ability to predict, plan and explain the world around us. Whether we are conscious of it or not, we respond to this in different ways. One response might be the immediate emotional and visceral reactions of fear and doubt, or a broader unspoken sense of discomfort and for some maybe queasy unease. However, there is an overlooked positive side to uncertainty.[18] It is a side which accommodates experiences of serendipity, surprise, excitement, discovery, hope, curiosity and yearning.

Uncertainty is not just felt but acted upon. Just as people differ in their awareness of and response to ignorance, there is a spectrum of possible reactions to uncertainty. Reactions can include the subtle but structured ways in which we try to foresee the unknown through our predictions about the future, other people and ourselves. We can also seek to create and use uncertainty to strategic ends, by drawing attention to ignorance in novel ways. Think, for example, of a creative commercial lawyer revisiting what appear to be established facts and law in order to assert a unique and unprecedented right for her client; or a criminal defence lawyer seeking to sow the seeds of reasonable doubt in a jury's mind.

Given that ignorance and uncertainty are present more often than we realize (or may willingly admit), we develop the approach taken by Smithson[19] as well as Vitek, Johnson and colleagues[20] to argue that it is neither desirable nor feasible to try to eliminate ignorance or to tame uncertainty. To try to do this would be to lose the many benefits of living in the unknown. Instead, the focus we are suggesting is to embrace and explore our own attitude and response to ignorance and uncertainty. A functional and flexible approach to the unknown may be necessary for wellbeing in legal professionals. A healthy orientation to uncertainty and ignorance can be taught and shaped through legal education and in the early stages of professional identity formation.

Working Well With Unknowns: Professionalism and Wellbeing

We do not seek to eliminate the scope of being and thinking like a lawyer, but to recognize it for what it is in practice. Good lawyers in practice are cognizant of the depth of complexity in the environments in which they practise and in the context of relating to other people. Recognizing ignorance and uncertainty in practice is not only a core aspect of ethical professionalism, but in our view is also inextricable from wellness in its fullest and proper sense.[21]

Fluency with ignorance and a tolerance of uncertainty within the demands of legal practice can act as a virtue or resource to equip (new) lawyers to survive and thrive in practice. In terms of ignorance, we would teach the ability to identify different types and scope of unknowns and become conscious of the limits of their current and possible knowledge. In terms of uncertainty, we would teach students to have a healthy and curious appreciation of uncertainty: not to be paralysed by it or simply to tolerate it, but to use the cues of uncertainty to foster inquiry, discovery, learning, good judgement and self-regulation and care.

Understanding Ignorance

To see ignorance as a resource requires taking a step back to be aware of the *process* of knowing and not knowing. This is a meta-cognitive stance: it requires the ability to reflect on the motivations, costs and value of that which is known and that which is unknown. It stands in contrast to the default assumption in legal education that knowledge and certainty are inherently desirable, attainable and psychologically cost-free.

Table 10.1 presents a version of a matrix used by Smithson, setting out in four simple quadrants a taxonomy of ignorance which may be helpful in challenging the common one-eyed view of the provenance of knowledge.[22] The first quadrant is the realm of *known knowns*. These are the things that we know that we know. It is not ignorance but its flipside, our explicit knowledge. For the lawyer, this would include not only the knowledge of legal rules and principles (knowing *that*), but also the procedural knowledge of how to perform certain tasks – such as drafting a contract – or how to acquire more knowledge or information through research or learning (knowing *how*). Seeking known knowns is a fundamental part of learning to 'think like a lawyer'. However, this quadrant occupies a much smaller space than we may be prepared to acknowledge. Legal rules change, processes evolve, facts remain to be discovered. We forget things and our memories become distorted almost from the moment they are created.[23] To the extent that this knowledge becomes inaccurate or invalid, it is no longer a 'known'.

The second quadrant, *known unknowns*, refers to our conscious ignorance: things we know we don't know. This type of ignorance is not inconsistent with the standard 'thinking like a lawyer' strategy. However, while the abstract problem-solving and answer-based reasoning taught by law school prepares lawyers well to address this kind of ignorance in specific instances, it is less useful when it is the only strategy generalized to respond to the infinite sea

Table 10.1 Quadrants of knowledge and ignorance

	Known	*Unknown*
Known	Known knowns *(what I know I know)*	Unknown knowns *(what I don't know I know)*
Unknown	Known unknowns *(what I know I don't know)*	Unknown unknowns *(what I don't know I don't know)*

of unknowns in the real world (rather than in tightly crafted law school problem scenarios). As Marlys Witte and her colleagues recognize, this 'explicit ignorance' is best addressed by first questioning assumptions or by challenging expectations, rather than unquestioningly absorbing information.[24] Nonetheless, there is an implicit message within the traditional strategy that known unknowns are the only kinds of unknowns that lawyers will face; that all other problems can be met with a singular solution based on information and knowledge. This message masks the presence of other forms of ignorance and colours the resultant uncertainty with negative overtones of fear and insecurity. Attempting to find exhaustive answers for all problems in the law and its practice is not only impossible, but psychologically exhausting.

Unknown knowns, or things we don't know we know, may at first appear to be a paradox. Such 'tacit' knowledge is surprisingly common, however, especially in the automatic, routine or gut-feeling actions of professional practice. There are many complex patterns of lawyer behaviours and decisions that cannot be easily explained or reduced to rules. Not knowing that we do, in fact, know something can be self-limiting and impose artificial barriers on our sense of competence, autonomy or relatedness – which, as self-determination theory (SDT) makes clear, are essential for 'human thriving',[25] particularly since it tends to be suppressed by the rational model of thinking. Recent research by Krieger and Sheldon which shows that these basic psychological needs tend to be impaired by legal education seems to confirm that traditional legal education and training leads students to underestimate their own resilience and capability as emerging legal professionals.[26] Unknown knowns are usually discovered (in retrospect, after they become consciously known) because they are unexpectedly useful in the face of marked uncertainty or adversity. When thrown into the 'deep end' of a situation where there is little recourse to rational knowledge, new lawyers may find themselves 'rediscovering' their developed skills and intuition.[27] Recognizing that these discoveries are valuable and useful can be wonderfully affirming, bridging the connections between different identities and sources of life experience. But denying students' and new lawyers' tacit knowledge, can detract from wellbeing, confidence and empathy.

Finally, there are *unknown unknowns*: things we don't know we don't know. This hidden ignorance (or meta-ignorance) is not in itself bad, but can be dangerous when juxtaposed with a worldview oriented only to certainty. The analytic, rational and rule-based models of 'thinking like a lawyer' can set up false expectations about one's preparedness for uncertainty. Taleb warns against this tendency:

> We humans, facing limits of knowledge, and things we do not observe, the unseen and the unknown, resolve the tension by squeezing life and the world into crisp commoditized ideas, reductive categories, specific vocabularies, and prepackaged narratives, which, on the occasion, has explosive consequences.[28]

Because rational thinking skills cannot be directly applied to unknown unknowns, this source of ignorance can only be addressed through experience. As such, we need to give law students early opportunities to experience these unknowns in a safe environment. The object of such learning is not to turn ignorance into knowledge, but to accommodate tacit knowledge and conscious ignorance as a springboard to be comfortable with its pervasiveness in practice.

Responding to Uncertainty

These forms of knowledge and ignorance give rise to a range of different experiences of uncertainty. Uncertainty can be not only aversive and unpleasant but also a positive and motivating experience. To meet the ignorance-laden demands of practice requires the management of uncertainty as a resource. This means both accepting and learning from the moments of discomfort and anxiety associated with ignorance, and also harnessing opportunities to exercise good judgement and make the most of unexpected turn of events.

Legal Practice as an Open System

A more realistic sense of the identity and role of a lawyer is best found in the 'ordinary, prosaic, Wednesday afternoon [of] law practice':[29] that is to say, the routine and everyday events of practice. This seemingly mundane depiction belies the fact that practice can be, and often is, behaviourally complex, intrinsically interpersonal and enmeshed in a network of interdependencies. James Boyd White, for example, sees that the law and its practice is:

> not at heart an abstract system or scheme of rules . . . nor is it a set of institutional arrangements . . . rather, it is an inherently unstable structure of thought and expression, built upon a distinct set of dynamic and dialogic tensions. It is not a set of rules at all, but a form of life. It is a process by which the old is made new, over and over again.[30]

If we accept this as referencing the micro level of practice we can see that a sizeable part of legal practice is *self-organizing*.[31] That is, the norms for the practice of law and the qualities of professionalism which govern that practice are created and recreated through little moments of action, reaction, imitation and informal learning in everyday events. Patterns of lawyer behaviour emerge and develop from unexpected origins in ways that cannot be simply subsumed into formal legal rules or checklist-based competency frameworks. Kirkland identified one such aspect of practice in large law firm lawyers' 'choice of norm rule'. This 'rule' (really a heuristic) she saw as being used by lawyers to determine how they should act in various situations. She observed that:

> [T]he appropriate norms to apply in a given situation are those of the people the lawyer is working for and with at the time. Because this choice of norm rule makes the partner or coterie a lawyer is working for at the time the source of norms, the lawyer asks, 'What norms would the partner or coterie I am working with follow in this situation?'[32]

This 'choice of norm' rule is but one example of a habit used to self-organize (probably unconsciously) a response to the uncertainty created by the lack of normative homogeneity in a large legal practice. Most if not all lawyers assess and adjust their practice style on a continual basis depending on the changing interpersonal dynamics of their particular niche in that practice environment.[33] It is through these adjustments within this particular community of practice that their own pattern of coherence will emerge, allowing them to manage some of the uncertainty that confronts them.[34]

The ability to recognize and positively use uncertainty in the interpersonal and ever-changing nature of practice is critical to learning to 'think like a lawyer'.[35] The ability to identify, respond to and participate in change will only become increasingly important in the context of major structural shifts currently underway in the legal profession.[36]

Uncertainty and Information Management

Lawyers' work is characterized by having to process large amounts of information under time pressure. Good professional judgement in these situations therefore includes the ability, when faced with the inherent uncertainty of complex and information-heavy situations, to remain *optimally ignorant*. It requires good judgement and an awareness of the limits of knowledge to say 'enough!' to research, preparation or polishing, and to be satisfied with a satisfactory outcome which meets professional and ethical requirements – though it may not be 'perfect'. Developing effective intuitive 'stopping rules' is vital for lawyers to be able to remain effective in their professional lives and not be paralysed by cognitive overload or crippling doubt about the adequacy of their performance.[37]

On the other hand, it is not only too much uncertainty or too much information which is a problem. Sometimes it is an insufficiency of uncertainty, where there is no challenge in the workplace. This can also be discomfiting and frustrating. It is equally important to know when to seek uncertainty by taking ethical but permissible risks, to look for new ways of solving problems, or even to consider whether or not to remain in a certain role.

Uncertainty Management as Key to Resilience and Adaptation

Engaging positively with uncertainty is therefore part of a necessary preparation for practice. Law students should see this skill and mindset as something which will prepare them for the many taxing and seemingly random aspects of practice. Smithson suggests that there are four kinds of situations, highly applicable to legal practice, where it is crucial to identify, invite and interact effectively with ignorance and uncertainty:

1. dealing with unforeseen threats and solving problems;
2. crafting good outcomes in a partially learnable world;
3. benefiting from opportunities for exploration and discovery; and
4. dealing intelligently and sociably with other people.[38]

Understanding that this ability to navigate with flexibility through this complexity and its unpredictability can be learned and developed is part of the development of professional judgement through what Carol Dweck labels a 'growth mindset'.[39] Specifically, an ability to converse with uncertainty presents opportunities for the new lawyer to meet the needs of autonomy, relatedness and competence identified as crucial to psychological wellbeing by SDT theory.[40] These concepts may serve as the core building blocks for lawyers to be fulfilled and healthy in a highly demanding line of work, and requires revisiting the premise of 'thinking like a lawyer'.

'Questioning Like a Lawyer': Towards a Pedagogy of Ignorance?

Our difficulty with 'thinking like a lawyer' is not with its use but its limitations. It excludes a whole category of 'other than analytic thinking', learning which we see as crucial. Wider approaches to managing uncertainty must become part of the core 'thinking like a lawyer' strategy. We argue that lawyers (especially new lawyers) do not make adequate use of their tacit knowledge and capacity for intuition and human warmth 'that are basic to us' but underappreciated in practice.[41] Core to revaluing these capacities is a stronger focus in legal education on experiential thinking through exposure to observations of 'real' practice, role plays and clinical experience where students can confront the pervasive uncertainty of law.

It is interesting to see how other professions deal with these challenges. Medical training in some jurisdictions has long recognized the need for strategies to address the 'transiency of [medical] knowledge and its mirror image – ignorance'.[42] The University of Arizona's College of Medicine has a programme that makes ignorance instruction explicit. It delivers a formal programme on the 'Curriculum on Medical Ignorance' (CMI), which it has offered since 1984.[43] The CMI runs in parallel to the 'traditional' knowledge-based medical curriculum, and recognizes that practising doctors and medical researchers have developed a broader ignorance management strategy than simply 'thinking like a doctor' to instead acquire the habit of 'questioning like a doctor'.[44]

Students are encouraged to acquire this habitual 'questioning approach' with their assumptions by 'pondering, puzzling, musing, sensing, intuiting' about medical problems. They are taught to structure all their professional dealings and engagements with patients and colleagues within a mode of active questioning and re-questioning in order to manage ignorance. The CMI was designed to develop such questioning habits which make explicit the unspoken uncertainty management we have outlined here. The aim is to prepare new clinicians to acquire skills and attitudes to deal productively with medical ignorance and uncertainty in their study and practice.[45]

Most importantly from our point of view is that their strategy gives explicit acknowledgement of the importance of using experiential knowledge (or perhaps *experiential ignorance*) acquired through clinical exposure to complement analytical thinking. The value of intuition and the use of tacit knowledge and skills (unknown knowns) are openly acknowledged in ways that do not take place in law schools. Their syllabus has developed strategies to deal with known unknowns (explicit or overt ignorance) using an approach which questioned fundamental assumptions ('if a problem has existed for an extended period of time, it means that experts probably don't have the right question'). Students are told to openly challenge expectations and 'search for surprises'.[46] They are encouraged to use a range of strategies to attempt to make their hidden ignorance overt, including using serendipity and happenstance as 'fecund sources [for discovering the existence] of unknown unknowns'.[47]

Legal education should learn from another profession's preparedness to embrace critical, experiential and honest questioning and thinking styles as means to prepare students for uncertainty and ignorance. The success of the CMI and similar programmes assures us that preparing lawyers in this way should take forms other than narrow analytical thinking.

Conclusion

If learning the 'thinking like a lawyer' strategy is to be more effective in preparing new lawyers to meet the challenges of ignorance and uncertainty, then legal education must undergo change. There needs to be a move away from a purely analytical approach to one that 'engineers back in' not only the affective[48] but also the unknown. We are not advocating that the resources of uncertainty and ignorance should be elevated above other skills which have traditionally been recognized in legal education. Rather, the fluency to work with the unknown and unpredictable aspects of legal practice is *one* part of a package of complementary ways of thinking and acting which can be drawn on flexibly in different situations. Such flexibility is required for psychologically sustainable, healthy and professional legal practice.

Our intention is to highlight the need to create a better fit between the uncertainty-laden demands of legal practice and the corresponding uncertainty and ignorance-based resources needed for that practice. Professional legal practice includes the need to be dispassionately argumentative and rational; but it also requires the ability to recognize the limits of rule-based logic and the boundaries of legal principles, and to show some simple human empathy. The sooner we expand the idea of 'thinking like a lawyer' to recognize the good, bad and difficult of knowing *and* not knowing, of being certain *and* being uncertain, the healthier the legal profession and its members can be.

Notes

* Dr Tony Foley is an Associate Professor at the Australian National University (ANU) College of Law; E: tony.foley@anu.edu.au. Stephen Tang is a lecturer and psychologist at the ANU Legal Workshop; E: stephen.tang@anu.edu.au.

1 Stephen Tang and Tony Foley, 'The Practice of Law and the Intolerance of Certainty' (2014) 37(3) *UNSW Law Journal* 1198.

2 Paul D Carrington, 'Of Law and the River' (1984) 34 *Journal of Legal Education* 222, 223; see also Elizabeth Mertz, *The Language of Law School: Learning to 'Think Like a Lawyer'* (Oxford University Press, 2007).
3 William M Sullivan et al, *Educating Lawyers: Preparation for the Profession of Law* (2007) 29ff ('Carnegie Report') 186.
4 Judith Wegner, 'Better Writing, Better Thinking: Thinking Like a Lawyer' (2004) 10 *Legal Writing* 9, 12–13.
5 Frederick Schauer, *Thinking Like a Lawyer: A New Introduction to Legal Reasoning* (Harvard University Press, 2009).
6 Jean Stefancic and Richard Delgado, *How Lawyers Lose Their Way* (Duke University Press 2005); Jess M Krannich, James R Holbrook and Julie J McAdams, 'Beyond "Thinking Like a Lawyer" and the Traditional Legal Paradigm: Toward a Comprehensive View of Legal Education' (2009) 86 *Denver Law Review* 381.
7 See also Michelle M Harner, 'The Value of "Thinking Like a Lawyer"' (2011) 70 *Maryland Law Review* 390.
8 Mertz, above n2, 56–7.
9 Molly Townes O'Brien, Stephen Tang and Kath Hall, 'Changing Our Thinking: Empirical Research on Law Student Wellbeing, Thinking Styles and the Law Curriculum' (2011) 20 *Legal Education Review* 45; Wendy Larcombe et al, 'Does an Improved Experience of Law School Protect Students against Depression, Anxiety and Stress? An Empirical Study of Wellbeing and the Law School Experience of LLB and JD Students' 35 *Sydney Law Review* 407.
10 Kate Galloway, 'Thinking Like a Lawyer' (2012) 37 *Alternative Law Journal* 298.
11 Jean Stefancic and Richard Delgado, *How Lawyers Lose Their Way* (Duke University Press 2005), 50–51.
12 Wegner, above n4; see also John Flood, 'Doing Business: The Management of Uncertainty in Lawyers' Work' (1991) 25 *Law and Society Review* 41.
13 See, e.g., E Scott Fruehwald, *Think Like a Lawyer: Legal Reasoning for Law Students and Business Professionals* (ABA Publishing, 2013).
14 Michael Smithson, 'The Many Faces and Masks of Uncertainty' in Gabriele Bammer and Michael Smithson (eds), *Uncertainty and Risk: Multidisciplinary Perspectives* (Earthscan, 2008) 13, 14–15.
15 Wendel Berry, 'The Way of Ignorance', in Bill Vitek and Wes Jackson (eds), *The Virtues of Ignorance* (University Press of Kentucky, 2008) 37, 45.
16 Anna L Peterson, 'Ignorance and Ethics' in Vitek and Jackson, ibid., 119, 126.
17 Bill Vitek and Wes Jackson, 'Introduction: Taking Ignorance Seriously' in Vitek and Jackson, ibid., 16.
18 Smithson, above n14, 18; see also Timothy D Wilson, David B Centerbar, Deborah A Kermer and Daniel T Gilbert, 'The Pleasures of Uncertainty: Prolonging Positive Moods in Ways People Do Not Anticipate' (2005) 88 *Journal of Personality and Social Psychology* 5.
19 Smithson, above n14.
20 Vitek and Jackson, above n15.
21 See Stephen Tang, Chapter 1 this volume.
22 Smithson, above n14; see also Ann Kerwin, 'None Too Solid: Medical Ignorance' (1993) 15 *Science Communication* 166. There is an echo of these categories in Donald Rumsfeld's well-known remarks that '[t]here are known knowns; there are things we know we know. We also know there are known unknowns; that is to say we know there are some things we do not know. But there are also unknown unknowns – the ones we don't know we don't know.' Press briefing by Donald Rumsfeld (US Secretary of Defense), 12 February 2002.

23 For instance, memory for complex information is easily distorted when it is verbalized: Jason M Chin and Jonathan W Schooler, 'Why Do Words Hurt? Content, Process, and Criterion Shift Accounts of Verbal Overshadowing' (2007) 20 *Journal of Cognitive Psychology* 396.
24 Marlys Hearst Witte et al, 'Lessons Learned from Ignorance: The Curriculum on Medical (and Other) Ignorance', in Vitek and Jackson, above n15, 254.
25 Edward L. Deci and Richard. M. Ryan, 'The "What" and "Why" of Goal Pursuits: Human Needs and the Self-Determination of Behavior' (2000) 11 *Psychological Inquiry* 227.
26 Kennon M. Sheldon and Lawrence S. Krieger, 'Does Legal Education Have Undermining Effects on Law Students? Evaluating Changes in Motivation, Values, and Well-Being' (2004) 22 *Behavioural Sciences and the Law* 261; Kennon M. Sheldon and Lawrence S. Krieger, 'Understanding the Negative Effects of Legal Education on Law Students: A Longitudinal Test and Extension of Self-Determination Theory' (2007) 33 *Personality and Social Psychology Bulletin* 883; Lawrence S. Krieger and Kennon M. Sheldon, 'What Makes Lawyers Happy? Transcending the Anecdotes with Data from 6200 Lawyers' (2015) 83 *The George Washington University Law Review* 554.
27 Vivien Holmes, Tony Foley, Stephen Tang and Margie Rowe, 'Practising Professionalism: Observations from an Empirical Study of New Australian Lawyers' (2012) 15 *Legal Ethics* 29, 42–9.
28 Nassim Nicholas Taleb, *The Bed of Procrustes*: *Philosophical and Practical Aphorisms* (Random House 2010), xii.
29 Thomas L Shaffer, *Christian Jurisprudence of Robert E Rodes Jr* (1997–98) 73 *Notre Dame Law Review* 737, 748.
30 James Boyd White, 'An Old-Fashioned View of the Nature of Law' (2011) 12 *Theoretical Inquiries in Law* 381, 382.
31 SH Strogatz, *Sync: The Emerging Science of Spontaneous Order* (Hyperion, 2003).
32 Kimberly Kirkland, 'Ethics in Large Law Firms: The Principle of Pragmatism' (2005) 4 *University of Memphis Law Review* 631, 638.
33 See also Leslie C Levin, 'Bad Apples, Bad Lawyers or Bad Decisionmaking: Lessons from Psychology and from Lawyers in the Dock' (2009) 22 *Georgetown Journal of Legal Ethics* 1549, 1556.
34 Leslie Levin, 'Guardians at the Gate: The Background, Career Paths, and Professional Development of Private US Immigration Lawyers' (2009) 34 *Law and Social Inquiry* 399; Michael Eraut, 'Informal Learning in the Workplace' (2004) 26 *Studies in Continuing Education* 247; Paula Baron and Lillian Corbin, 'Thinking Like a Lawyer/Acting Like a Professional: Communities of Practice as a Means of Challenging Orthodox Legal Education' (2012) 46 *Law Teacher* 100.
35 Michael Eraut, 'Non-Formal Learning and Tacit Knowledge in Professional Work' (2000) 70 *British Journal of Educational Psychology* 113.
36 Richard Susskind, *The End of Lawyers? Rethinking the Nature of Legal Services* (Oxford University Press, revised ed, 2010); Bernard A Burk and David McGowan, 'Big But Brittle: Economic Perspectives on the Future of the Law Firm in the New Economy' [2011] *Columbia Business Law Review* 1. See also Ronit Dinovitzer and Bryant G Garth, 'Lawyer Satisfaction in the Process of Structuring Legal Careers' (2007) 41 *Law and Society Review* 1.
37 See, e.g., Gerd Gigerenzer, *Rationality for Mortals: How People Cope with Uncertainty* (Oxford University Press 2008) 5–6.
38 Smithson, above n14.
39 Carol S Dweck, *Mindset: The New Psychology of Success* (Ballantine, 2007); see also Carrington, above n2.
40 Krieger and Sheldon, above n26.
41 Kerwin, above n22, 180.

42 Marlys Hearst Witte, Ann Kerwin and Charles L Witte, 'A Curriculum on Medical Ignorance' (1989) 63 *Journal of Medical Education* 793; see also Renée C Fox, 'Training for Uncertainty' in Robert K Merton et al (eds), *The Student-Physician* (Harvard University Press 1957) 207.

43 <http://www.ignorance.medicine.arizona.edu/curriculum.html>.

44 There is a parallel argument for valuing ignorance in scientific research: see Martin A Schwartz, 'The Importance of Stupidity in Scientific Research' (2008) 121 *Journal of Cell Science* 1171.

45 Witte et al, above n42, 795.

46 Witte et al, above n24, 251.

47 Robert Root-Bernstein, 'I Don't Know!' (2008) in Vitek and Johnson, above n15, 233, 243.

48 See Paul Maharg and Caroline Maughan (eds), *Affect and Legal Education* (Ashgate, 2011).

11 Balance and Context

Law Student Well-Being and Lessons From Positive Psychology

*James Duffy**

Introduction

Balance. In addressing the nexus between legal education and decline in law student well-being, it is important to think about balance. When levelling criticism at the content and pedagogy of twenty-first century legal education, we speak of adversarialism, pessimism, rationality and professional detachment in pejorative tones. We shouldn't. The phrase 'thinking like a lawyer' has become a euphemistic 'catchcry' for the almost schizoid detachment of feeling and affect from legal reasoning.[1] It shouldn't be. In the public eye there is a disconnect between the role of lawyers and the resolution of conflict. There shouldn't be. In this context law students are being asked to feel good about themselves and the future profession that they are entering. It is little wonder that many do not.

The field of positive psychology has lessons to offer the discipline of law in terms of the importance of balance. The field of positive psychology itself is a balance to other areas of psychology which focus on damage, weakness and pathology. Perhaps one answer to the law student well-being challenge is reflected in positive psychology's contribution to the greater field of psychology: a focus that goes beyond fixing what is wrong, to include a strengthening of what is going right. Adversarialism, pessimism, rational cognition and detachment represent incredibly important skillsets and mindsets for the law student and the legal practitioner. That said, they are context specific and should not be equated with what it 'means to be a lawyer' (whatever that means). Adversarialism should be balanced with alternative dispute resolution, pessimism with optimism and the cognitive with the affective. Striving towards these balances may help to address the imbalance of psychological distress experienced by law students.

Positive Psychology

One of the main purposes of this chapter is to promote the role that positive psychology might play in addressing the well-being of law students. Positive psychology has been described as a subfield of psychology with a 'very long past, but only a very short history'.[2] What this means is that many of the issues that fall under the banner of positive psychology have been considered and debated for hundreds of years. However, the field of positive psychology has a short history because it was only formally named/created in 1998 by Martin Seligman, the then president of the American Psychological Association. The main thrust of the positive psychology movement is that the scientific study of what goes right in life is just as important as the study of mental illness and what goes wrong in life. According to psychology Professor Christopher Peterson, since World War II the field of psychology has adopted a disease model of human nature where 'people are seen as flawed and fragile, casualties of cruel environments or bad genetics, and if not in denial then at best in recovery'.[3] Positive psychology was introduced to correct this balance and consider how average (and not so average) people can live better and more fulfilling lives.

Relying upon positive psychology as the theoretical basis for this chapter involves certain normative assumptions about law student well-being and the purpose of groups like the Wellness Network for Law in Australia. First is that law student psychological distress currently exists at levels that warrant intervention. Second, legal academics (and not just psychologists) have a role to play in preventing/ameliorating law student psychological distress. Third, the steps we take to improve well-being should not be limited to, or specifically directed at, those who are suffering high levels of psychological distress. Interventions should apply to all students, in an attempt to improve the psychological well-being of everyone. Fourth, where possible our interventions should be preventative, rather than reactive.

In brief, evidence suggests that law student psychological distress does currently exist at alarming levels, and therefore warrants intervention. Empirical studies in the United States since the 1980s were suggestive of this phenomenon,[4] and Australian research has confirmed that law student psychological distress is a problem there also.[5] The 2009 report *Courting the Blues: Attitudes towards Depression in Australian Law Students and Legal Practitioners* concerningly showed that 35.2 per cent of law students were suffering either high or very high levels of psychological distress.[6] These findings have been empirically supported by research at the University of New South Wales,[7] the University of Adelaide,[8] Monash University,[9] the Australian National University[10] and the University of Melbourne.[11] This evidence base is unavoidable and justifies action.

Legal academics must have a role to play in combating law student psychological distress. The empirical work referred to above suggests that what we teach at law school and how we teach it are contributing factors to declines in well-being. These factors are, to a degree (acknowledging the Priestly 11 requirements for legal curricula), within the control of the legal academy, and it is important that the academy recognizes its agency in supporting the psychological well-being of law students.[12]

Consistent with the message of positive psychology, I believe that the steps we take to improve law student well-being should be aimed at all students – not just those suffering from psychological distress. If 35 per cent of law students are suffering from high levels of psychological distress, then 65 per cent are not. The argument here is that we should consider studying those students who succeed and thrive at law school. Given the competitive pressures and stressors that we know are attendant upon legal study, how do these students cope, succeed and potentially do so with a degree of happiness? To date, this has not been a focus of the wellness in law movement in Australia or overseas. By broadening the wellness agenda of legal education, we send the message to students that everybody can improve their psychological well-being – regardless of their current well-being base level. By considering what goes right for many law students, we can begin to identify those factors or characteristics that may buffer these students from stress, anxiety and depression.[13]

Finally, where possible our wellness interventions should be proactive and preventative, rather than reactive. At the 2014 Wellness Forum for Law (hosted at the Queensland University of Technology), legal academic and psychologist Stephen Tang asked other legal academics, 'what are we trying to do' with respect to law student well-being? Are we trying to promote well-being or prevent distress? Are we hoping to be proactive about law student psychological distress or reactive (taking steps after we know it is occurring)? One view, consistent with positive psychology, is that our goal should be to *promote* the psychological well-being of all law students. A consequence of promoting well-being is that we may *proactively prevent* psychological distress. If our goal is simply the *prevention* of distress (be it proactive or reactive), we risk subscribing to the disease model of human nature (law students are flawed and fragile) and ignoring what is going right with many law students. Through our research, conversations and interventions with law students we are at risk of marginalizing the majority if our sole focus is on law student psychological distress and what is going wrong. We need to reframe the challenge. Psychological well-being is more than just the absence of mental illness – it is the promotion of positive emotion, positive character and positive institutions.[14] This is a message that is applicable to all law students and legal practitioners.

Adversarialism and Alternative Dispute Resolution (ADR): Avoiding Zero-Sum Games

Very few connections between positive psychology and the law have been made in academic literature. Seligman himself has suggested that one of the causes of lawyer unhappiness is their continual involvement in zero-sum games.[15] A zero-sum game is one in which any gain by one player/party is counterbalanced by a corresponding loss by the other player/party. If my wife and I are deciding how to divide a pizza up to eat, and I take 75 per cent of the pizza, my wife then loses 75 per cent of the pizza. If one party gains 75 per cent and the other party loses 75 per cent, the result is a net sum of zero. According to Seligman, Verkuil and Kang, we should avoid zero-sum games because they lead to negative emotions such as anger, anxiety and sadness.[16]

The adversarial/court system in Australia and other common law countries is a zero-sum game for plaintiffs and defendants, appellants and respondents. A judge will rule in favour of one party and the other party loses. The message from positive psychology would be that to optimize well-being we should avoid zero-sum games wherever possible. This has implications for both the practice of law and the content of legal education. Tertiary legal education places an enormous weight upon adjudication (particularly appellate decisions) as the predominant form of conflict resolution. Students are taught how to work within and manipulate this adversarial system. Either wittingly or unwittingly, students are being indoctrinated into the zero-sum world of adversarial litigation, and their 'standard philosophical map'[17] regarding the appropriate fit between conflict and court-based adjudication is constantly being shaped.[18]

For a law student, a win in litigation means a judgment in their (imaginary) client's favour. The goal of winning a zero-sum game invites competition and adversarialism and suppresses cooperation. Substantive and procedural law must be used to defeat an opponent so your client can achieve their legally desired outcome and your opponent cannot achieve theirs. Why would you help or cooperate with the other party, knowing that your help advantages them (to your detriment) in a zero-sum game? Such an environment does little to encourage empathy and compassion towards another party in a dispute.

The complete avoidance of zero-sum games in legal practice and education is neither possible nor desirable. Litigation is an essential part of our justice system, and essential where conflict is entrenched; parties are unwilling to negotiate; a precedent needs to be set; or where the topic matter of the dispute demands court-based adjudication (for example criminal law). Those cases aside, a focus on alternative forms of dispute resolution (where possible) is consistent with the principles of positive psychology, because such a focus promotes the expression of positive human emotions and traits in legal actors. Alternative dispute resolution options such as negotiation, mediation and conciliation are not zero-sum games, and that impacts upon how lawyers and law students can think and behave with respect to situations of conflict. As King et al. have stated:

> For many lawyers, the ability to practise without having to adopt the aggressive persona of the litigator is a liberating experience, as no doubt there is a vast number of lawyers whose self image as a professional does not follow the traditional adversarial model. Non-adversarial practices allow lawyers to cast off the shackles of adversarial behaviour, providing them with an opportunity to reinvent themselves (and their image) as more caring and helpful.[19]

Positive psychology has three central areas of interest: the study of positive emotions, positive character traits and positive (enabling) institutions.[20] When writing about zero-sum games, Seligman pointedly observes that negative emotions evolve from zero-sum games and positive emotions flow from non-zero sum games.[21] Attitudes and actions of cooperation, collaboration, mutual respect and mutual problem solving underpin the philosophy behind ADR. It is not difficult to see how these actions/attitudes lead to lawyers experiencing a range of positive emotions: *pleasure* in finding common ground between disputing parties; *gratification* when a matter is settled without going through the expense and emotional turmoil of litigation; *satisfaction* and *contentment* that legal knowledge and skills have been used in a non-adversarial forum to facilitate the efficient resolution of a dispute.

ADR as a non-zero sum game approach to conflict may also promote the flourishing of positive human traits. Peterson and Seligman's list of character strengths and virtues includes many traits that are often expressed by lawyers (and law students when conducting role plays) when engaged in ADR forums:

- Creativity – thinking of novel and productive ways to conceptualize and do things.
- Open-mindedness – thinking things through and examining them from all sides.
- Perspective – being able to provide wise counsel to others.
- Authenticity/integrity – presenting oneself in a genuine way.
- Bravery – not shrinking from threat, challenge, difficulty or pain.
- Kindness – doing favours and good deeds for others.
- Social intelligence – being aware of the motives and feelings of self and others.
- Fairness – treating all people the same according to notions of fairness and justice.
- Team work – working well as a member of a group or team.
- Prudence – being careful about one's choices; not saying or doing things that might later be regretted.
- Self-regulation – regulating what one feels and does.
- Hope – expecting the best and working to achieve it.[22]

An approach to dispute resolution informed by positive psychology would likely enhance these character strengths, rather than increasing anxiety by focusing only on risks and weaknesses. ADR forums allow these traits to be expressed more openly and completely when compared to zero-sum litigation. Deep down, it may be that these are the traits that many lawyers and law students want to possess and express. The difficulty for law students and practitioners (and of potential impact to their psychological well-being) is that these positive traits are not often associated with lawyers. The media and popular discourse more generally does not always portray lawyers in a positive light. This has flow-on effects to the general public and law students themselves, who are susceptible to accepting negative stereotypes of lawyers, without a full appreciation of the functional utility (and social good) that is part of any lawyering role. With respect to lawyer and law student psychological well-being, positive psychology researchers have shown that the human strengths and traits mentioned above 'act as buffers against mental illness'.[23] If lawyers and law students can gain an appreciation of what their signature character strengths are, and act in accordance with them, this action may not simply ward off mental illness, but actually improve well-being.[24] This assertion is supported by Seligman, who claims that 'authentic happiness' results when people use their 'signature strengths' on a daily basis.[25]

Finally, ADR is a positive institution within the wider justice system. The word 'institution' is used broadly in positive psychology to encompass things like family, school, work, religion. It is also used narrowly to refer to groups of people, and bricks and mortar organizations. A positive institution is one that provides a sense of meaning and purpose to those who are involved with it – it relates to 'civic virtues and the institutions that move individuals toward better citizenship'.[26] Peterson uses the phrase 'enabling institution' interchangeably with 'positive institution', because in his view 'positive institutions facilitate the development and display of positive traits, which in turn facilitate positive subjective experiences'.[27] ADR forums are enabling in a literal sense in that they allow access to justice for many people who simply do not have the resources (money, time etc.) to engage with the court system. In a positive psychology sense, ADR processes are enabling in that they are undergirded by values associated with well-being. Voluntariness, non-adversarialism, self-determination, autonomy and consensuality of outcomes have all been identified as values of ADR processes[28] – values that sometimes lie in stark contrast to the operation of court-based adjudication.

In summary, litigation is often a zero-sum game, and repeat exposure to zero-sum games negatively impacts upon psychological well-being. In the legal context, ADR processes provide constructive alternatives to zero-sum games, and the message from positive psychologists is to pursue non-zero sum games wherever possible. Litigation is an essential part of our legal system, but current legal education places a disproportionate emphasis upon court adjudication, compared to its prevalence in practice.[29] There is a need to redress this imbalance. An increased focus on ADR instruction in law school[30] would allow our students to envisage different modes of legal practice that are more consonant with positive human emotion[31] and the expression of positive character traits. Curbing the intensity of law student (and lawyer) non-zero sum behaviour through the positive/enabling institution of ADR has positive well-being implications for all involved, regardless of their baseline level of mental health.

Pessimism and Optimism/Hope

I have written elsewhere that the goal of legal education should be to produce happy, healthy, competent professionals, in law or otherwise.[32] This goal has the twin benefits of being easy to understand and being quite ambitious; and it will sometimes be the case that legal educators fall short of achieving this end with their students. Holistic legal education goals must admit to gradation, but we should not tolerate educational practices that cause net harm. In this respect, law schools should borrow the principle from medicine and healthcare to do no harm (*primum non nocere*/non-maleficence). Much has been written about law student and lawyer thinking styles, often euphemistically referred to as 'thinking like a lawyer'. Teaching law students to think like a lawyer has the potential to cause psychological harm to law students because this thinking style is pessimistic and sometimes negative.[33] According to Krieger,

> Thinking like a lawyer is fundamentally negative; it is critical, pessimistic, and depersonalising. It is a damaging paradigm in law schools because it is usually conveyed, and understood, as a new and superior way of thinking, rather than an important but strictly limited legal tool.[34]

Contrary to the thoughts of Krieger, there are reasons to believe that teaching students to think like a lawyer is not *necessarily* damaging, but I would place a caveat on this response. Some of the cognitive thinking skills we teach and model to our students *are* pessimistic and depersonalizing; and, to that extent, students need to be made aware that pessimism is adaptive in some contexts but maladaptive in others.[35] Secondly, pessimism in the law degree needs to be counterbalanced (and ideally counteracted) with optimism/hope.

Given the high levels of workload and stress that are attendant upon studying law, the fact that many students remain happy and quite successful is no mean feat. The field of positive psychology urges us to consider how these students thrive under such conditions. Empirical research on hope and optimism continues to be an important part of positive psychology, and this research has extended to the benefits of hope for undergraduate students (including undergraduate law students).[36]

Hope can be described as a 'cognitive model of human motivation which explains goal related thinking'.[37] Snyder's model of hope suggests that hope can be understood in terms of three key elements: goals, pathways thinking and agentic thinking.[38] A goal is a mental endpoint or destination that an individual or group is trying to achieve, and can be short term or long term. Pathways thinking involves 'the production of plausible routes to a goal as well as a sense of confidence in these routes'.[39] Agency/agentic thinking is 'the perceived capacity to initiate and sustain movement along a pathway until the goal is reached'.[40] We could therefore say that a law student has high hopes when they are motivated and have strong willpower (agentic thinking) to generate a range of strategies (pathways thinking) for achieving a goal (an endpoint).[41]

Optimism has been variously defined in the psychological literature, but many writers refer to anthropologist Lionel Tiger's definition of optimism as 'a mood or attitude associated with an expectation about the social or material future – one which the evaluator regards as socially desirable, to his [or her] advantage, or for his [or her] pleasure'.[42] In plain language, optimists expect good things to happen and pessimists expect bad things to happen.[43] The concept of optimism is slightly different to the concept of hope. Whilst the concepts both relate to a desired state of affairs, hope relates to outcomes that an individual can influence, or take steps to achieve. Optimism involves a person expecting good things to happen, where the outcome is outside the individual's control.[44] For example, Martin and Rand suggest that a student could be hopeful about getting good grades (an outcome a student can influence by studying hard), compared to a person being optimistic that it won't rain today (an outcome beyond their control).[45]

When legal academics are teaching their students about thinking styles that will be essential to their future careers, they introduce students to instrumentally useful skills:

- non-assumptive thinking
- critical thinking
- emotional detachment
- tolerance of ambiguity
- rational analysis
- intellectual flexibility (being able to argue both sides of a case)
- problem spotting and risk detection.[46]

The negative flipside of some of these thinking skills is that they can be described as pessimistic. In particular, law students and lawyers are trained to find problems and assign blame in scenarios that have already occurred. They are asked to identify risk, and predict downsides and catastrophes that might eventuate in future legal transactions. They are constantly asked to look for, expect and then plan for worst-case scenarios. They are trained to take a pessimistic view, over and over again. This pessimism is said to be adaptive in a legal context because clients are often interested in understanding their worst-case scenario, and how they can hedge against future risks. The ability to extrapolate forward and anticipate future problems and their legal consequences is one of the chief ways that a lawyer adds value for their client. Law students are being trained to operate effectively in this problem-focused environment.

Wisely, Seligman, Verkuil and Kang comment 'that the qualities that make for a good lawyer [and law student], however, may not make for a happy human being'.[47] Studies confirm that pessimism generally leads to decreased coping skills[48] and is a significant cause of depression and learned helplessness.[49] Legal educators are therefore left with a tricky task – to preserve the functionally adaptive aspects of pessimism within their students,[50] but to do so in a way that is balanced (with optimism/hope) and context appropriate. This means that we need to have explicit conversations with our students about pessimistic thinking styles leaking into their personal lives, and the deleterious effects this may have upon their well-being. Pessimism and risk aversion may be appropriate in some legal contexts, but there will also be many scenarios in a legal setting where pessimism may be counterproductive. A lawyer, when assuming the worst-case scenario for their client, may premise their communications and procedural advice on the basis that a matter is destined for litigation. In this way, opportunities for constructive negotiation and early settlement of a matter may be overlooked.

It may sound glib to suggest that hope is a powerful way to increase law student well-being. Snyder's conception of hope theory, however, provides us with a definition and partial operationalization of hope that (in my opinion) makes the construct far less abstract – goals, pathways thinking and agentic thinking. Positive psychology literature on hope (as it pertains to law students) has shown that hope predicts academic performance and psychological well-being in law school.[51] More generally, Rand and Martin note that:

> Hope has been shown to positively correlate with self-esteem, perceived problem-solving abilities, perceptions of control, and positive affect. High-hope persons tend to experience better mental health, greater pain tolerance, and better recovery from illness and injury . . . Hope has [also] correlated positively with social competence and pleasure in getting to know others.[52]

Whilst this chapter has focused on theoretical connections between positive psychology and law student well-being, it is important that this knowledge can actually be translated into the classroom. Martin and Rand have identified five ways that legal educators can instil hope in their students:

1 Help law students formulate appropriate goals.
2 Increase law students' autonomy.
3 Model the learning process.
4 Help law students understand grading as feedback rather than pure evaluation.
5 Model and encourage agentic thinking.[53]

I would add to this list by suggesting that encouraging law students to develop a positive legal professional identity can also increase their levels of hope. A legal professional identity focuses on how an individual views themselves in a legal professional role. A legal professional identity is shaped by the way a person defines and views their legal role, and the expectations and behaviours they possess (and adopt) when thinking about their professional role.[54] Simply put, if a law student is working towards a goal that has meaning for them (being a happy, healthy, competent professional) they are likely to be more motivated and determined (agentic thinking) in finding multiple routes (pathways thinking) to achieving that goal. Legal educators do not have to be passive bystanders in this process. Legal practitioners are somewhat maligned in the eyes of the public, and legal educators can remind law students about the social importance and public good that underpins the lawyering role. We can help students appreciate the many different types of lawyering roles that exist. We can help students identify modes of legal practice that may resonate with their own personalities, values and signature strengths. Positive psychology tells us that acting upon signature strengths promotes psychological well-being and happiness. In essence, we can facilitate the emergent development of a student's professional identity, and the concomitant mental health boost that accompanies a student who has high hope for their future career.

Conclusion

This chapter has suggested that the field of positive psychology has a lot to offer in terms of how we address law student and lawyer psychological health. The legal academy's focus on law student psychological distress to date has been well intentioned, but we may only be doing half the job we should be doing. In addition to considering what may be going wrong with law students, we should also consider what is going right, and how we can improve the psychological well-being of all students, regardless of their base level of mental health. This approach to law student well-being is inclusive and represents a positive reframing of the challenge we face with respect to law students and their mental health. Promoting law student psychological well-being in a proactive manner may require us to do more of certain things, and less of others, in our legal curricula. This chapter has suggested the importance of balance in what we do – balancing our focus on litigation (zero-sum game) with increased instruction in alternative dispute resolution, supplementing some of the pessimistic traits we encourage and reward in law school with instruction and facilitation of hope and optimistic traits (including the development of positive professional legal identities). If 35 per cent of our law students are suffering from high levels of psychological distress, then 65 per cent are not. It is time to take our knowledge of what allows individuals to thrive, flourish and be happy, and apply it to 100 per cent of our law students.

Notes

* BCom/LLB (Hons)(UQ), LLM (QUT), Lecturer, Queensland University of Technology Law School; james.duffy@qut.edu.au.

1 Paul Maharg and Caroline Maughan (eds), *Affect and Legal Education: Emotion in Learning and Teaching the Law* (Ashgate, 2011) 1.

2 Christopher Peterson, *A Primer in Positive Psychology* (Oxford University Press, 2006) 4.

3 Ibid. 5.

4 Stephen B Shanfield, G Andrew and H Benjamin, 'Psychiatric Distress in Law Students' (1985) 35 *Journal of Legal Education* 65; G Andrew et al, 'The Role of Legal Education in Producing Psychological Distress among Law Students and Lawyers' (1986) 11(2) *Law and Social Inquiry* 225.

5 For a summary of this research, see Rachael Field and James Duffy, 'Better to Light a Single Candle than to Curse the Darkness: Promoting Law Student Well-Being through a First Year Law Subject' (2012) *Queensland University of Technology Law and Justice Journal* 133.

6 Norm Kelk et al, *Courting the Blues: Attitudes towards Depression in Australian Law Students and Lawyers* (Brain and Mind Research Institute [BMRI], 2009), available at http://www.cald.asn.au/docs/Law%20Report%20Website%20version%204%20 May%2009.pdf. See also Norm Kelk, Sharon Medlow and Ian Hickie, 'Distress and Depression among Australian Law Students: Incidence, Attitudes and the Role of Universities' (2010) 32 *Sydney Law Review* 113.

7 Massimiliano Tani and Prue Vines, 'Law Students' Attitudes to Education: Pointers to Depression in the Legal Academy and the Profession?' (2007) 19(1) *Legal Education Review* 3.

8 Catherine Leahy et al, 'Distress Levels and Self-Reported Treatment Rates for Medicine, Law, Psychology and Mechanical Engineering Students: Cross-Sectional Study' (2010) 44(7) *Australian and New Zealand Journal of Psychiatry* 608.

9 Natalia Antolak-Saper, Lloyd England and Anthony Lester, 'Health and Wellbeing in the First Year: The Law School Experience' (2011) 36(1) *Alternative Law Journal* 47.

10 Kath Hall, Molly Townes O'Brien and Stephen Tang, 'Developing a Professional Identity in Law Schools: A View from Australia' (2010) 4 *Phoenix Law Review* 19; Molly Townes O'Brien, Stephen Tang and Kath Hall, 'No Time to Lose: Negative Impact on Law Student Well-Being May Begin in Year One' (2011) 2(2) *International Journal of the First Year in Higher Education* 49; Molly Townes O'Brien, Stephen Tang and Kath Hall, 'Changing our Thinking: Empirical Research on Law Student Well-Being, Thinking Styles and the Law Curriculum' (2011) 21(2) *Legal Education Review* 149.
11 Wendy Larcombe et al, 'Does an Improved Experience of Law School Protect Students against Depression, Anxiety and Stress? An Empirical Study of Well-Being and the Law School Experience of LLB and JD Students' (2013) 35 *Sydney Law Review* 407; Wendy Larcombe and Katherine Fethers, 'Schooling the Blues? An Investigation of Factors Associated with Psychological Distress among Law Students' (2013) 36 *University of New South Wales Law Journal* 390; Wendy Larcombe, Ian Malkin and Pip Nicholson, 'Law Students' Motivations, Expectations and Levels of Psychological Distress: Evidence of Connections' (2012) 22 *Legal Education Review* 71.
12 Field and Duffy, above n5.
13 Todd David Peterson and Elizabeth Waters Peterson, 'Stemming the Tide of Law Student Depression: What Law Schools Need to Learn from the Science of Positive Psychology (2009) *Yale Journal of Health Policy, Law, and Ethics* 357, 362.
14 Martin Seligman and Mihaly Csikszentmihalyi, 'Positive Psychology: An Introduction' (2000) 55 *American Psychologist* 5, 5.
15 Martin Seligman, Paul Verkuil and Terry Kang, 'Why Lawyers Are Unhappy' (2005) 10 *Deakin Law Review* 49.
16 Ibid. 60.
17 Leonard Riskin, 'Mediation and Lawyers' (1982) 43 *Ohio State Law Journal* 29, 49–50.
18 Molly Townes O'Brien, 'Facing Down the Gladiators: Law School's Hidden Adversarial Curriculum' (2011) 37(1) *Monash Law Review* 43.
19 Michael King et al, *Non-Adversarial Justice* (Federation Press, 2009) 230.
20 Martin Seligman et al, 'Positive Psychology Progress' (2005) 60(5) *American Psychologist* 410, 410.
21 Seligman, Verkuil and Kang, above n15, 60.
22 Seligman et al, above n20, 412.
23 Seligman and Csikszentmihalyi, above n14, 7.
24 Colin James, 'Law Student Wellbeing: Benefits of Promoting Psychological Literacy and Self-Awareness Using Mindfulness, Strengths Theory and Emotional Intelligence' (2011) 21(1/2) *Legal Education Review* 217, 224–30.
25 Martin E Seligman, *Authentic Happiness* (Free Press, 2002) xi. Surveys that identify an individual's character strengths and virtues are available free online. The best known of these is Peterson and Seligman's 'Values in Action' character strengths survey, available at http://www.viacharacter.org/www/The-Survey.
26 Seligman and Csikszentmihalyi, above n14, 5.
27 Peterson, above n2, 20. See also Peter Huang and Jeremy Blumenthal, 'Positive Institutions, Law, and Policy' in Shane J Lopez and CR Snyder (eds), *The Oxford Handbook of Positive Psychology* (Oxford University Press, 2nd ed, 2009) 589.
28 Laurence Boulle, *Mediation: Principles, Process, Practice* (LexisNexis, 2011) 62–91.
29 See James Duffy and Rachael Field, 'Why ADR Must Be a Mandatory Subject in the Law Degree: A Cheat Sheet for the Willing and a Primer for the Non-Believer' (2014) 25(1) *Australasian Dispute Resolution Journal* 9, 10. It has been estimated that the number of commenced civil actions that culminate in adjudication is less than 5 per cent; Michael King et al, *Non-Adversarial Justice* (Federation Press, 2009) 9, 90. Compare Hon Justice Michael Kirby AC CMG, 'Foreword to the Second Edition' in Peter Condliffe, *Conflict Management: A Practical Guide* (LexisNexis, 3rd ed, 2008) v–vi.

30 See Rachael Field, ALTC Teaching Fellowship entitled *Stimulating Strategic Change in Legal Education to Address High Levels of Psychological Distress in Law Students*. Summary available at http://www.olt.gov.au/resource-promoting-law-student-well-being-through-curriculum.

31 Dr Colin James at the University of Newcastle law school has written frequently on the value of positive emotion and emotional intelligence generally for law students and legal practitioners. See Colin James, 'Lawyer Dissatisfaction, Emotional Intelligence and Clinical Legal Education' (2008) 18 *Legal Education Review* 123; Colin *James, 'Seeing Things As We Are: Emotional Intelligence and Clinical Legal Education' (2005) 6 International Journal of Clinical Legal Education 123.*

32 See Rachael Field and James Duffy, 'Law Student Psychological Distress, ADR and Sweet-Minded, Sweet-Eyed Hope' (2012) 23(3) *Australasian Dispute Resolution Journal* 195.

33 See Hall, O'Brien and Tang, 'Developing a Professional Identity', above n10.

34 Lawrence Krieger, 'Institutional Denial about the Dark Side of Law School, and Fresh Empirical Guidance for Constructively Breaking the Silence' (2002) 52 (1–2) *Journal of Legal Education* 112, 117.

35 Seligman, Verkuil and Kang, above n15, 56.

36 Allison Martin and Kevin Rand, 'The Future's So Bright, I Gotta Wear Shades: Law School through the Lens of Hope' (2010) 48 *Duquesne Law Review* 203, 207.

37 Ibid. The general description of hope theory in this paragraph has been adopted from Field and Duffy, 'Law Student Psychological Distress', above n32, 199. Hope is also one of the 24 character strengths identified above in Peterson and Seligman's character strengths and values list.

38 CR Snyder, 'Hypothesis: There is Hope', in CR Snyder (ed), *Handbook of Hope: Theory, Measures, and Applications* (Academic Press, 2000) 9.

39 Kevin Rand, 'Hope and Optimism: Latent Structures and Influences on Grade Expectancy and Academic Performance' (2009) 77(1) *Journal of Personality* 231, 233.

40 Ibid.

41 Snyder, above n38, 10–11.

42 Lionel Tiger, *Optimism: The Biology of Hope* (Simon & Schuster, 1979) 18.

43 Michael Scheier and Charles Carver, 'Optimism, Coping and Health: Assessment and Implications of Generalised Outcome Expectancies' (1985) 4 *Health Psychology* 219, 223.

44 Martin and Rand, above n36, 209.

45 Ibid. Further discussion of hope and optimism can be found in Rachael Field, James Duffy and Anna Huggins, *Lawyering and Positive Professional Identities* (LexisNexis Butterworths, 2014) Chapter 3.

46 This list has been drawn (and modified) from Michelle Sanson, Thalia Anthony and David Worswick, *Connecting with Law* (Oxford University Press, 2010), 10–11.

47 Seligman, Verkuil and Kang, above n15, 56.

48 Rand, above n39, 235.

49 Peterson and Peterson, above n13, 240.

50 Satterfield et al. explain that the quality of prudence may be an aspect of pessimism that is useful for both law students and lawyers alike: 'Perhaps under the more rigorous demands and specific intellectual requirements of law school, diligent students who develop a sense of healthy scepticism are the highest achievers. In fact, careful attention to detail, considering all sides of an argument, seeing all potential pitfalls or catastrophes, attention to precedent rather than salutary creativity and thoroughness are typically seen as important traits for the successful lawyer': Jason Satterfield, John Monahan and Martin Seligman, 'Law School Performance Predicted by Explanatory Style' (1997) 15 *Behavioural Sciences and the Law* 95, 103.

51 Martin and Rand, above n36, 205.
52 Ibid, 204–15 (citations omitted).
53 Martin and Rand, above n36.
54 Field, Duffy and Huggins, above n45, 10.

12 Connecting Law Students to Health and Wellbeing

Molly Townes O'Brien[*]

This chapter re-examines law school student wellbeing from a remedial standpoint. It does not claim to have all the remedies. Instead, it considers student discomfort, some possible remedial options, and makes some recommendations to promote a positive law student culture in order to graduate a group of engaged, connected and confident lawyers.

Looking at the available data, it is apparent that many students find law school to be stressful.[1] Surveys administered at the Australian National University (ANU) showed that students entered law school with very few symptoms of depression, stress and anxiety; but by the end of the year their distress scores were substantially higher, not only than the beginning-of-year students, but also higher than the general population. By the end of the first year, approximately one-third of students had levels of psychological distress which could cause substantial impairments in educational, interpersonal or occupational functioning.[2] The ANU surveys were followed by a weekend dialogue retreat for a group of students and faculty at ANU's Kioloa coastal campus. Participants were provided with informal opportunities to describe, discuss and re-imagine law school.[3]

While there are many possible reasons that law school may increase psychological distress,[4] this chapter will focus on what students cited in dialogue as their chief grievances. Students described law school as a transformative journey in which they addressed complex and confusing cases but avoided or ignored the personal impact of law. They found law school to be a place that made them more rational, competitive, adversarial, arrogant and elitist. For some students, mental distress was relieved by the encouragement and assistance of friends, mentors and lecturers. Other students pointed out the isolation, disconnection and intolerance of law school. When asked to re-imagine their law school experience, students explained that their ideal law school experience would have been more connected – to mentors, to other students and to the real-world impact of law.[5] With regard to the content of the law degree, there was a consensus that law study could be made more interesting and contextual. Some students re-imagined the law school as a place that would do more to engage with the political and practical side of law.[6]

In other words, students associated their lack of social connections and/or engagement in social justice issues with their loss of wellbeing. They also pointed to the infrequent use of their developing problem-solving skills. The student complaints do not, however, dictate the steps a law school should take to foster positive relationships and nurture student wellbeing. In sum, this chapter asks, and attempts to answer, two difficult questions: What changes in the law school curriculum would promote a 'more connected' and more engaged experience? And, more importantly, how can the lawyer's role as problem solver be thoroughly incorporated into the legal curriculum?

To provide more complete answers to these questions, further research on student wellbeing is needed. Nevertheless, in trying to answer these questions, ANU has not simply wrung its hands. It has made an effort to implement steps that promote student engagement and connection. These steps focus on the development of a positive culture. They promote law students' thriving and doing good in the world. In summary, the steps are to:

1 have an explicit mission that makes students central;
2 recruit students who value work and get a chance to try several job placements or part time jobs;
3 support student activism and fund it;
4 have an active learning curriculum;
5 build a faculty who respect the practice of law and who value students and their health;
6 foster an open-minded approach.

Although the steps and methods sound diverse, the anticipated result of adopting them is singular: a group of thriving, value-oriented and confident law students and future legal practitioners.

The Mission

Every law school has a mission. It may be to 'train well-rounded, critical, and socially conscious thinkers and doers'[7] or 'to be a nationally and internationally recognized leader in the development and dissemination of legal knowledge'[8] or '[to train] . . . lawyers . . . to serve their clients and the public; to lead our profession; and to help solve the problems of our nation and our world'.[9] Whatever the law school claims its mission to be, a *mission statement* is a statement of the fundamental reason for an organization's existence. It tells something about the organization's strengths, its public image and its core values.[10]

In the US, the American Bar Association (ABA) requires every accredited law school to have a mission statement.[11] Similarly, in 2009 the Council of Australian Law Deans (CALD) adopted a set of standards that requires every law school to state its mission.[12] Nevertheless, despite the CALD decision, very few Australian law schools have published a mission statement. While most US law schools make their mission statement available on the web, sometimes the mission is treated as a formality, or not made clear to the faculty, the students or the public.[13] In failing to enunciate a mission, some law schools miss an opportunity to test out strategic plans; to establish a sense of community; to prepare for changes in the structure of legal education; or to state a deeply shared vision and values in terms of 'serving students, faculty, society, sponsor, or other constituency'.[14] The connection between a mission statement and student wellbeing is about trying to address the student questions: What is the meaning of law school? Why am I doing this? If the law school isn't clear about the use and meaningfulness of law studies, how can the student be?

Each law school has a personality, created by the personalities and specialties of its faculty. The mission statement should reflect that personality. Drafting a mission statement is difficult because the mission aspires to state the core reason for the organization's existence and because writing it requires the agreement of many people throughout the organization. The mission statement can encapsulate the organization in terms of its aspirations, its commitments, its philosophy, its self-concept, its image or its techniques.[15] Mission statements can communicate important ideas to the public and to students. They can provide a clear and compelling description of 'the road ahead, of how the organisation defines success and of important shared values and beliefs'.[16]

In other words, a mission statement can inform a student of what is considered to be important for success at the law school. It can tell a student what the key ingredients of successful law study are. A mission statement can tell a student how important their training is and how crucial their future role will be to the implementation of justice. The mission statement can let the student know that his or her education is fundamental to the existence of the law school. Having a philosophy that is stated and that is centred on students and their success could be crucial to the students' feeling connected to the school. It could make a student feel significant and welcome. It should function like a welcome mat or an inviting menu at a restaurant.

Students Who Value Work

When I first decided to attend law school, I did not know even one lawyer. I was not sure what legal practice would entail – even though I had seen episodes of *Perry Mason* and *Law and Order*. The practice of law was a mystery to me, as it is to many of our beginning students. Most law students enter law school without understanding much about the practice of law. For those students who end up practising law, however, working with clients – advising them, representing them, negotiating for them and being their legal counsel – will occupy most of their time. They need opportunities to work in law-related positions while they are still in law school. Working in a law office or in a law-related position will give them experience, confidence, connections and insight into how they plan to use their law degree.[17] It can also convince them that the law is not for them.

Although law students cannot go out and practise law during law school, they can do some closely allied jobs in law offices and in legal clinics. Of course, they can have hands-on learning experiences, explore different areas of the law and hone their legal skills in class. But more than any other activity, working at a law-related job will help them determine where they would like to apply their talents, and to build skills that will allow them to step confidently into the legal career of their choice. As a law student, I worked at four different law-related jobs. I spent several weeks, for example, at a large firm that specialized in insurance defence. I learned both the intricacies of discovery work and the certainty that I would never again work at an insurance defence firm.

Like me, as students work or volunteer at a law-related job, they can experience what various kinds of practice are like. They can see for themselves how they can be a peacemaker, a healer, a problem-solver,[18] facilitator for companies trying to navigate labyrinthine tax law, or even defender of the wealthy. They can be mentored by practising lawyers and gain insight into various fields. A law school should employ a number of practising lawyers and encourage students to do clinical classes. Many students work at law-related jobs during the semester. Law-related work helps them polish their legal skills and allows them to develop connections in their potential field of interest.

Working in a law-related job puts theory into practice. When students volunteer to work in legal service clinics or do practical tasks associated with their classes, the law comes to life. I have gone to a prison with a group of students on a Prison Issues Project. The volunteer work exposes the students to some real and difficult problems. It also opens an avenue for them to share their legal learning.

Students need to explore avenues for addressing problems with the law. When students collaborate with full-time practising lawyers, they contribute to the resolution of actual cases for real clients. They also enrich their coursework. Law becomes meaningful to students as they use it to help someone solve a problem. Law is no longer just abstract words and theory. It becomes practice. It is something that they know in a way that is not just a philosophy or a guideline. It becomes a useful tool.

Using the law to solve problems or generate action is deeply satisfying. It is rewarding to the students as people. As they use the skills they have acquired, they make an impact in a professional sense. They can try out a variety of areas of practice and gain confidence in their decision to study law.

Support and Fund Student Activism

In 2008 the ANU College of Law appointed its first Director of Law Reform and Social Justice to promote activity and awareness, and to teach students not only the law as it is, but also how the law came to be, and how it could be different. As the inaugural Director, Professor Simon Rice organized his way around the difficulties of running an outreach programme at a major university. Other law schools can take positive steps toward supporting student activism. Many teachers can make themselves accessible to students by keeping their door open; by supervising law reform honours projects; and by encouraging the highly motivated honours students to investigate their ideas for making law better.

In other words, you can encourage activism by encouraging your students to follow their feelings. When presented with naive untrained pathos from a student, we law professors can either help educate, direct and encourage the pathos; or we can (more easily) discourage the student by saying: 'It's more complicated than that' or 'It's not that simple'. As law teachers we are in an enviable position to inspire legal change. If we don't stifle student initiatives, we can encourage them and help facilitate their role as potential agents of legal reform.

Law schools should recognize and encourage academic staff to research not only the technical aspects of law's operation, but also law's connection to community engagement. Law students should explore who uses law, who is affected by it, whether it operates fairly and what the options are for its operating differently. Students at ANU have been actively encouraged to participate in devising and running voluntary social justice programmes.[19] A group of students put together an ANU Law Reform and Social Justice page on Facebook.[20] Student-run web pages at ANU have shown how law students can keep track of visiting scholars and join various projects involving prison issues, global power, human rights, animal rights and others.

These initiatives led to increased student activism and participation in law reform and social justice internships.[21] The law reform and social justice website helped by recording the student projects, the interested faculty, the events and the work groups open for students to join.

Over a few years, the ANU College of Law expanded its role in sharing its knowledge, skills and values through engagement with the community. Law reform and social justice became parts of the ANU College of Law. Through teaching, research, public events and social justice initiatives, the law school enhances law's role in society and the part that lawyers play in promoting both social change and stability. In fact, the student programme attracted high numbers of volunteers and developed projects to include community legal education, a human rights project, a prison issues project, a global power project and a project to get ready for a referendum on the constitutional recognition of indigenous peoples.[22]

Faculty members work with students on each project to assure that the work done is high quality. About 30 faculty members also submit papers to parliamentary inquiries or work with overseas law reform agencies.[23] Sometimes this work inspires a student to become involved. One student, for example, recently completed an honours project that considered the topic of one of my parliamentary submissions: education in a child's mother tongue.

In addition to participating in the student social justice projects, students at the ANU College of Law have a range of study opportunities in which they can explore the relationship between law and social justice through clinics and internships. Many of the internships can be undertaken as courses for credit. For example, ANU Green,[24] an on-campus environmental action group, offers a range of internships. Some are offered for course credit and are available to all students. These include the highly competitive International Alliance of Research Universities sustainability internships.[25] The Aurora Project offers law students and graduates internships and career opportunities in native title, policy, social justice and indigenous affairs.[26] Overseas internships are also available.[27]

By supporting and fostering various methods of student activism, ANU creates a community where the importance of the social good is acknowledged. Students can participate in one or more projects and know that they are learning to do good in the world. They can also continue working toward social justice when they return from internships to full-time study (law students) or to practice (graduates).

An Active Learning Curriculum

It is not enough to want to do good. Students need to have opportunities to put their ideals into action. Passive listening may, in fact, be a poor way to learn anything.[28] Transforming information into operational knowledge (an internalized understanding) is an active and interactive process.[29] It is an active process in that it requires students, at a minimum, to listen or read and understand. Students are more likely to understand and recall information, however, if they have engaged in applying, extending, interrogating, analysing or using it to make decisions and solve problems. Learning is also interactive in that new information must be integrated into the students' existing frameworks for understanding.[30] Learning involves not only absorbing new information but also integrating and revising existing information and assumptions.[31]

When students talk about what they are learning, write about it, relate it to past experiences and apply it to their daily lives, they are learning actively. They are also in a position to question their prior notions of social justice. Active learning puts students in a position to learn more and to learn differently. It is possible to engage in active learning in the law school classroom.[32] A course can employ hypothetical problems, video, online questions, mock debates, client simulations, negotiations, strategic planning etc. as ways to engage students in active learning in the classroom.[33] There is no reason for students to listen idly while a teacher reads a lecture. Students can be actively involved in learning, focused on a simulated or virtual client and engaged in a client-centred curriculum during a regularly scheduled class. Active, engaged students learn more.

Teaching rooms full of actively engaged learners will mean that sometimes teachers will need to make the transition from 'I don't know and that's not important' to 'I don't know, let's find out'. The main reluctance law professors (and academics in general) have in initiating these types of learning conditions is lack of confidence and the fear of not knowing something they should. We need to be reassured that saying 'I don't know, let's find out' is the only legitimate way to deal with a free-flowing, give-and-take with student participation. Students are not horrified when they ask a question and I say, 'I don't know the answer. How would you find out the answer?' They see that I am not dodging the question or leaving them without an answer. Instead, I am showing them how to drive pathways to knowledge.

In teaching a large Evidence course, I employ slide-based trivia-style contests. I divide the class into teams of five students each, to answer multiple choice questions. The questions require the students to read and interpret the rules of evidence in class, to discuss them with their peers, and to come up with what they think is the best answer. Teams record their answers on a sheet which is then exchanged with another team's at the end of each round. Each team scores the answer sheet of another team as the best or 'correct' answers are discussed. The answers to several of the questions are arguable – and I leave plenty of room for argument. As the game progresses students seem to forget that they are in a law lecture. Instead of listening with their heads down, they interject to defend their team's answers. They articulate legal concepts; they offer arguments in support of their views. The game has changed the social dynamic and made arguing a legal point more acceptable and fun.

When the faculty recently had a symposium to discuss integrating technology into the classroom, a two-hour session was not enough to hear all the different things that teachers were trying. Some engaged with students in another part of the world, for example in online discussion. Some used online surveys to test students and provide instant feedback during class.

A Faculty Who Respect the Practice of Law and Who Value Students and Their Health

Some law school faculties have teachers who practised law for a short time, disliked it and came back to a place where they were more comfortable – university. This pattern may be comfortable for some teachers; but if the faculty of a law school has many such teachers, the school may project hostility to the practice of law and may be a negative factor in students' sense of wellbeing.

Teacher attitude is important to the emotional climate of the classroom. Positive emotions help learning. Teacher warmth and support are vital to student success in law school.[34] The academic material is difficult. There are many legal questions without objectively correct answers.[35] Many law students do not know what they are going to do with their lives.[36] Many students enter law school with little interest in ever practising law. They may spend their time doing things that are not healthy or productive: procrastinating, playing games online or watching television. They may be unmotivated to study law, but may perceive law to be a relatively easy way to earn a degree that will confer status, respectability and a good salary.[37]

Meanwhile, law students' habits do not promote their wellbeing. A recent study at the University of Western Australia revealed that most students spent very little time exercising, but that students who exercised had better mental health results than those who did not.[38] As I observe what happens in most law schools, I am surprised at how little is done to encourage healthy living habits. Oh, we offer counsellors and physicians for the sick. But where are the cues for health? Where are the law school teams and intra-mural sports competitions? Maybe we should remind students to eat and sleep regularly.

These things are not difficult to change. For example, I spend a few minutes in a class actively encouraging my students to exercise and to look out for their health. Before exams, I remind students that they need to eat well, rest and sleep regularly during exam week. Students have contacted me years after graduating to tell me that they survived law school on my advice. I have recently begun having my office hours for students on foot – either running or walking. To my surprise, students have been appearing at my door and are keen to go. On the trail, they open up about issues that bother them. I listen and voice my encouragement or advice. Sometimes I just listen.

Law teachers' attitudes should reflect respect for students[39] and for the practice of law. Teachers should also be connected to, and positive about, healthy living.

Foster an Open-Minded Approach

Law school teachers need to create a respectful environment in the law school. In a respectful environment teachers and students accept each other as individuals, explore ideas and solve problems creatively. Intimidation, denigration, alienation and humiliation are absent. Teachers like and respect the students; and students like and respect each other and the teacher.[40] The teacher allows the students to get to know him or her by sharing some of their thoughts and stories.[41] For example, I often share stories with students about my most difficult clients or most difficult cases. The stories that generate the most animated reaction, however, are stories that generate ethical questions – like the story about the time a sex-offence defendant put the underwear of his rape victim on my office desk.[42]

Throughout the course, teachers can demonstrate respect for students, colleagues, lawyers, judges and the law. Teachers can incorporate and encourage a variety of student perspectives in their teaching. They can collaborate with students in goal setting, listen carefully to students' comments and challenge all students to meet high expectations.[43]

Each law student brings a unique set of perspectives and experiences to the classroom. Teachers can cultivate a respectful atmosphere by allowing for and listening to a variety of points of view. Law students will be appropriately stressed or distressed at some points in the semester. Sadness, disgust or anger can and probably should be felt in the face of gross injustice or harm of the kind that students are exposed to in their reading or clinical legal experience. Respectful teachers should give students opportunities to voice their negative feelings aloud in class, and to address them in terms of meaningful action in and beyond the classroom.

Negative emotions are an unavoidable part of human experience and the study and practice of law. They need to be processed reflectively and turned into values-congruent action, rather than internalized in destructive ways.[44] Awareness of emotion ought to be complemented with opportunities to respond and act in healthy and appropriate ways. Law students, like other students, need to have their values and judgements recognized and encouraged, especially when they are faced with the reality of struggle. No struggle is too difficult if it is made meaningful by association with a valuable goal. Assisting students to process their emotions may help to fulfil the basic psychological needs of autonomy, competence and relatedness.[45]

A good struggle is one that is motivated by meaning. Engaging with the complexity and challenge of law school in a way that is connected with the students' own motivations and values, rather than drowning them with experience-erasing abstraction, is essential for psychological health and wellbeing. By engaging in meaningful struggle with supported autonomy, a law student may immunize himself or herself to the psychological distress caused by disengagement, isolation, hopelessness and helplessness.

Conclusion

In spite of the data revealing law student psychological distress, law schools attract and graduate highly intelligent, motivated and passionate people. The majority of students stay psychologically healthy, and go on to highly active practice in their post-law school lives. While recognizing the need to address systemic wellbeing-impairing problems in the law school environment, we also need to focus on positive goals. A promotion-focused goal is concerned with the need to prevent further harm, eliminate negatives and promote a culture of safety, security and responsibility.[46] The goal is not to produce relaxed and superficially happy lawyers, but to produce competent lawyers and problem solvers who have the skills and the creativity to address legal and social problems and make a positive difference. Legal education should be experientially and emotionally grounded, so that lawyers can embrace the idea of struggle and change.

While the data collected at the ANU College of Law has been extremely valuable, the research process is just as important. It may be valuable to embrace the idea of empirical research as reflective conversation. It may be necessary to take steps that are compatible both with academic excellence and student wellbeing. The six steps outlined in this chapter encompass the law student's law school career from start to finish. The mission statement will make the student feel welcome and important. Recruiting students who value work and have an opportunity to try out several law-related jobs will inspire classroom work and will generate community connections. Law school support for law reform, social justice and student activism will create a community where the importance of social good is acknowledged and appreciated. An active-learning curriculum will ensure that the students engage with the substance of the material taught. If the law school faculty demonstrate respect for the practice of law and advocate healthy living habits, law students may feel healthier. And, finally, by fostering respect and an open-minded approach, law teachers can ensure that any struggle the students encounter is confronted in a positive and supported way.

These six steps do not resolve the problems of law student psychological distress. The ANU College of Law is actively researching what can be done to better support and connect its students. More research is needed before specific programmes to address law student wellbeing can be constructed. In the meantime, however, all of the steps I have outlined are likely to contribute positively to student wellbeing and to the success of the law school.

Notes

* Molly Townes O'Brien, AB JD LLM, is an Associate Professor at the ANU College of Law, Australian National University. This chapter is based on a talk delivered at the 2013 National Wellness for Law Forum, 21 February, University of Melbourne Law School.

1 A Brain and Mind Research Institute ('BMRI') report concluded that lawyers and law students generally exhibit higher levels of psychological distress and depression than their peers in the community: Norm Kelk et al, *Courting the Blues: Attitudes towards Depression in Australian Law Students and Legal Practitioners* (Brain and Mind Research Institute, 2009) 42. Norm Kelk, Sharon Medlow and Ian Hickie, 'Distress and depression among Australian law students: Incidence, attitudes and

the role of universities. (2010) 32 *Sydney Law Review*, 113–22; Wendy Larcombe, Ian Malkin and Pip Nicholson, 'Law Students' Motivations, Expectations and Levels of Psychological Distress: Evidence of Connections' (2012) 22 *Legal Education Review*, 71–98.

2 Molly Townes O'Brien, Stephen Tang and Kath Hall, 'Changing Our Thinking: Empirical Research on Law Student Wellbeing, Thinking Styles and the Law Curriculum' (2011) 21 *Legal Education Review*, 149–82.

3 Molly Townes O'Brien, 'Walking the Walk: Using Student-Faculty Dialogue to Change an Adversarial Curriculum' (2011) 4 *Journal of the Australasian Law Teachers Association*, 129–35.

4 A recent study suggests, for example, that students may feel better if they exercise more and spend more time with friends and family. Natalie Skead and Shane L Rogers, 'Stress, Anxiety and Depression in Law Students: How Student Behaviours Affect Student Wellbeing' (2014) 40(2) *Monash University Law Review*, 1–24.

5 O'Brien et al, above n2, 155–7.

6 Ibid. 162.

7 The Educational Mission of the Law School (2013), available at http://www.law.uchicago.edu/school/mission.

8 Law School Mission (2013), available at http://www.law.ucdavis.edu/about/law-school-mission.html.

9 The History of Stanford Law School (2013), available at http://www.law.stanford.edu/history.

10 Gordon Butler, 'The Law School Mission Statement: A Survival Guide for the Twenty-First Century' (2000) 50 *Journal of Legal Education* 240, 240.

11 ABA Standards for Approval of Law Schools 2012–2013, Standard 202, Self Study, states, in part: 'the dean and faculty of a law school shall develop a written self-study, which shall include a mission statement'.

12 See 'The CALD Standards for Australian Law Schools' at http://www.cald.asn.au/docs/CALD%20-%20standards%20project%20-%20final%20-%20adopted%2017%20November%202009.pdf.

13 Bethany Rubin Henderson, 'Asking the Lost Question: What Is the Purpose of Law School' (2003) 50 *Journal of Legal Education* 48, 53.

14 Butler, above n10, 242.

15 Ibid. 243–60.

16 Ibid. 246.

17 Angela McCaffery, 'The Healing Presence of Clients in Law School' (2003) 30 *William Mitchell Law Review* 87.

18 Ibid., 88.

19 A list of the current programmes is found at http://law.anu.edu.au/lrsj/studentsocialjusticeinitiative.

20 See ANU Law Reform and Social Justice, http://www.facebook.com/pages/ANU-Law-Reform-and-Social-Justice/488124584558320.

21 The expansion of the number and types of social justice projects can be seen on the ANU Law Reform and Social Justice website, http://law.anu.edu.au/lrsj/studentsocialjusticeinitiative.

22 A continuous update of the student social justice projects is available at http://www.law.anu.edu.au/lrsj/studentsocialjusticeinitiative. Indigenous issues are also addressed by the National Centre for Indigenous Studies, located at the law school: http://ncis.anu.edu.au/.

23 A list of law reform submissions by the ANU law faculty is accessible at http://www.law.anu.edu.au/lrsj/law-reform-submissions-anu-college-law-staff.

24 Read more about ANU Green at http://sustainability.anu.edu.au/.

25 For more information about campus sustainability projects, see International Alliance of Research Universities, 2013 at http://www.iaruni.org/about-us/iaru.

26 The Aurora Project, at http://www.auroraproject.com.au/node/76.

27 See, for example, the Bridges Across Borders Southeast Asia Community Legal Education Initiative, at https://www.babseacle.org; *Commonwealth Human Rights Initiative*, www.humanrightsinitiative.org.
28 The fact that active learning methods are more effective than passive ones is so well known that it is no longer considered to be a topic for research: Roy Stuckey et al, *Best Practices in Legal Education* (Clinical Legal Education Association, 2007) 90.
29 Paul L Caron and Rafael Gely, 'Taking Back the Law School Classroom: Using Technology to Foster Active Student Learning' (2004) 54 *Journal of Legal Education* 551, 552–3.
30 David A Kolb, *Experiential Learning: Experience as the Source of Learning and Development* (Prentice Hall, 1984) 27.
31 Susan Sturm and Lani Guinier, 'The Law School Matrix: Reforming Legal Education in a Culture of Competition and Conformity' (2007) 60 *Vanderbilt Law Review* 515, 550.
32 While there are many descriptions of active learning law school classrooms, see for example: Molly Townes O'Brien, 'An Active Learning Smorgasbord for Teaching Evidence' (2011) *Journal of the Australasian Law Teachers Association*, 31–40.
33 Ibid.
34 James B. Levy, 'As a Last Resort, Ask the Students: What They Say Makes Someone an Effective Law Teacher' (2006) 58 *Maine Law Review* 49, 61.
35 Ibid., 63.
36 Our surveys of law students showed a large minority were attending law school because they 'didn't know what else to do'. O'Brien, Tang and Hall, above n2, 150. See also Paul T. Wangerin, 'Objective, Multiplistic, and Relative Truth in Developmental Psychology and Legal Education' (1988) 62 *Tulane Law Review* 1237, 1255–6.
37 Timothy Terrell, 'A Tour of the Whine Country: The Challenge of Extending the Tenets of Lawyer Professionalism to Law Professors and Law Students' (1994) 34 *Washburn Law Journal* 1–8.
38 Skead and Rogers, above n4.
39 Gerald Hess, 'Heads and Hearts: The Teaching and Learning Environment in Law School' (2002) 52 *Journal of Legal Education* 75, 87.
40 Ibid., 88.
41 Ibid., 89.
42 Students often express surprise that I could not ethically leave it on my desk, hide it or tell the prosecution about it. At the time, I had to telephone an ethics hotline before I could decide what to do with the underwear.
43 Hess, above n39, 90.
44 Scott L. Rogers, 'The Mindful Law School: An Integrative Approach to Transforming Legal Education' (2012) 28 *Tauro Law Review* 1189–205.
45 Edward Deci and Richard Ryan, *Handbook of Self-Determination Research* (University of Rochester Press, 2002); Kennon M. Sheldon and Lawrence S. Krieger, 'Does Legal Education Have Undermining Effects on Law Students? Evaluating Changes in Motivation, Values and Well-Being (2004) 22 *Behavioral Science and Law*, 261–86.
46 E. Tory Higgins, 'Beyond Pleasure and Pain' (1997) 52 *American Psychologist* 1280–300.

13 Contemplative Practice in the Law School

Breaking Barriers to Learning and Resilience

Prue Vines and Patricia Morgan[*]

Abstract

In this chapter we argue that the increasing use of contemplative practices in law schools is significant not just in relation to enhancing resilience and diminishing stress and depression, but in that they also have major benefits in the development of traditional legal roles. However, there is an attitudinal barrier that needs to be overcome, as law students and legal academics have commonly been resistant to the use of these practices. It is interesting and somewhat ironic, therefore, that just as we are developing some level of openness to practices that often seem alien to those in the law, we also find evidence that they indeed enhance capacities for legal and educational practice such as level of focus, ability to prioritize, the optimization of objectivity, higher-order thinking and so on. Further, the management of ethical issues of professional practice, which are frequently triggers for depression, may also be improved by contemplative practices as they enhance students' and lawyers' ability to articulate their personal and professional ethics. In turn, this knowledge can be used to help break down remaining barriers to the use of contemplative practices within the legal academy. To reiterate, until recently the supposition was that the remedial benefits of contemplative practices ameliorated negative aspects of legal education and practice. However, now it appears that the enhancement may also be linked to a direct correspondence between contemplation and the law.

Introduction

The rise of depression in society generally,[1] and disproportionately in legal education and practice,[2] has become increasingly significant. In this chapter we discuss one response in tertiary legal education: the use of contemplative practices in order to help to combat this seeming epidemic.

> I think it is just getting worse and worse and as a society we put such a value on multi-tasking, which is just the opposite of mindfulness. So you know if I'm answering 3 emails at once, and talking on the phone, and trying to write a legal brief, and dealing with my secretary, and someone's got a problem in the office, and thinking about some personal problems, and all of the

> appointments that I have, and my personal emails – how do you do it all? You can't possibly be healthy if you do that.[3]

This comment, made by a legal academic and lawyer in Los Angeles in 2009, is illustrative of the pressures underpinning the practice of law in the US. We know that lawyers and law students suffer disproportionally high levels of psychological distress and depression, and the accompanying substance abuse and high rate of suicide. This has been apparent in the United States for some time[4] and the pattern has now been confirmed in Australia.[5] Although there are many differences between legal practice and legal education in the United States and Australia, it is apparent that in this field findings in the United States are very often replicated in Australia. For this reason we draw on both US and Australian literature in this chapter. Lawyers came second only to patent attorneys in unhappiness in a 2006 survey of 7,000 Australian professionals in which 45 per cent of young lawyers wanted to leave their job within two years and 9 per cent planned to leave law altogether.[6] A survey of 741 law students in 13 Australian law schools, as well as 924 solicitors and 756 barristers across Australia, confirmed these findings, showing that over 35 per cent of law students and almost a third of solicitors and one-fifth of barristers had elevated levels of psychological distress.[7]

Before they enter law school there appear to be no differences in well-being between law students and the general population.[8] Indeed law students may enter law school with feelings of well-being higher than the rest of the student population, feeling that they have done extremely well to be offered a place. However, we also know that approximately a third of law students begin to suffer elevated levels of psychological distress within 6–12 months of beginning their studies.[9] Why this is so remains unclear, and at present a number of theories about its cause exist. They include the idea that law students may select themselves into a highly stressful profession because of a personality that aims to please others rather than themselves. There is some force in this, and the literature is highly persuasive.[10] Another line of thought emphasizes what happens in law school and in the profession.[11] This is also very persuasive. For example, Riskin in his discussion of these issues in the US observes:

> The most prominent reasons are that law schools tend to over-emphasize analytical reasoning at the expense of developing interpersonal skills, and they incline students to seek satisfaction from external sources such as 'winning' in general, and especially through grades, awards, and prestigious jobs – rather than from internal sources, such as a secure sense of self.
>
> . . . Much of our discomfort is a by-product of assumptions and attitudes commonly shared within the law school and attorney communities. These assumptions revolve in significant part around the notions that only the 'best' will reliably find success in their lives, and that performance and appearances are crucially important. Such beliefs undermine the ability to have satisfying and healthy lives as lawyers by generating stress and anxiety as baseline life experiences for many of us.[12]

A further line of thought notes the significant changes in the legal profession over the later part of the twentieth century, with its increasing emphasis on the commercial and a lesser emphasis on the role of professional.[13] Anthony Kronman, in his book *The Lost Lawyer*, has emphasized the damage to the profession created by the loss of the ideal of the 'lawyer statesman',[14] a person who exercises greater ethical judgement and wisdom than the business lawyer model. If a profession is, as Roscoe Pound claims, 'a group . . . pursuing a learned art as a common calling in the spirit of a public service',[15] then the lessening of a sense of this 'calling' may be an important factor in the distress law professionals suffer. Whatever the cause of this distress, what is needed is ethically resilient lawyers[16] who have turned to what has been termed an older vision of the lawyer:

> Leaders in the legal community have called for a return to older visions of the lawyer . . . the nineteenth-century ideal of the 'lawyer-statesman', a person of good judgement and 'prudence' or practical wisdom . . . there is a need for a special kind of ability to deliberate, which includes both compassion and detachment.[17]

The Integration of Contemplation Into Legal Study and Practice

As noted above, one argument is that the high rates of stress and depression lawyers and law students suffer is in part due to the 'adversarial mind-sets that tend to dominate the way most lawyers think and most legal education is structured'.[18] To ameliorate this Riskin[19] proposes the use of mindfulness meditation, and details a range of law schools and firms in the USA that are currently integrating contemplative practices into their programmes and activities.[20] Although the contemplative movement in legal education can be said to have started in the USA it is rapidly spreading to other countries. Currently in Australia there are a number of programmes considering the wellness of law students, including law schools at the Universities of Wollongong,[21] UNSW,[22] ANU,[23] Newcastle,[24] Queensland University of Technology (QUT),[25] University of Technology Sydney (UTS) and Macquarie, and the Tristan Jepson Memorial Foundation,[26] which is working to decrease the causes of depression and anxiety in the legal profession. These and other programmes in Australia and the USA engage in a range of contemplative practices, though many focus on mindfulness meditation. Mindfulness meditation is a secularized version of Buddhist Vipassana or Insight Meditation, which was introduced to the West in the early 1970s by Western Buddhist practitioners and scholars. The Berkeley Law School's Initiative for Mindfulness in Law defines mindfulness as:

> being fully present in the moment, in a state of clarity and receptiveness. In the legal profession, with its culture of speed and adversarial energy, mindfulness – cultivated most commonly through meditation – can offer a source of inner calm in the midst of intense intellectual and emotional pressure.

> It is a method to create and, when lost, to regain a grounded and centered state of being amidst the often contentious and stressful nature of the legal profession.[27]

Increasingly, law students and practitioners are turning to mindfulness and other contemplative practices for these remedial benefits. They were the initial focus of the contemplative law movement, though theorists in this area[28] are now finding other links between contemplative practices and some of the necessary roles of lawyers. The varying ways that contemplation can support lawyers as analysts, fact-finders, counsellors, negotiators, problem-solvers and advocates[29] are introduced by the following sketch of the positive physiological and psychological outcomes of contemplation.

Physiological and Psychological Benefits of Contemplation

The last 40 years of neuroscience, psychology and meditation research has provided evidence for the benefits of contemplation generally, and specifically in education. This section introduces some of that research, starting with the positive impacts of meditation on stress, anxiety and depression described by Riskin[30] and Hart.[31] These contemplative theorists have found that meditation lowers stress by lowering cortisol levels. In addition it lowers blood pressure and heart rate, and positively impacts chronic migraines, depression and heart disease.[32] These findings provided the initial impetus for teaching contemplative practices to law students and lawyers. However, Riskin contends that they also enhance the capacity to relax, deal with anxiety and improve the ability to concentrate, and increase performance not just in ordinary life but also on tasks involving high levels of mental functioning, such as the study and practice of law.[33]

The educational psychologist Tobin Hart supports Riskin's propositions with findings from neuroscience and psychoneuroendocrinology research.[34] These results outline some of the detrimental impacts of the hyperarousal of the hypothalamic–pituitary–adrenal axis[35] and the elevated levels of the hormone cortisol produced by chronic stress. These effects include obesity, loss of memory and the underlying neurobiology of suicide. He claims that 'chronic stress or corticosterone treatment induces pathological alterations [in the brain], such as dendritic atrophy in hippocampal neurons . . . which are paralleled by cognitive deficits'.[36] The results he cites also suggest that meditation can provide physiological relaxation; lower stress and anxiety symptoms; slow metabolism; produce feelings of calm; improve concentration, empathy, perceptual acuity; and provide heightened self-awareness or metacognition. These benefits of mindfulness meditation are being reported by a range of research psychologists studying meditation, who describe it as a counterbalance to the exponential growth of stress and stress-related diseases.[37]

In a comprehensive review of meditation in higher education, Shapiro and her colleagues drew on four decades of meditation and education research identifying similar physiological benefits. However, they were only one aspect of three key findings, discussed under the titles: cognitive and academic performance; mental health and psychological well-being; and what they term the development of the 'whole person'.[38] In the first category they found that meditation can improve the ability to maintain preparedness, orient attention and improve the ability to process information quickly and accurately, and that over time it may have a positive impact on academic achievement.[39] In the second category, related to mental health, Shapiro et al. found that meditation can decrease stress, anxiety and depression, and that it supports better regulation of emotional reactions and the cultivation of positive psychological states.[40],[41]

These findings confirm Hart's proposition that meditation can increase students' ability to focus, retain and retrieve information. These skills are important for law students who rely heavily on memory and recall,[42] as well as on the ability to objectively analyse situations and arguments. The development of these skills is due, he suggests, to 'physiological coherence', a state in which the physiological, cognitive and emotional systems and neural communication networks become aligned.[43] The physiological relaxation that results is said to positively impact emotional response, cognition and learning. Research such as Hart's is currently being augmented in the contemplative law movement by neuroscience research specific to law.[44] Evidence from this field is now being referenced in law schools, such as Berkeley and Florida in the US and UNSW and the University of Wollongong in Australia to name just a few, as they use mindfulness meditation to cultivate focus, concentration and the capacity to pay attention.

Intrinsic Links Between Contemplation and Law

> It seems incongruous: lawyers – whose professional work tends to focus on the external and to rest on thinking, judging and action – are engaging in a practice that, in contrast, focuses on the internal and rests on *not* thinking, *not* judging, and *not* acting.[45]

Why would lawyers and law students seek out a practice that seems so inconsistent with what is generally assumed to be their rationalist and externalist focus? Possibly because, paradoxically, the non-thinking and non-doing of meditation can heighten lawyers' ability to 'think' and 'do', as it can remedy the negative physiological and affective issues that may block their analytical skills.[46]

In his reflection on Riskin's work, the legal theorist Steven Keeva describes the outcome for lawyers who routinely maintain a combative rationalist approach, as their 'living above the surface alone'.[47] He suggests that this results from a life profoundly out of balance. Discourse related to the imbalance in law students' and lawyers' lives has until recently been focused on lawyers' 'outer lives', as Keeva describes it – the 'thinking, judging and action' of the legal life. He outlines recent attempts to rectify the imbalance in some law students' and lawyers' lives, such as the development of programmes to support work–life balance. However, Keeva believes this is not enough, for:

> the fundamental problem of imbalance cannot be addressed by merely rearranging the furniture, so to speak, of one's life so that it comports with some externally agreed-upon ideal. Instead, it is only by observing that 'furniture' clearly and non-judgementally through the *inner* experience of awakened mindfulness that lawyers or law students are able to see their situations for what they are and then redress this crucial, but often overlooked, lack of balance.[48]

To return balance Keeva suggests that lawyers practise from the 'inside out', which involves giving equal attention to their 'outer' and 'inner' or subjective worlds by engaging in contemplative practices. He is not suggesting that lawyers discard linear, rational or analytical thinking. Rather, through contemplation law students and lawyers can learn to 'tether [the mind] to its moorings',[49] which is the calm, balanced, interior space that can be found in contemplative reflection. Keeva claims that the practice of mindfulness allows law students and lawyers to watch their thoughts, make choices about how they react or identify with them, and use 'specific thoughts, or types of thought – legal analysis being one example – as *tools*, rather than allow them to be tyrants'.[50] This awareness of thoughts – otherwise known as 'metacognition', arising from contemplation – is, according to Keeva, currently being sought by many law students and lawyers.

Such self-awareness is a valuable tool for lawyers whose practice often requires them to make arguments for a person whose moral values may not be theirs, and to be in an adversarial situation without becoming combative. Metacognition allows them to take a metaphorical step away from the situation so that they can more effectively analyse their situation and manage the different perceptions of reality which might exist in a legal dispute, and determine their best approach. It allows them to perceive their emotional responses clearly, to provide an 'inner' reflective space so that a comprehensive understanding of the situation under investigation can be gained. This metacognition, because it allows a space to stand aside from emotional responses and observe situations acutely and realistically, also allows the practitioner to make better ethical and personal evaluations.

Contemplation and Lawyers' Roles: Hyman's Model

Hyman has given one of the clearest accounts of the value of contemplative practices in law through his re-examination of legal roles.[51] He has shown how metacognition arising from contemplative practice can rework the adversarial and stressful nature of legal practice. Hyman describes metacognition as being 'awake' in many of the situations lawyers find themselves in.[52] Specifically, he emphasizes that meta-awareness underpins the roles of a mindful lawyer, including legal analyst, fact-finder, counsellor, negotiator and advocate. As a 'legal analyst' the lawyer not only needs to know the legal rules but also their subtleties and lacunae. For instance those lawyers who are uncomfortable with a lack of clear rules may make hasty or incorrect analyses in order to provide themselves with certainty. Hyman provides the example of lawyers who rush to a conclusion, or who, in wanting to ingratiate themselves with their clients, may lead them to believe that their case is stronger than it is. Mindfulness can be a useful 'inner tool' in these instances, for it assists lawyers to recognize thought patterns and processes that can alert them to underlying emotions driving faulty analyses.

The second role Hyman outlines is the lawyer as 'fact-finder', where in creating legal strategy they need to identify and develop a comprehensive understanding of the facts involved in their cases. Lawyers distracted by 'mental static' and/or unconscious preconceptions are more likely to be misled by incorrect information that is intentionally or negligently provided by clients, witnesses and others. The mindful lawyer, who has less mental static and a heightened awareness of their habitual patterns, is more likely to bring a clear and empirical attitude to investigating the 'facts' that are presented to them. Lawyers trained in mindfulness can see past their limiting beliefs or behaviours, so making them more effective as fact-finders. Before this training they may have failed to delve deeply enough into their clients' stories, not wanting to intimidate them; or, conversely, missed important information because of an overly aggressive approach. Hyman notes that rather than directing the mindful lawyer, meditation heightens metacognition and facilitates a calm attitude, which helps them clarify the 'pushes and pulls' of the situation.[53]

The lawyer as 'counsellor', the third role in Hyman's schema, refers to the work lawyers do to support their clients' informed decision making. This can be stressful, as the lawyer-counsellor is frequently navigating an environment of uncertainty. In some instances the approach that needs to be taken in a case is unclear, while in others the merits of alternative approaches have to be outlined. The anxiety that this produces may result in the lawyer falling back on habitual mental patterns. However, lawyers trained in mindfulness learn to be present in the moment, which can inhibit their reversion to old, possibly redundant, mental patterns. Through the practice of mindfulness, or moment-to-moment awareness, mindful lawyers are able to apply professional detachment in their roles as counsellors. This provides the 'psychological space'[54] from which the required insight can arise.

Engaging mindfulness in the fourth role of 'legal negotiator' can help lawyers avoid becoming trapped in negative thought patterns and – overcome rigidity, inflexibility, resistance and aggression. The metacognition they develop through mindfulness meditation supports awareness of their reactivity, making it less likely for them to become embroiled in combative situations where they respond in kind to aggressive statements by opposing counsel. Riskin alludes to this issue in his engagement with research relating to mindfulness and lawyers' problem solving abilities. He claims that meditation helps 'lawyers negotiate better, enabling them to enhance their awareness of, and distance from limiting mind-sets and habitual behaviours associated with negotiation and the impulses, assumptions and cravings that support them'.[55] Both Riskin and Hyman ask us to engage with the concept that the mindful legal negotiator attempts to remain open to a range of possible solutions and creative approaches, which can lead to them becoming a more successful legal negotiator or deal-maker.

The role of legal advocate, the last of the roles considered by Hyman, can be very stressful for lawyers, with the anxiety arising from speaking on behalf of a client often described as akin to stage fright. When the legal advocate is required to respond immediately and precisely it can lead to them falling back on rote responses, or possibly freezing. Mindfulness can support lawyers to overcome this kind of anxiety because of the equanimity, calm and flexibility of mind that can develop through its practice. These relaxed states then help lawyers become mindful advocates and more readily think on their feet. The reduction of stress and anxiety, and the development of equanimity and metacognition that mindful lawyers experience, can support them in their roles as advocates, negotiators, counsellors, fact-finders and analysts.

Using Contemplative Practices in Legal Education

Law schools are beginning to recognize that contemplative practices may be useful in assisting students with their greater levels of anxiety and depression.[56] However, there is some resistance to what is often initially seen as irrational, 'touchy-feely', 'new age' material, which has no place in the tough and 'survival of the fittest' world of the law school.[57] So it is ironic that just as we are developing some level of openness to a practice which seems alien to us, we also find evidence that this practice indeed greatly enhances essential legal roles and skills. In turn, this knowledge can be used to help break down the barriers to the use of contemplative practices within the legal academy. Indeed in our own work with first year students in law school, we have found that giving this information to students greatly reduces their resistance to contemplative practices.

The ability of contemplative practices to enhance the capacity to articulate personal and professional ethics is another significant reason to use them in legal education – specifically because ethical dilemmas are known to frequently be the trigger for people dropping out of law school or the profession.[58]

The positive impacts of contemplation in supporting an ethical stance and its remedial effects have until recently supported the argument that these practices enhance legal life and learning. However, now it appears that the enhancement may also be related to a direct correspondence between contemplation and the law.

Conclusion

This chapter has considered how contemplative practices might be used to help develop greater resilience to depression and anxiety in law students and lawyers. Although the 'non-thinking' and 'non-doing' emphasized in these embodied, calm and reflective states of consciousness appear contrary to common assumptions about the sharpness of the analytical legal mind, the evidence shows that mindfulness can not only reduce stress and anxiety, but also enhance and complement many of the roles, analyses and judgments of lawyers. Legal theorist Rhonda Magee argues that the contemplative movement in law:

> does much more than merely specify skills missing from traditional legal education that are crucial to effective and sustainable lawyering . . . The movement goes much further, suggesting a new approach to the foundation of legal education – one which may better instil in young lawyers an abiding sense of an inspiring professional identity, embodying self-reflective civic engagement and practical, ethical judgement by broadening their ways of learning what they need to know to practice and to lead effectively in a changing world.[59]

There is good reason to think, as Magee does, that the use of contemplative practices in legal education can benefit students well beyond the reduction of stress. The process of self-reflecting, better focus and concentration, and the increase in metacognition may indeed develop in our students an ability to reflect on themselves, their values, ethics and their practice, which moves them further towards Anthony Kronman's 'lawyer-statesman' and away from his 'lost lawyer'.[60]

Notes

* Prue Vines is Professor, Faculty of Law, UNSW. Patricia Morgan, School of Humanities, UNSW, recently completed her PhD on the use of contemplation in higher education.

1 R Eckersley, *Well and Good: Morality, Meaning and Happiness* (2nd ed, Text, 2005); R Eckersley, 'Is Modern Western Culture a Health Hazard?' (2006) 35 *International Journal of Epidemiology* 252; Australian Bureau of Statistics, 'Mental Health' in *Australian Social Trends* 4102.0 (2009), <http://www.ausstats.abs.gov.au/ausstats/subscriber.nsf/LookupAttach/4102.0Publication25.03.094/$File/41020_Mentalhealth.pdf.>.

2 W Larcombe and K Fethers, 'Schooling the Blues? An Investigation of Factors Associated with Psychological Distress among Law Students' (2013) 36 *University of New South Wales Law Journal* 390.

3 Unpublished transcript from fieldwork conducted for Patricia Morgan, *Learning Feelings: Foundations of Contemplative Practice* (PhD Thesis, UNSW 2013).

4 William Eaton et al., 'Occupations and the Prevalence of Major Depressive Disorder' (1990) 32 *Journal of Occupational Medicine* 1079, 1083; G Andrew H Benjamin, Elaine Darling and Bruce Sales, 'The Prevalence of Depression, Alcohol Abuse and Cocaine Abuse among United States Lawyers' (1990) 13 *International Journal of Law and Psychiatry* 233, 240; Martin Seligman, Paul Verkuil and Terry Kang, 'Why Lawyers are Unhappy' (2005) 10 *Deakin Law Review* 1, 5; Martin Seligman, *Authentic Happiness* (Nicholas Brearley, 2004) 177; American Bar Association, *At the Breaking Point: The Report of a National Conference on the Emerging Crisis in the Quality of Lawyers' Health and Lives –Its Impact on Law Firms and Client Services* (1991); Amiram Elwork, *Stress Management for Lawyers: How to Increase Personal and Professional Satisfaction in the Law* (Vorkell Group, 2007.

5 Below, n8.

6 Beaton Consulting, *Annual Professions Survey 2007: Short Report* (2007), 2, 2.

7 Norm Kelk et al, *Courting the Blues: Attitudes towards Depression in Australian Law Students and Legal Practitioners'* (Brain and Mind Research Institute, 2009) 14, 42; Colin James, 'Lawyer Dissatisfaction, Emotional Intelligence and Clinical

Legal Education (2008) *Legal Education Review* 123, 124. See also Kath Hall, Molly Townes O'Brien and Stephen Tang, 'Developing a Professional Identity in Law School: A View from Australia (2010) 4 *Phoenix Law Review* 21; Norm Kelk et al, 'Distress and Depression among Australian Law Students: Incidence, Attitudes and the Role of Universities (2010) 32 *Sydney Law Review* 113; Wendy Larcombe et al, 'Does an Improved Experience of Law School Protect Students against Depression, Anxiety and Stress?' (2013) 35 *Sydney Law Review* 407; Larcombe and Fethers, above n3.

8 G. Andrew H Benjamin et al, 'The Role of Legal Education in Producing Psychological Distress among Law Students and Lawyers'(1986) *American Bar Foundation Research Journal* 225, 240; Kennon M. Sheldon and Lawrence S. Krieger, 'Does Legal Education Have Undermining Effects on Law Students? Evaluating Changes in Motivation, Values and Well-being' (2004) 22 *Behavioural Science and Law* 261, 262; Kennon M Sheldon and Lawrence S Krieger, 'Understanding the Negative Effects of Legal Education on Law Students: A Longitudinal Test of Self-Determination Theory' (2007) 33 *Personality and Social Psychology Bulletin* 833, 890–91.

9 Above n8 and Ann Iijima, 'Lessons Learned: Legal Education and Law Student Dysfunction' (1998) 48(4) *Journal of Legal Education* 524,526; Benjamin et al, above n9, 241.

10 Massimiliano Tani and Prue Vines, 'Law Students Attitudes' to Learning: A Pointer to Depression in the Legal Academy and the Profession? (2009) 19 *Legal Education Review* 3, 39; S Daicoff, *Lawyer Know Thyself: A Psychological Analysis of Personality Strengths and Weaknesses* (American Psychological Association, 2004).

11 Seligman, Verkuil and Kang, above n5, 5.

12 Leonard Riskin, 'Contemplative Lawyer: On the Potential Contributions of Mindfulness Meditation to Law Students, Lawyers, and their Clients' (2002) 7 *Harvard Negotiation Law Review* 1, 10.

13 LS Krieger, 'The Inseparability of Professionalism and Personal Satisfaction: Perspectives on Values, Integrity and Happiness' (2005) 11 *Clinical Law Review* 425. See also Rachael Field, James Duffy and Anna Huggins, *Lawyering and Positive Professional Identities* (LexisNexis Butterworths, 2014).

14 Anthony T Kronman, *The Lost Lawyer: Failing the Ideals of the Legal Profession* (Harvard University Press, 2003).

15 Roscoe Pound, *The Lawyer from Antiquity to Modern Times* 5 (1953) cited in Thomas D Morgan, 'Creating Life as a Lawyer' (2003) 38 *Valparaiso University Law Review* 37–64, 45.

16 Colin James has argued this comprehensively: Colin James, 'Lawyer Dissatisfaction, Emotional Intelligence and Clinical Legal Education (2008) *Legal Education Review* 123; see also Patrick J Schiltz, 'On Being a Happy, Healthy, and Ethical Member of an Unhappy, Unhealthy, and Unethical Profession' (1999) 52 *Vanderbilt Law Review* 871–951.

17 Riskin, above n13, 8, 19.

18 Ibid. Molly Townes O'Brien, 'Facing Down the Gladiators: Addressing Law School's Hidden Adversarial Curriculum' (2011) 37(1) *Monash University Law Review* 43.

19 Leonard Riskin, 'Contemplative Practices in Law Schools: A Search for Balance in the Whirlwind of Law School' (2005) <http://www.aals.org/am2006/program/balance/riskin.outline.pdf>, 37–41.

20 Riskin lists the for-credit courses at Yale and Columbia, Denver, Hastings, Miami, Missouri-Columbia, North Carolina, Stanford and Suffolk; non-credit courses at the University of Missouri-Columbia and the University of North Carolina; and the meditation groups at Harvard, Yale, Columbia and Berkeley Schools of Law, many other contemplative law programmes in the USA; and refers to the expansion of initiatives and literature in the area: Riskin, above n13, 8.

21 'Vitality for Life and Law', UOW <http://lha.uow.edu.au/law/vitality/index.html>.

22 Vines has developed a number of mentoring programmes and the website 'Surviving and Thriving in Law School', and Vines and Morgan have conducted a number of

seminars and lectures on resilience, mindfulness and the study of law. <http://www.law.unsw.edu.au/current-students/surviving-thriving-law-school>.

23 Associate Professor Kath Hall, Professor Molly O'Brien and Stephen Tang at the Australian National University (ANU) in Canberra have been conducting research into issues of well-being for law students through the 'Student Wellbeing' programme Learning Communities, ANU, <http://students.anu.edu.au/studentlife/learning-communities.php>.

24 Kate Lindsay and Sher Campbell working with first year students, Newcastle University, NSW.

25 Rachael Field, Teaching Fellowship to Reduce Law Students' Distress, QUT: Report, <http://www.olt.gov.au/resource-promoting-law-student-well-being-through-curriculum>. She has also established the Wellness Network for Law through the Fellowship, <http:wellnessforlaw.com/>. See also Rachael Field and James Duffy, 'Better to Light a Single Candle than to Curse the Darkness: Promoting Law Student Well-Being through a First Year Law Subject' (2012) *Queensland University of Technology Law and Justice Journal* 133.

26 Tristan Jepson Memorial Foundation, <http://www.tjmf.org.au/>.

27 Berkeley Law, *Berkeley Initiative for Mindfulness in Law* (2012), <http://www.law.berkeley.edu/mindfulness.htm>.

28 As a fast-growing theoretical area it is impossible to name all the current researchers, though they include: Douglas Codiga, 'Reflections on the Potential Growth of Mindfulness Meditation in the Law (2002) 7 *Harvard Negotiation Law Review* 109; Susan Daicoff, 'Law as a Healing Profession: The Comprehensive Law Movement' (2005) *Pepperdine Dispute Resolution Law Journal* 6; Steven Keeva, 'Practicing from the Inside Out' (2002) 7 *Harvard Negotiation Law Review* 97; Larry Spain, 'Collaborative Law: A Critical Reflection on Whether a Collaborative Orientation Can Be Ethically Incorporated into the Practice of Law' (2004) 56 *Baylor Law Review* 141.

29 J. Patton Hyman, 'The Mindful Lawyer: Mindfulness Meditation and Law Practice' (2007) *Vermont Bar Journal* 40.

30 Riskin, above, n13.

31 Tobin Hart, 'Interiority and Education: Exploring the Neurophenomenology of Contemplation and its Potential Role in Learning' (2008) 6 *Journal of Transformative Education* 235, 250.

32 Craig Cormack, 'Lawyers Turn to Meditation to Fight Stress and Improve Performance' (23 March 2009) *Canadian Lawyer* 1.

33 Riskin above n13.

34 Hart, above n32, 250.

35 The hypothalamic–pituitary–adrenal axis is a complex of interactions between the hypothalamus in the brain with the pituitary and the adrenal glands. It is the part of the neuroendocrine system that controls reactions to stress and many bodily processes.

36 Hart, above n32, 246.

37 John Miller, Ken Fletcher and John Kabat-Zinn, 'Three-Year Follow-up and Clinical Implications of a Mindfulness Meditation-Based Stress Reduction Intervention in the Treatment of Anxiety Disorders' (1995) 17 *General Hospital Psychiatry* 192–200; Putai Jin 'Efficacy of Tai Chi, Brisk Walking, Meditation and Reading in Reducing Mental and Emotional Stress' (1992) 36 *Journal of Psychosomatic Research* 361; Vidya Anderson et al, 'The Effects of Meditation on Teacher Perceived Occupational Stress, State and Trait Anxiety, and Burnout (1999) 14 *School Psychology Quarterly* 3.

38 Shauna Shapiro, Kirk Brown and John Astin, 'Toward the Integration of Meditation into Higher Education: A Review of Research' (2008) 113 *Teachers College Record* 493, 528.

39 Ibid.

40 Ibid.

41 Shamini Jain et al, 'A Randomized Controlled Trial of Mindfulness Meditation Versus Relaxation Training: Effects on Distress, Positive States of Mind, Rumination, and Distraction' (2007) 33 (1) *Annals of Behavioral Medicine*, 11.

42 Steve Wilson and Phillip Kenny, *The Law Student's Handbook* (Oxford University Press, 2007).
43 The correlates of physiological coherence include a regular heart rhythm; decreased sympathetic nervous system activation; increased parasympathetic activity; and increased heart–brain synchronization. The sympathetic nervous system basically stimulates the 'fight or flight' distress system in the body, while the parasympathetic nervous system manages resting and digesting. Both are part of the autonomic system which automatically regulates the body.
44 See 'Neurolaw', <http://www.neulaw.org/>. Henry Greely, 'Law and the Revolution in Neuroscience: An Early Look at the Field' (2009) 42 *Akron Law Review* 687, 716; Thomas Scott, 'Neuroscience May Supersede Ethics and Law' (2012) 18 *Science and Engineering Ethics* 1,5; Michael Freeman, *Law and Neuroscience* (Oxford University Press 2011); Brent Garland, *Neuroscience and the Law: Brain, Mind, and the Scales of Justice: A Report on an Invitational Meeting Convened by the American Association for the Advancement of Science and the Dana Foundation* (Dana Press, 2004); Pauline Tesler, 'Neuro-Resolution', presented at *Practical Neuro-literacy: Where Divorce Practice, Neuroscience, and Legal Conflict Resolution Intersect* (2012), Concord, New Hampshire, <http://cuttingedgelaw.com/blog/practical-neuro-literacy-where-divorce-practice-neuroscience-and-legal-conflict-resolution-intersect>.
45 Riskin, above n13.
46 Ingrid Loreen, 'Therapeutic Jurisprudence and the Law School Asylum Clinic' (2004) 17 *St Thomas Law Review* 835, 844.
47 Keeva, above n29, 97.
48 Ibid., 97, 99, 107.
49 Ibid.
50 Ibid., 100.
51 Hyman, above n30.
52 Ibid. 42.
53 Ibid. 43.
54 Ibid.
55 Riskin, above n13, 57. See also Leigh Thompson, Janice Nadler and Peter Kim, 'Some Like it Hot: The Case for the Emotional Negotiator', in Leigh Thompson, John Levine and David Messick (eds), *Shared Cognition in Organizations: The Management of Knowledge* (Psychology Press, 1999) 139, 156.
56 See above, n29.
57 The experience of Prue Vines in discussing these issues with the members of the Committee of Australian Law Deans is illustrative. Initial resistance, based on the view that it is not the job of academics to deal with the mental health of law students, gave way to recognition that mental health was closely connected to legal education. See also Christine Parker, 'The Moral Panic over Psychological Wellbeing in the Legal Profession' (2014) 37(3) *University of New South Wales Law Journal* 1103.
58 Schiltz, above, n17.
59 Rhonda Magee, 'Educating Lawyers to Meditate' (2010) 79 *University of Missouri Kansas City Law Review* 535, 593, 538.
60 Kronman, above, n15.

14 Harnessing the Law Curriculum to Promote Law Student Well-Being, Particularly in the First Year of Legal Education

Rachael Field[1]

Introduction

The study of law can have serious effects on the psychological health of law students.[2] Scholarship in the US has long established that the psychological well-being of law students is a concern.[3] We now know (and the chapters of this work affirm) that concern is also justified in Australia. It is well recognized that the 2009 Report of the Brain and Mind Research Institute (BMRI) of the University of Sydney was one of the first projects to provide rigorous empirical evidence that Australian law students suffer disproportionately high levels of psychological distress.[4] The BMRI found that more than one-third (35 per cent) of law students suffer high to very high levels of psychological distress.[5] At the time of the release of the report, these levels of psychological distress were 17 per cent higher than those recorded for medical students, and more than 20 per cent higher than those found in the general population.[6]

Since the publication of the BMRI Report, Australian scholarly work in the field has grown, and there have been many important developments. As other chapters in this work explain, a number of Australian legal and psychology scholars have independently interrogated the BMRI findings by empirically investigating the psychological well-being of students at a range of Australian law schools.[7] This body of research again confirms that law students suffer concerningly high levels of psychological distress after their first year of law school.

In 2009, shortly after the release of the BMRI Report, Kath Hall published a piece in the *QUT Law and Justice Journal* entitled 'Do We Really Want to Know? Recognising the Importance of Student Psychological Wellbeing in Australian Law Schools'.[8] Hall noted that:

> For law school staff, cognitive dissonance and rationalisation can affect our reactions to the research on student wellbeing. In particular, cognitive dissonance may arise when we become aware of the negative impact law school can have on our students. It may be hard to acknowledge that what we do can create a high risk of student distress. There can also be discomfort in

> knowing that we are involved in perpetuating a system that has been shown to have a detrimental impact on many of our students' goals and public service aspirations.[9]

This piece motivated me to reflect on the ethical responsibility that we have as legal educators – particularly when we have evidence that we may be contributing to student psychological distress – and to advocate for legal academics to work to ameliorate that distress, to create positive learning experiences for our students and to 'do no harm' through legal education. Hall's work inspired me to act by applying for an Australian Learning and Teaching Council (ALTC) Teaching Fellowship, which was awarded in 2010. The Fellowship worked on curriculum renewal in legal education to strategically harness the curriculum, and to use the teaching of dispute resolution in particular, to address law student psychological distress.[10] The Fellowship's programme of activities sought to provide national leadership on this issue with three programme goals: first, to raise awareness in the legal academy about the importance of law student psychological well-being;[11] second, to persuade the legal academy to accept the need for strategic change in legal education;[12] and third, to design model curriculum and assessment practice to promote law student well-being through engaging, motivating and supporting law student learning.[13] This chapter discusses the importance of intentionally designing the law curriculum to promote law student well-being, and argues that this work is particularly important in the context of the first year experience of legal education.

The Importance of Intentional Curriculum Design for Promoting Law Student Well-Being

There are many potential causes for the elevated levels of psychological distress experienced by students at law school.[14] For example, Daicoff has highlighted research suggesting that students who choose to study law may have a predisposition to pessimism and depression (which can be associated with academic high achievers).[15] However, the very fact of being at law school cannot be ignored as a contributing cause.[16] The extant research confirms the important impact on student well-being of the learning experience at law school.[17] It suggests that the way we design the legal education curriculum is an important part of the problem. However, it also suggests, perhaps more significantly, that the curriculum is an important part of the solution.

The law school learning experience therefore warrants scrutiny in terms of the ways in which it might potentially contribute to the elevated levels of psychological distress experienced by law students. The BMRI Report tentatively pointed to the highly competitive nature of the learning environment at law school,[18] noting that law students experience high levels of competition in relation to their peers (competing not only for good grades, but also for limited jobs upon graduation).[19] Other literature suggests that students may experience law school as an adversarial, intimidating and competitive environment – one that can cause them to feel isolated, inferior, inadequate, anxious, alienated, paranoid and depressed.[20]

Iijima noted in 1998 that 'typical law school pedagogy does nothing to mitigate the students' isolation',[21] because 'the focus is on individual effort' and 'teaching methods that encourage students to collaborate, such as role playing and small-group exercises, are used very little in traditional courses'.[22] Hess has also argued persuasively that 'the narrow [law] curriculum contributes to alienation'.[23]

Students may also struggle with a range of stressors common to the experience of law school. For example, the heavy, demanding and time-intensive learning workload; the (often) difficult and complex content; the use of traditional teacher-centric teaching methods; pressures to keep up and perform; a lack of feedback (particularly a lack of positive feedback); and a lack of opportunity through the curriculum to develop life skills to contextualize the learning of law.[24] Many students find it difficult that they have significantly less time for family, friends and recreation than they experienced in their life before attending law school.[25] Segerstrom has argued that an actual or perceived loss of control that follows from the experience of such stressors leads to feelings of helplessness, and contributes to high levels of stress and anxiety amongst law students.[26]

Additionally, the BMRI Report suggested that legal thinking styles, which are taught from the first year of law school – and are pessimistic by nature (adversarial, risk adverse, searching for a problem, focused on the negatives of a situation, and contemplating worst case scenarios) – may not only compound over the course of years of legal studies but may also transfer into the realms of everyday life, exacerbating psychological distress.[27] This analysis is supported by work on the relevance of legal thinking styles to law student and lawyer well-being conducted by O'Brien, Hall and Tang at the Australian National University.[28]

US scholars in particular have noted that the way we teach students how to think at law school minimizes the development of their interpersonal skills, such as their capacity to build relationships and engender the confidence of others – skills which have been labelled as 'critical for law practice'.[29] Law schools require students to think predominantly in rigorously analytical ways, rewarding intellectual excellence at the expense of other qualities which might support well-being, such as values and character.[30] Hess argues that the law curriculum 'teaches that tough-minded analysis, hard facts, and cold logic are the tools of a good lawyer, and it has little room for emotion, imagination, and morality'.[31] Indeed, learning how to 'think like a lawyer' has been said to ask students to abandon their 'ideals, ethical values, and sense of self'.[32]

With this in mind, it is problematic that the emotional dimension of the law and the reality of its connection with the rigours and stresses of the practice of law are rarely addressed in the content of what we teach at law school, or in the discussions in our classrooms. Silver has argued that a lack of emotional intelligence in law students contributes to their disproportionately high levels of stress, substance abuse and depression.[33] Law students are also taught to favour objectivity and impartiality in their approach to advocacy, and to put aside their own conscience and personal responses. To achieve this, students are taught to compartmentalize values and feelings. This can result in their becoming disconnected from their sense of self, which in turn has a detrimental impact on their well-being.[34]

In addition, the adversarial nature of both the law curriculum and the culture at law school, and the general lack of a concentration on holistic and reflective practice are also considered relevant to the high levels of psychological distress experienced by law students.[35] For this reason the BMRI Report recommended a greater emphasis in the legal curriculum on positive and collaborative lawyering through less adversarial approaches to legal problems and problem solving.[36]

It is the collective impact of some (or all) of these issues at law school which, it has been suggested, encourages students to wear a 'social mask' – one which projects an image of strength, confidence, action and enthusiasm – to veil the reality that on an intrapersonal level they are in fact experiencing strong feelings of insecurity, lack of confidence and uncertainty.[37] These experiences in many cases will impact negatively on student values and their capacity to engage with the law school learning environment, as well as on their levels of motivation for learning.[38]

A fairly dim picture of the nature of the law school learning and teaching environment, and of the student experience of it, emerges from this empirical scholarship. However, this perspective can be reframed for a constructive purpose – to inform intentional curriculum design to work to prevent a decline in student well-being at law school. For this to be possible, law teachers need to view the curriculum, including approaches to formative and summative assessment, as an important location for influencing and guiding students in ways that help promote well-being.[39] We need to avoid the limited, traditional notions of the legal curriculum as a collection of (often) complex doctrinal tenets of substantive law, and instead embrace the curriculum as a critical opportunity to facilitate and support student learning motivation and engagement.[40]

There are many different ways law teachers can harness the law curriculum and take advantage of it as a place of critical connection with students for the promotion of well-being. For example, the curriculum can be used to support the development of a positive professional identity,[41] particularly through instruction about, and reflection on: the positive contribution lawyers make to society as upholders of the rule of law; as advocates for the vulnerable and less powerful; as resolvers of disputes and conflict; and as ethical members of an honourable profession.[42] Law teachers can use the curriculum to teach students, intentionally and explicitly, to be reflective, resilient and life-long learners;[43] to think constructively as lawyers; to engage with their emotions; to communicate well; to have empathy; and to work collaboratively.[44] Further, Howieson's research at the University of Western Australia provides evidence that teaching dispute resolution knowledge, skills and attitudes can support student well-being, particularly by creating in students a sense of belonging to their law school.[45] By way of the direct connection with students that occurs through our management and design of the curriculum, we can encourage students to actively deal with their stress and anxiety levels; to seek support if they see signs of depression; to be aware of their signature strengths;[46] to be conscious of the efficacy for well-being of approaches such as mindfulness;[47] and even to adopt simple strategies such as exercising, eating and sleeping well.

Approaches such as these are affirmed by the Threshold Learning Outcomes (TLOs) for legal education, which were developed through the Australian Learning and Teaching Council (ALTC) in 2010.[48] The TLOs provide a holistic and comprehensive view of the required elements of focus for the law curriculum, through the lens of six learning outcomes. The TLOs articulate the knowledge, skills and attitudes that a law graduate should be expected to have on graduating with an Australian law degree. The six TLOs relate to: knowledge; ethics and professional responsibility; thinking skills; research skills; communication and collaboration; and, importantly, self-management.[49] The self-management TLO states that: 'Graduates of the Bachelor of Laws will be able to (a) learn and work independently, and (b) reflect on and assess their own capabilities and performance, and make use of feedback as appropriate, to support personal and professional development.'[50] The notes accompanying TLO 6 confirm that it is intended to 'encompass the affective dimensions of student learning with the intention of supporting students to become careful, efficient, concerned, and curious learners'.[51] The notes also emphasize the importance of emotional intelligence and self-awareness skills and attitudes for law graduates.[52]

A number of other important international and Australian reports on legal education confirm that working with the curriculum provides significant opportunities to engage, motivate and support student learning.[53] The corollary of this, and one that is supported by self-determination and other positive psychology theories,[54] is that students who are engaged, motivated and supported in their learning arguably have a better chance of avoiding a decline in their psychological well-being. The curriculum content and the pedagogy of a subject are spaces where law teachers have the potential to connect with and guide their students. It is where they can address, or at least work to ameliorate, many of the aspects of legal education noted above that may be damaging for student well-being. Harnessing the curriculum to promote student well-being allows legal academics to go to where the student is. As Kift has said, 'a truly integrative approach to law curriculum renewal may deliver a viable way forward in a time of dynamic change for both the legal and higher education sectors'.[55]

It has been emphasized a number of times throughout this chapter that the current available empirical evidence, in both Australia and the US, shows that law student psychological well-being starts to decline in the first year of law school.[56] For this reason the preventative and proactive strategies for intentional curriculum design should rightly begin in the first year of legal education. Using the curriculum in the first year experience of law also sits well with Kift's 'transition pedagogy'.[57] This was developed through an ALTC Senior Teaching Fellowship, to provide a conceptual framework for approaches in the first year curriculum designed to assist students to 'transition from their previous education experience to the nature of learning in higher education, learning in their discipline and to life-long learning'.[58] Kift identified through the transition pedagogy that curriculum design should support first year students to develop: 'independent learning and academic agency', 'self-belief and academic confidence', 'guided reflection on the way in which they learn' and an 'understanding of the cognitive and affective hierarchy' of learning.[59] Kift also argued that the first year curriculum should enact 'an engaging and involving curriculum pedagogy' that enables 'active and collaborative learning',[60] supports 'opportunities for peer-to-peer collaboration and teacher-student interaction'[61] and provides timely and constructive feedback.[62]

It is arguable, however, that legal academics have not capitalized on the opportunities presented by the curriculum to address the high levels of psychological distress experienced by law students.[63] The use of curriculum and assessment as tools to promote student well-being is yet to be widely adopted around Australia. For this reason, my ALTC Fellowship Report offers a philosophical framework for intentional curriculum design to promote student well-being, as well as a model first year unit on dispute resolution and non-adversarial legal practice, and a set of dispute resolution motifs for integration in each of the Priestly 11 core curriculum units for law (these are core units that are required for admission to legal practice in Australia).[64]

Conclusion

The law curriculum offers law teachers an opportunity to strategize for important change in legal education by addressing the currently high levels of psychological distress experienced by law students. Law student well-being must be promoted through the curriculum if law students are to be effectively supported to engage in effective learning of law, particularly in the first year of legal education. Some members of the legal academy may feel reluctant to acknowledge that the law curriculum and pedagogy may contribute to causing law students to experience psychological distress. However, the law curriculum is not only a part of the problem; it is also potentially an important part of the solution to student well-being. It is our ethical obligation as legal educators to do no harm to our students. Addressing law student well-being through the law curriculum offers an optimistic future for law students – and, as a consequence, an optimistic future for the legal profession.

Notes

1 This chapter is developed from the final report of Field's 2010 Australian Learning and Teaching Council (ALTC) Fellowship, entitled *Stimulating Strategic Change in Legal Education to Address High Levels of Psychological Distress in Law Students* (published 2014); see http://www.olt.gov.au/resource-promoting-law-student-well-being-through-curriculum. Support for the production of that report was provided by the Australian Government's Office for Learning and Teaching. The views expressed in that report do not necessarily reflect the views of the Australian Government's Office for Learning and Teaching. That report drew from the following works and others cited later by the author and colleagues, published as part of the Fellowship research outcomes: Rachael Field and James Duffy, 'Law Student Psychological Distress, Alternative Dispute Resolution, and Sweet-Minded, Sweet-Eyed Hope' (2012) *Australasian Dispute Resolution Journal* 195; Rachael Field and Sally Kift, 'Addressing the High Levels of Psychological Distress in Law Students through Intentional Assessment and Feedback Design in the First Year Law Curriculum' (2010) 1(1) *International Journal of the First*

Year in Higher Education 65. In particular, parts of the report were developed from: Rachael Field and James Duffy, 'Better to Light a Single Candle than to Curse the Darkness: Promoting Law Student Well-being through a First Year Law Subject' (2012) 12(2) *QUT Law and Justice Journal* 133; Kathy Douglas and Rachael Field, 'Teaching Non-Adversarial Practice in the First Year of Law: A Proposed Strategy for Addressing High Levels of Psychological Distress in Law Students', 14th Pacific Rim First Year in Higher Education Conference, Fremantle, 28 June–1 July 2011; and Judith McNamara, Rachael Field and Catherine Brown, 'Learning to Reflect in the First Year of Legal Education: The Key to Surviving Legal Education and Legal Practice', 12th Pacific Rim First Year in Higher Education Conference, Townsville, 29 June–1 July 2009.

2 Judy Allen and Paula Baron, 'Buttercup Goes to Law School: Student Well-Being in Stressed Law Schools' (2004) 29(6) *Alternative Law Journal* 285; Colin James, 'Seeing Things as We Are: Emotional Intelligence and Clinical Legal Education' (2005) 8 *Clinical Legal Education* 123; Martin Seligman, Paul Verkuil and Terry Kang, 'Why Lawyers are Unhappy' (2005) 10(1) *Deakin Law Review* 49; Massimiliano Tani and Prue Vines, 'Law Students' Attitudes to Education: Pointers to Depression in the Legal Academy and the Profession?' (2007) 19(1) *Legal Education Review* 3; Catherine Leahy et al, 'Distress Levels and Self-Reported Treatment Rates for Medicine, Law, Psychology and Mechanical Engineering Students: Cross-Sectional Study' (2010) 44(7) *Australian and New Zealand Journal of Psychiatry* 608; Kath Hall, Molly Townes O'Brien and Stephen Tang, 'Developing a Professional Identity in Law Schools: A View from Australia' (2010) 4 *Phoenix Law Review* 19; Molly Townes O'Brien, Stephen Tang and Kath Hall, 'No Time to Lose: Negative Impact on Law Student Well-being May Begin in Year One' (2011) 2(2) *International Journal of the First Year in Higher Education* 49; Molly Townes O'Brien, Stephen Tang and Kath Hall, 'Changing our Thinking: Empirical Research on Law Student Well-being, Thinking Styles and the Law Curriculum' (2011) 21(2) *Legal Education* Review 149; Natalia Antolak-Saper, Lloyd England and Anthony Lester, 'Health and Well-being in the First Year: The Law School Experience' (2011) 36(1) *Alternative Law Journal* 47; Beaton Research & Consulting, *2011 Annual Business and Professions Study*, http://www.beatonglobal.com/pdfs/2011_Annual_Business_and_Professions_Study.pdf.

3 Andrew S Watson, 'The Quest for Professional Competence: Psychological Aspects of Legal Education' (1968) 37 *Cincinnati Law Review* 93; Lawrence Silver, 'Anxiety and the First Semester of Law School' (1968) *Wisconsin Law Review* 1201; G Andrew H Benjamin et al, 'The Role of Legal Education in Producing Psychological Distress among Law Students and Lawyers' (1986) 11(2) *American Bar Foundation Research Journal* 225; Susan Daicoff, *Lawyer, Know Thyself: A Psychological Analysis of Personality Strengths and Weaknesses* (American Psychological Association, 2004); Susan Daicoff, 'Lawyer, Know Thyself: A Review of Empirical Research on Attorney Attributes Bearing on Professionalism' (1997) 46 *American University Law Review* 1337; Ruth Ann McKinney, 'Depression and Anxiety in Law Students: Are We Part of the Problem and Can We Be Part of the Solution?' (2002) 8 *Legal Writing: The Journal of the Legal Writing Institute* 229.

4 Norm Kelk et al, *Courting the Blues: Attitudes towards Depression in Australian Law Students and Lawyers* (Brain and Mind Research Institute, 2009), http://www.cald.asn.au/docs/Law%20Report%20Website%20version%204%20May%2009.pdf. See also Norm Kelk, Sharon Medlow and Ian Hickie, 'Distress and Depression among Australian Law Students: Incidence, Attitudes and the Role of Universities' (2010) 32 *Sydney Law Review* 113. The Tristan Jepson Memorial Foundation (http://www.tjmf.org.au) funded this research.

5 Kelk et al, above n4, 11.

6 Ibid. 12.

7 See Hall, O'Brien and Tang, above n2; O'Brien, Tang and Hall, 2011, above n2; Antolak-Saper, England and Lester, above n2. Wendy Larcombe et al, 'Does an Improved

Experience of Law School Protect Students against Depression, Anxiety and Stress? An Empirical Study of Wellbeing and the Law School Experience of LLB and JD Students' (2013) 35 *Sydney Law Review* 407–32; W Larcombe and K Fethers, 'Schooling the Blues? An Investigation of Factors Associated with Psychological Distress among Law Students' (2013) 36 *University of New South Wales Law Journal* 390–436; W Larcombe, I Malkin and P Nicholson, 'Law Students' Motivations, Expectations and Levels of Psychological Distress: Evidence of Connections' (2012) 22 *Legal Education Review* 71–98; Adele Bergin and Kenneth Pakenham, 'Law Student Stress: Relationships between Academic Demands, Social Isolation, Career Pressure, Study/Life Imbalance and Adjustment Outcomes in Law Students' (2014) *Psychiatry, Psychology and Law* 1.

8 Kath Hall, 'Do We Really Want to Know? Recognising the Importance of Student Psychological Wellbeing in Australian Law Schools' (2009) 9(1) *QUT Law and Justice Journal* 1–12.

9 Ibid., 10. See also Nick James, Chapter 16 in this work, and Nick James, '"How Dare You Tell Me How to Teach!": Resistance to Educationalism within Australian Law Schools' (2013) 36(3) *University of New South Wales Law Journal* 779.

10 Field, above n1.

11 The Fellowship has built, and continues to build, a community of practice through the Wellness Network for Law. The Network's website is at http://www.wellnessforlaw.com, its Twitter presence is @WellnessForLaw, and the Network also has a listserv with more than 100 members. Colleagues from the Network – in particular Kate Galloway, Melissa Casten and Stephen Tang – support the Network by administering these communication tools.

12 The Fellowship funding supported me to make more than 40 presentations at law schools (face-to-face meetings, seminars, workshops and facilitated discussions) around Australia and at more than five international conferences. Under the auspices of the Fellowship, three Wellness for Law Forums were held in 2012, 2013 and 2014 in conjunction with (and with the financial support of) the law schools of RMIT University, Melbourne University and Queensland University of Technology. The fourth forum was held in 2015 with the financial and organizational support of the ANU Legal Workshop, and will be held in 2016 at College of Law, Sydney.

13 See Field, above n1.

14 See, for example, Daicoff, above n3.

15 Daicoff, 2004, above n3, 117.

16 Larcombe et al, above n7; Larcombe and Fethers, above n7; Larcombe, Malkin and Nicholson, above n7.

17 See above nn1, 2.

18 Kelk et al, above n4.

19 Ibid. See also Helen Stallman, 'Embedding Resilience within the Tertiary Curriculum: A Feasibility Study' (2011) 30(2) *Higher Education Research and Development* 121; Helen Stallman, 'A Qualitative Evaluation of Perceptions of the Role of Competition in the Success and Distress of Law Students' (2012) 31(6) *Higher Education Research and Development* 891.

20 Benjamin et al, above n3, 236; P Lake, 'When Fear Knocks: The Myths and Realities of Law School' (2000) 29 *Stetson Law Review* 1015; Susan Grover, 'Personal Integration and Outsider Status as Factors in Law Student Well-Being' (2008) 47 *Washburn Law Journal* 419.

21 Ann L Iijima, 'Lessons Learned: Legal Education and Law Student Dysfunction' (1998) 48 *Journal of Legal Education* 524, 528.

22 Ibid.

23 Gerald F Hess, 'Heads and Hearts: The Teaching and Learning Environment in Law School' (2002) 52 *Journal of Legal Education* 75, 78.

24 Lawrence S Krieger, 'Institutional Denial about the Dark Side of Law School, and Fresh Empirical Guidance for Constructively Breaking the Silence' (2002) 52 *Journal of Legal Education* 112. See also Bergin and Pakenham, above n7.

25 SC Segerstrom, 'Perceptions of Stress and Control in the First Semester of Law School' (1996) 32 *Willamette Law Review* 593, 602.
26 Ibid.
27 Kelk et al, above n4, 46.
28 Hall, O'Brien and Tang, above n2; O'Brien, Tang and Hall, 'Changing our Thinking', above n2; O'Brien, Tang and Hall, 'No Time to Lose' above n2.
29 Hess, above n23, 78.
30 Lawrence S Krieger, 'What We're Not Telling Law Students – and Lawyers – That They Really Need to Know: Some Thoughts-in-Action toward Revitalizing the Profession from Its Roots' (1998–1999) 13 *Journal of Law and Health* 1, 24. See also Chapter 11 of this book, where Duffy considers the importance of law students acting upon their character strengths and values to promote their psychological well-being.
31 Hess, above n23, 78–9.
32 Ibid. 79.
33 Marjory Silver, 'Emotional Intelligence and Legal Education' (1999) 5(4) *Psychology, Public Policy and Law* 1173–203.
34 Krieger, above n30, 25.
35 Stephen Reich, 'California Psychological Inventory: Profile of a Sample of First-Year Law Students' (1976) 39 *Psychology Reporter* 873, 874. See also Molly Townes O'Brien, 'Facing Down the Gladiators: Addressing Law School's Hidden Adversarial Curriculum' (2011) 37(1) *Monash University Law Review* 43.
36 Kelk et al, above n4, 46–7.
37 Reich, above n35.
38 See for example, Hess, above n23; Kennon M Sheldon and Lawrence S Krieger, 'Does Legal Education Have Undermining Effects on Law Students? Evaluating Changes in Motivation, Values, and Well-Being' (2004) 22 *Behavioural Science and Law* 261; Lawrence S Krieger, 'The Inseparability of Professionalism and Personal Satisfaction: Perspectives on Values, Integrity and Happiness' (2005) 11 *Clinical Law Review* 425; Lawrence S Krieger, 'Human Nature as a New Guiding Philosophy for Legal Education and the Profession' (2008) 47 *Washburn Law Journal* 247; Lawrence S Krieger, 'The Most Ethical of People, the Least Ethical of People: Proposing Self-Determination Theory to Measure Professional Character Formation' (2011) 8 *University of Saint Thomas Law Journal* 168. Hall, O'Brien and Tang, above n2, 21.
39 Sally Kift, '21st Century Climate for Change: Curriculum Design for Quality Learning Engagement in Law' (2008) 18(1/2) *Legal Education Review* 1. See also Sally Kift and Rachael Field, 'Intentional First Year Curriculum Design as a Means of Facilitating Student Engagement: Some Exemplars', 12th Pacific Rim First Year in Higher Education Conference, Townsville, 29 June–1 July 2009; Field and Kift, above n1.
40 Kift, above n39, 2; James Duffy, Rachael Field and Melinda Shirley, 'Using Student Engagement Strategies to Promote the Psychological Wellbeing of Law Students' (2011) 36 (4) *Alternative Law Journal* 250.
41 See for example, Rachael Field, James Duffy and Anna Huggins, *Lawyering and Positive Professional Identities* (LexisNexis Butterworths, 2014).
42 See Ibid.
43 See Rachael Field, James Duffy and Anna Huggins, 'Supporting Transition to Law School and Student Well-Being: The Role of Professional Legal Identity' (2013) 4(2) *First Year in Higher Education International Journal* (online); Rachael Field, James Duffy and Anna Huggins, 'Independent Learning Skills, Self-Determination Theory and Psychological Well-Being: Strategies for Supporting the First Year University Experience', 17th International First Year in Higher Education Conference, Darwin, 6–9 July 2014; Rachael Field and James Duffy, 'Using Reflective Practice Assessment in the First Year of Law to Encourage a Positive Professional Identity and Promote Law Student Well-Being', 15th International First Year in Higher Education Conference, Brisbane, 26–29 June 2012; Anna Huggins, Sally Kift and Rachael Field, 'Implementing the Self-Management Threshold Learning Outcome for Law: Some

Intentional Design Strategies from the Current Curriculum Toolbox' (2011) *Legal Education Review* 183; Penelope Watson and Rachael Field, 'Promoting Student Wellbeing and Resilience at Law School' in S Kift et al (eds), *Excellence and Innovation in Legal Education* (LexisNexis, 2011), 389.

44 Nick James and Rachael Field, *The New Lawyer* (Wiley, 2013).

45 Jill Howieson and William Ford, 'Teaching and Learning skills: Increasing a Sense of Law School Belongingness' in Student Engagement: Proceedings of the 16th Annual Teaching Learning Forum, Perth, January 2007; Jill Howieson, 'ADR Education: Creating Engagement and Increasing Mental Well-Being through an Interactive and Constructive Approach' (2011) 22 *Australasian Dispute Resolution Journal* 48. For a discussion of the importance of dispute resolution in the law curriculum see, for example, National Alternative Dispute Resolution Advisory Committee (NADRAC), *The Resolve to Resolve: Embracing ADR to Improve Access to Justice in the Federal Jurisdiction* (AGPS, 2009); NADRAC, *Teaching Alternative Dispute Resolution in Australian Law Schools* (AGPS, 2012); James Duffy and Rachael Field, 'Why ADR Must Be a Mandatory Subject in the Law Degree: A Cheat Sheet for the Willing and a Primer for the Non-Believer' (2014) 25(1) *Australasian Dispute Resolution Journal* 9–19; Tania Sourdin, 'Not Teaching ADR in Law Schools? Implications for Law Students, Clients and the ADR Field' (2012) 23 *Australasian Dispute Resolution Journal* 148; C Brabazon and S Frisby, 'Teaching Alternative Dispute Resolution Skills' in C Sampford, S Blencowe and S Condlin (eds), *Educating Lawyers for a Less Adversarial System* (Federation Press, 1999); Kathy Douglas, 'Shaping the Future: The Discourses of ADR and Legal Education' (2008) 8(1) *QUT Law and Justice Journal* 118–38; Kathy Douglas, 'The Teaching of ADR in Australian Law Schools: Promoting Non-Adversarial Practice in Law' (2011) 22 *Australasian Dispute Resolution Journal* 49–57; Judy Gutman, Tom Fisher and E Martens, 'Why Teach Alternative Dispute Resolution to Law Students Part 1: Past and Current Practices and Some Unanswered Questions' (2006) 16 *Legal Education Review* 125–51.

46 Christopher Peterson and Martin EP Seligman, *Character Strengths and Virtues: A Handbook* (Oxford University Press, 2004).

47 Joel Orenstein, 'Mindfulness and the Law: A Different Approach to Sustainable and Effective Lawyering' (2014) 14(1) *QUT Law Review* 106; Leonard L Riskin, 'Contemplative Lawyer: On the Potential Contributions of Mindfulness Meditation to Law Students, Lawyers, and Their Clients' (2002) 7 *Harvard Negotiation Law Review* 1.

48 Sally Kift, Mark Israel and Rachael Field, *Learning and Teaching Academic Standards Project: Bachelor of Laws Learning and Teaching Academic Standards Statement December 2010* (ALTC, 2011).

49 See Anna Huggins, 'The Threshold Learning Outcome on Self-Management in the Discipline of Law: A Proposed Focus for Teaching Strategies in the First Year Law Curriculum' (2011) 2(2) *International Journal of the First Year in Higher Education* 23–34; Anna Huggins, *Strategies for Learning, Teaching and Assessing Self-Management in Australian Legal Curricula*, Master of Laws by Research Thesis, QUT 2012; Judith Marychurch, *Good Practice Guide: Threshold Learning Outcome 6 Self-Management* (Working Paper, ALTC, 30 September 2011); Judith May Marychurch et al, 'Graduate Capabilities Assessment Rubric for Self-Management Standards in the Bachelor of Laws' (Wollongong Faculty of Law Research Papers, 2011).

50 Kift, Israel and Field, above n48, 22.

51 Ibid. 23.

52 Ibid.

53 W Sullivan et al, *Educating Lawyers: Preparation for the Profession of Law* (Jossey-Bass, 2007); R Stuckey et al, *Best Practices for Legal Education: A Vision and A Road Map* (Clinical Legal Education Association, 2007); Richard Johnstone and Sumitra Vignaendra, *Learning Outcomes and Curriculum Development in Law: A Report Commissioned by the Australian Universities Teaching Committee* (AUTC, 2003).

54 See Duffy at Chapter 11. See also Krieger, above n38.
55 Kift, above n39, 1.
56 For a summarized discussion of many of these studies see Field and Duffy, 'Better to Light a Single Candle', above n1.
57 Sally Kift, 'A Transition Pedagogy for First Year Curriculum Design and Renewal', Keynote Address to the *FYE Curriculum Design Symposium 2009*, Brisbane, http://www.fyecd2009.qut.edu.au/resources/PRE_SallyKift_5Feb09.pdf; Queensland University of Technology (QUT), *Protocols for First Year Experience*, https://cms.qut.edu.au/__data/assets/pdf_file/0004/183874/first-year-experience-protocols-20110801.pdf.
58 QUT, above n57, 3.
59 Ibid.
60 Ibid.
61 Ibid. 7.
62 Ibid. See also Paul Ramsden, *Learning to Teach in Higher Education* (Routledge, 2nd ed, 2003), 96.
63 Hess, above n23.
64 See LJ Priestley, *Uniform Admission Requirements: Discussion Paper and Recommendations*, Centre for Legal Education, Sydney, 1994. See also Field, above n1.

15 Beyond the Curriculum

The Wellbeing of Law Students Within Their Broader Environment

*Helen M. Stallman and James Duffy**

There is growing international concern with the increasing prevalence[1] and severity[2] of mental health problems experienced by university students. The reluctance to seek professional support; the high level of disability associated with psychological distress;[3] the limited on-campus treatment options;[4] and the cost of non-intervention[5] all provide strong rationales for considering the broader context of student wellbeing. Mental health and wellbeing result from an interaction of biological, psychological and social factors. As the primary part of a university student's psychological and social experience for a number of years, most frequently at a critical developmental period of young adulthood, the entirety of the university environment influences health and wellbeing.

Introduction

The mental health of tertiary students is affected by the ongoing reciprocal interaction between the student and the physical and social environment of the university. This chapter examines the impact of tertiary education policy, university characteristics and student characteristics on the mental health and wellbeing of law students. It will discuss how modifiable university-wide practices and interventions have the potential to positively influence the self-management and self-regulation skills of law students. It explores the relationship between these personal skills and both learning and graduate outcomes. Implications for policy and practice are reviewed, including challenges to the implementation of universal wellbeing strategies.

Personal achievement, social competence and emotional resilience are influenced by a student's sense of self-efficacy and self-worth, social connectedness, health beliefs and having clear standards.[6] Proximal social and physical environments, including the learning environment, affect the ongoing development of the student as a person. The enrolling student has their own developmental history that includes protective factors and vulnerabilities for their wellbeing. The university plays a role in their ongoing development through its community reputation, student recruitment strategies, physical and virtual environments, and teaching. In order to promote law student wellbeing, these systemic influences need to align with factors that are known to support psychological health.

Systemic Influences on Student Mental Health and Wellbeing

In the late 1990s and early 2000s academic commentary arose highlighting the changing nature of university education. The corporatization of higher education was said to have shifted tertiary education from an educational *opportunity* to a *commodity*, with the student as consumer.[7] This business model of university, driven largely by competitive pressures, means much of the focus of universities rests upon student recruitment and retention.[8] Recruitment and retention therefore become the university's focus, and metrics to measure success (such as using customer satisfaction, rather than learning progress) are altered towards these goals.

An *opportunity* model of tertiary education puts the emphasis on the university to provide learning environments that foster curiosity, critical thinking and substantive/doctrinal competence. The responsibility for utilizing this opportunity lies with the student. The educational experience is not served on a platter for students, and requires a rethink about how university degrees are marketed:

> 'You can have it all' (University of Tasmania)
> 'USQ Hero' (University of Southern Queensland)
> 'The University of You' (University of Queensland)

Perhaps incongruously, we need to turn to Disney films to find the opportunity model of education marketed to would-be students (monsters): 'Are you talented, driven, intelligent, and ready for an adventure? . . . Opportunity is knocking.'[9] Such an approach changes the focus towards striving and being part of something bigger than yourself, rather than the more narcissistic 'it's all about you' rhetoric. The *commodity* approach fails to connect students with the purpose and meaning of being a university student, and reflects the broader problem within western culture of failing to provide a sense of belonging and purpose to young adults through which they can develop a sense of meaning and self-worth.[10]

Self-determination theory (SDT) places these issues into theoretical context.[11] Students who are intrinsically motivated to study law at a particular institution, rather than choosing it for externally controlled reasons, are more likely to have greater interest, excitement and confidence that are associated with enhanced learning, persistence and creativity.[12] As a consumer product, the tertiary degree may actually undermine intrinsic goals associated with mental health and wellbeing, such as personal growth; striving to reach goals; and resilience gained from experiences, setbacks and overcoming them. The pursuit of a degree because it is a product/asset involves extrinsic motivation, and acting pursuant to external drivers is known to decrease intrinsic motivation towards a task.[13]

Factors that occur prior to coming to university influence how a student may approach and be affected by their university studies. Law students each come with their own genetic make-up and vulnerabilities. They have high academic abilities and may be predisposed to high levels of perfectionism and competition.[14] They may have been influenced by their families and friends, their perceptions of others, their social and language skills and/or their definitions of success in making the decision to study law. The university they choose to study at may begin to impact on how they view themselves within the university context long before they enrol as a student. The choice of law school is affected by advertising and the community perception and reputation of the school.[15] The student identity is subsequently developed around how they view themselves within the reputation of their chosen school.[16] Students then arrive at university with their unique aims and expectations. Some, for example, may not even want to be there, but find themselves propelled along a pathway paved by their entrance score and family expectations.[17] Whilst law students are often the most academically capable in secondary school – a big fish in a small pond experience – once they reach university they can feel like a small fish in a big pond, challenging their own self-image as they find themselves competing with other law students for what might seem to be only one prize: a job at the most prestigious law firm upon graduation.[18] Individual risk factors combined with the stress associated with law studies, social comparisons and competition[19] can contribute to the development or maintenance of mental health problems in law students.

This knowledge and understanding necessitates a shared rethink about what a successful career looks like in the law, and how this might be explained and promoted to law students. Success needs to be defined broadly, and opportunities highlighted throughout a degree programme, so that each student has realistic expectations of the diverse career pathways available to them upon graduation, as well as an awareness of their own personal strengths and how they might utilize their law degree to achieve job and life satisfaction.[20] Regular seminars in the first year of law school could be held, where a range of professionals talk about how they used their law degree to end up in their particular professional role. The aim of such an intervention would be to highlight the many different types of legal practice that exist, and the steps these professionals took to end up where they are. Discussions of career possibilities need to highlight both positive and negative aspects of each job, and how each may impact on an employee's life experience. This will enable students to identify jobs that fit with their strengths, values and life goals outside of work.

Social connections and relatedness to others are strong protective factors for mental health and wellbeing.[21] Law students in particular may have well-developed skills to argue, compete and dominate others, which may be useful in certain legal contexts. Legal education implicitly and explicitly fosters these skills.[22] Outside of these contexts, these same strengths are not conducive to warm, supportive and ongoing social relationships. An important skill law students need to develop is the ability to isolate competitiveness and debate to certain contexts, whilst maintaining and developing good social and relational skills. The Threshold Learning Outcomes (TLOs) for the discipline of law speak to the importance of context-appropriate communication and collaboration with others, while the Priestly 11 guidelines remain silent on the importance of these skills.[23] With more and more content being available online, and lectures being recorded, students are at greater risk of having no connections with their university teachers or peers. Such an outcome poses threats to psychological wellbeing because it reduces one of the three basic psychological needs that humans must satisfy to remain well – relationships/relatedness to others.[24]

Communication and connectedness in the twenty-first century presents a challenge to the mental health of both staff and students. Large class sizes, massive open online courses (MOOCs) and recorded lectures increasingly disconnect students from other students and staff.[25] Email can undermine students' abilities to self-regulate and problem-solve, and provides students with the illusion that there are staff waiting around the clock to answer their every question. It is much quicker to send an email when you have a thought, rather than to first consider and research the problem yourself. These are the very skills needed for an independent, creative and problem-solving graduate. Having students make an appointment to see a lecturer, for example (rather than firing off a quick email) allows them to think more deeply about things; consider if they can solve the problem themselves before seeking help; and teaches students delayed gratification by having to wait a few days or even a week to discuss the issue. Such a simple step can promote student independence and autonomy, which are associated with increased levels of psychological wellbeing.[26]

An increasing problem for students is workload management. In a large study on Australian university student mental health, 47 per cent of students reported being full-time students and working more than 10 hours per week.[27] Optional or recorded lectures, MOOCs and other strategies that provide flexibility for students may also create the impression that students can work part time, carry a full-time academic load *and* achieve excellent grades. Clear pathways (including the marketing and normalizing of part-time study) are needed for students who, because of financial, carer or other commitments, do not have adequate time to study a full course load.

To manage workload issues, we know anecdotally that some/many law students will cut back on the amount of sleep they have. We know empirically however that the quality and quantity of sleep affects student learning and academic performance.[28] Sleep is critical to learning processes and memory consolidation.[29] Sleep loss effects are primarily evident on higher cognitive functions such as attention, memory and problem-solving – those processes needed for learning. Sleep habits such as later bedtimes and wake-up times,[30] and short duration of sleep are associated with lower Grade Point Averages. Sleep-deprived students actually inaccurately rate their performance on cognitive tasks significantly higher than non-sleep deprived students, suggesting that students are not aware of the extent to which sleep deprivation actually affects their cognitive ability.[31] Despite the evidence for sleep being fundamental to learning outcomes, the university environment can undermine its importance through 24-hour access to buildings and facilities, and online assignment deadlines set at 11:59pm or 9am. A 4pm deadline for assignments, for example, ensures most students do not stay up all night completing the assignment, and enables them to access staff in a timely manner if they have problems submitting.

Poor nutrition and excess alcohol are often associated with the university experience.[32] Nutrition and alcohol are major problems on campus, as they are in society in general. The ubiquitous vending machine provides access to chocolate, crisps and carbonated drinks at any time. Less prevalent on campuses are low-cost, nutrient-dense food options for students and staff. Despite national and international guidelines on nutrition,[33] most universities find it challenging to apply them within the university community context. Links have been drawn between nutrition and psychological wellbeing. Empirical studies conducted in a number of different countries suggest that people with healthier diets are less likely to experience depression.[34] The UK, as an example of good practice (through its Public Health Responsibility Deal),[35] recognizes the potential for businesses and organizations to contribute to improving public health by creating healthy environments.

Why a Whole of University Approach?

There is a strong rationale for universities to take an active role in promoting the protective factors, and decreasing the risk factors, associated with mental illness. In contradistinction to many physical conditions, the disabling consequences of many mental illnesses begin early in life.[36] Roughly half of all lifetime mental disorders have first onset by mid-adolescence and nearly three-quarters by the mid-20s.[37] Early detection and intervention of initially mild disorders can therefore have large ripple effects in the latter wellbeing of law graduates. Universities are well suited to a population approach to mental health for a number of reasons:[38]

- There is a high[39] and increasing prevalence of mental health problems among university students.[40]
- Mental health is associated with many other important outcomes and factors in this population, including educational attainment, economic productivity and social connectedness.
- A treatment approach alone has proven inadequate.
- The typical population age (18–25 years) encompasses the average age of first onset for many mental disorders, providing a natural opportunity for early intervention.[41]
- Campus settings are typically integrated communities with substantial human and organizational resources that can be leveraged to enact change for entire student communities.

What Is Student Success?

It is important to define what we mean by student success because our perception of success influences where efforts go to help students be successful, and what we measure to demonstrate that students are successful. Consideration of the systemic university influences on mental wellbeing (above) can potentially be dismissed if they are not seen to be important to student success. Some law academics, for example, consider a competitive spirit to be an important attribute for graduates working successfully within a competitive law environment; others consider it to be a potentially negative characteristic.[42] If achieving the highest grade in the cohort means 'success', competition will be an important activity for staff to nurture. In contrast, if we consider attainment of the skills needed for life-long professional and personal success of law graduates, we might define success as mental health and wellbeing in addition to knowledge and skills. Activities that nurture all these components of success would therefore be important. Universities generally, and law faculties more specifically, need to ask themselves what student success looks like. More importantly, they need to articulate this vision to their students. An example of this is the QUT Law School, where Field and Duffy have described a successful law school experience as producing, happy, healthy, competent professionals – in the law or in another discipline.[43] Such an articulation places psychological wellbeing and legal knowledge and skills *together*, as important components of student success.

Healthy University Communities

Just as the mental health and wellbeing of the student cannot be delineated from the physical health of the student, a healthy university necessarily involves all of its students and staff; its physical and virtual environment; its explicit and implicit messages; and its learning, teaching, support and social activities. A healthy university requires attention to policy, procedures and practices and their individual impact on the health of its students and staff.

Prevention activities relating to psychological wellbeing are most cost effective when matched with a student's level of risk. Universal interventions target the entire university population rather than individual students who are at risk of developing problems (selected intervention) or students who are showing signs or symptoms of psychological or behavioural problems (targeted intervention).[44] Universal interventions to promote a healthy university would include an emphasis on developing protective factors for general health and wellbeing, such as sleep, nutrition, physical activity, connectedness and resilience.

The *Work Health and Safety Act 2011* (Cth) requires businesses to manage risks associated with health and safety through governance, prevention, response, managing hazards and recovery. While there is mandatory workplace training for employees within universities, little attention is given to workplace health and safety for students (non-employees) beyond those on high-risk courses. A healthy workplace for students needs to be one that is aware and responsive to them throughout their enrolment. Some interventions can form part of the general work environment, such as accessible and affordable nutrition, incidental exercise (for example, by placing an emphasis on stairs rather than elevators) or the opening hours of facilities. Others, such as awareness-raising interventions, may be delivered universally across the student population at the beginning of enrolment or each academic year: for example, training in ergonomics, academic integrity, workload expectations and self-management. Other selected interventions for those experiencing problems need to be available when each particular student needs it, such as for managing depression, anxiety, stress, relationships or support in academic areas such as studying or writing.

Universal Interventions

Universal interventions that target the psychological wellbeing of all students within a university (or law faculty) have several advantages:

- They send the message that health and wellbeing is an essential part of being a successful student and graduate.
- They demonstrate that health and wellbeing is valued by the university.
- They model how to incorporate health and wellbeing into everyday life.
- The emphasis is not placed solely on the student to recognize they have a problem, identify relevant resources of services and prioritize time to get help.
- Generally, it is significantly more cost effective at the individual, institutional and societal level to prevent mental health problems than to treat them.[45]

There are a number of universal interventions that demonstrate how health and wellbeing activities can simply be incorporated into law schools. It is important to recognize that not all students need (or want) one-on-one interventions with a counsellor or academic adviser. The modality of delivery for interventions is therefore an important consideration, not just in terms of economics but also in ensuring it is providing scaffolding to (rather than undermining) a student's own strengths and capabilities. Effectiveness, efficiency, stigma, access, uptake and developmental needs of students all warrant consideration in the implementation of interventions. A stepped-care approach is an efficient and effective model for the provision of minimally sufficient interventions. The following paragraphs provide an overview of four universal interventions that can be utilized in law schools in order to improve law student mental health and wellbeing.

thedesk

thedesk[46] is a web-based programme developed specifically to support the mental health and wellbeing of university students. *thedesk* is promoted as a resource for successful students rather than as a mental health intervention, with both the design and content of the website normalizing common student experiences and supporting the development of learning and wellbeing skills. An active skills framework enables students to be active in learning new strategies and skills to manage their wellbeing. PowerPoint slides are available to teaching staff for inclusion in their own lecture slides at relevant points throughout the semester to link students with relevant and timely modules and tools, such as the *Managing Stress* module at high-stress times in the course, or the *Using Feedback* tool after assignments are returned. *thedesk* is a free resource that can be utilized by students or staff at any time.

On Track to Success

On Track to Success,[47] a tool within *thedesk*, enables students to reflect on whether they are achieving their organismic needs – important for achieving goal-related pursuits. It is based on Maslow's Theory of Human Motivation.[48] *On Track to Success* differs from many measures because:

- It is strengths focused, looking at what students are doing rather than what they are not doing.
- It focuses on behaviours rather than feelings and symptoms. In this way it increases awareness of behaviours students could change to be more successful.
- It is pictorial and provides immediate feedback. Being a web-based tool, students can repeat the quiz regularly to get feedback on their progress. The *On Track to Success* tool lends itself to being a universal intervention during orientation week to raise student awareness of the importance of meeting all their needs to achieve wellbeing and success at university.

The Success and Wellbeing Seminar

The Success and Wellbeing Seminar[49] is an example of a low-intensity intervention that improves student knowledge of mental health strategies and promotes help-seeking. The programme focuses on the student goal of *success* rather than the institutional goal of improving mental health. The seminar is delivered in class to all students around week 4 or 5 of the academic semester, at a time when students are often feeling stressed – thereby providing a *just-in-time* intervention. It is delivered by counselling service staff, which has the benefit of putting a human face (or faces) to university counselling services. One aim of the success and wellbeing seminar is to reduce some of the anxiety that students may have in seeking professional help for the first time. The seminar also provides practical strategies that students can implement independently to promote their own psychological wellbeing.[50]

The Learning Thermometer

The Learning Thermometer[51] is an example of a web-based screening and referral tool. The tool consists of four surveys completed independently by students at intervals throughout the semester that encourage them to reflect on their motivation; their progress towards achieving learning outcomes; the usefulness of course resources and learning environment; and their personal wellbeing. Students receive tailored online feedback and suggestions to help them improve if needed. The recommendations are provided in a hierarchy from most autonomous to least autonomous: starting with strategies students can do on their own; followed by self-help resources students can access; and lastly people who can assist the student. This approach maximizes student autonomy and self-sufficiency. Students are prompted to select two or three things they can do differently to promote their learning. Those details are then emailed to the student in a personalized Learning Plan. At the beginning of the subsequent survey, students are prompted to reflect on how they went about implementing their Learning Plan, reinforcing their problem-solving and reflection skills. Used as a compulsory learning activity in at least one core subject across a programme of study, *The Learning Thermometer* ensures that all students are linked with relevant and useful strategies, resources and services if and when they are personally relevant and useful to them. The student's individual data is not accessible to anyone else, apart from themselves. At a higher level of intervention, where faculty are involved in making special considerations for students, the Learning Plan could be used (with the student's permission) to discuss the student's progress, and in making changes necessary to improve their learning performance.

Conclusion

Mental health and wellbeing cannot be separated from the physical health of the law student; the environment that the student studies within; the staff that the student interacts with; or the everyday practices and experiences involved in being a student. Mental health cannot be promoted through the work of a single service, curriculum change or mental health awareness day, whilst the everyday university experience continues to run counter to these initiatives. Improving the mental health of law students therefore requires a holistic approach to wellbeing that relies upon broader university policies and procedures. Universities are in a unique position to influence the health and wellbeing of their students. Students with health and wellbeing knowledge and skills will not only affect the vibrancy of law schools, but will also (hopefully) take these skills into their working and personal lives. These graduates become synecdochic representations of a broader university environment that understands systemic tertiary influences, engages in universal interventions and articulates its holistic understanding of student success.

Notes

* Helen M Stallman, BSc, BPsych(Hons), CertMedEd, DClinPsych, PhD, Senior Lecturer University of South Australia; James Duffy, BCom/LLB (Hons) (UQ), LLM (QUT), Lecturer Queensland University of Technology Law School.

1 Jean M Twenge et al, 'Birth Cohort Increases in Psychopathology among Young Americans, 1938–2007: A Cross-Temporal Meta-Analysis of the MMPI' (2010) 30(2) *Clinical Psychology Review* 145; Helen M Stallman, 'Psychological Distress in University Students: A Comparison with General Population Data' (2010) 45(4) *Australian Psychologist* 286; Daniel Eisenberg et al, 'Prevalence and Correlates of Depression, Anxiety, and Suicidality among University Students' (2007) 77(4) *American Journal of Orthopsychiatry* 534.

2 RP Gallagher, *National Survey of College Counseling Centers 2013, Section One: 4-Year Directors* (International Association of Counseling Services, 2014).

3 David Richards and Mark Whyte, *Reach Out: National Programme Student Materials to Support the Delivery of Training for Psychological Wellbeing Practitioners Delivering Low Intensity Interventions* (National Health Service, 2009); Stallman, above n1.

4 Helen. M. Stallman, 'University Counselling Services in Australia and New Zealand: Activities, Changes, and Challenges' (2011) 47(4) *Australian Psychologist* 249; Gallagher, above n2.

5 Daniel Eisenberg, Ezra Golberstein and Justin Hunt, 'Mental Health and Academic Success in College' (2009) 9(1) *B.E. Journal of Economic Analysis and Policy* Article 40.
6 Stephen Zubric, Sven Silburn and Margot Prior, 'Resources and Contexts for Child Development: Implications for Children and Society' in Sue Richardson and Margot Prior (eds), *No Time to Lose: The Wellbeing of Australia's Children* (Academy of the Social Sciences in Australia and Melbourne University Press, 2005) 161–200.
7 Bill Readings, *The University in Ruins* (Havard University Press, 1996); Margaret Thornton, 'Among the Ruins: Law in The Neo-Liberal Academy' (2001) 20 *Windsor Year Book of Access to Justice* 3; Margaret Thornton, 'Law as Business in the Corporatised University' (2000) 25(6) *Alternative Law Journal* 269; Jim Jackson, 'The Marketing of University Courses under Sections 52 and 53 of the Trade Practices Act 1974' (2002) 6 *Southern Cross Law Review* 106.
8 Mantz Yorke and Bernard Longden, *Retention and Student Success in Higher Education* (Open University Press, 2004); Commonwealth of Australia, *A Sustainable Higher Education System* <http://education.gov.au/sustainable-higher-education-system>.
9 Disney Interactive Media Group, *Monsters University* <http://monstersuniversity.com/edu/>.
10 Richard Eckersley, 'Failing a Generation: The Impact of Culture on the Health and Well-Being of Youth' (1993) 29 *Journal of Paediatrics and Child Health* S16.
11 Edward Deci and Richard Ryan, *Intrinsic Motivation and Self-Determination in Human Behavior* (Plenum, 1985).
12 Kennon M. Sheldon and Lawrence S. Krieger, 'Does Legal Education Have Undermining Effects on Law Students? Evaluating Changes in Motivation, Values, and Well-Being' (2004) 22 *Behavioral Sciences and Law* 261; Massimiliano Tani and Prue Vines, 'Law Students' Attitudes to Education: Pointers to Depression in the Legal Academy and the Profession?' (2009) 19(1) Legal Education Review 3.
13 Richard Ryan and Edward Deci, 'Intrinsic and Extrinsic Motivations: Classic Definitions and New Directions' (2000) 25 *Contemporary Educational Psychology* 54, 59.
14 Susan Daicoff, 'Lawyer, Know Thyself: A Review of Empirical Research on Attorney Attributes Bearing on Professionalism' (1997) 46 *American University Law Review* 1337.
15 Tani and Vines, above n12.
16 For information on law student and legal practitioner identity more generally, see Rachael Field, James Duffy and Anna Huggins, *Lawyering and Positive Professional Identities* (LexisNexis Butterworths, 2014).
17 Tani and Vines, above n12, 24.
18 Helen M. Stallman, 'A Qualitative Evaluation of Perceptions of the Role of Competition in the Success and Distress of Law Students' (2012) 31(6) *Higher Education Research and Development* 891.
19 Ibid.
20 Stallman, above n18.
21 Edward Deci and Richard Ryan, 'The "What" and "Why" of Goal Pursuits: Human Needs and the Self-Determination of Behavior' (2000) 11 *Psychological Inquiry* 227.
22 Molly Townes O'Brien, 'Facing Down the Gladiators: Law School's Hidden Adversarial Curriculum' (2011) 37(1) *Monash Law Review* 43.
23 Sally Kift, Mark Israel and Rachael Field, 'Bachelor of Laws Learning and Teaching Academic Standards Statement' (Australian Learning and Teaching Council, 2010).
24 Basic psychological needs theory (BPNT) is one component of broader self-determination theory. Under BPNT, human beings require regular experiences of autonomy, competences and relatedness to maintain psychological wellbeing. See Deci and Ryan, above n21.
25 See generally Sally Kift, Karen Nelson and John A. Clarke, 'Transition Pedagogy: A Third Generation Approach to FYE' (2010) 1(1) *International Journal of the First*

Year in Higher Education 4; James Duffy, Rachael Field and Melinda Shirley, 'Engaging Law Students to Promote Psychological Health' (2011) 36(4) *Alternative Law Journal* 250.

26 Deci and Ryan, above n21.

27 Stallman, above n1.

28 Giuseppe Curcio, Michele Ferrara and Luigi De Gennaro, 'Sleep Loss, Learning Capacity and Academic Performance' (2006) 10(5) *Sleep Medicine Reviews* 323.

29 Ibid. See also Carlyle Smith, 'Sleep States and Memory Processes in Humans: Procedural Versus Declarative Memory Systems' (2001) 5(6) *Physiological Review* 491.

30 Mickey Trockel, Michael Barnes and Dennis Egget, 'Health-Related Variables and Academic Performance among First-Year College Students: Implications for Sleep and Other Behaviors' (2000) 49 *Journal of American College Health* 125.

31 June Pilcher and Amy Walters, 'How Sleep Deprivation Affects Psychological Variables Related to College Students' Cognitive Performance' (1997) 46(3) *Journal of American College Health* 121.

32 See Field, Duffy and Huggins, above n16, Chapter 8.

33 National Health and Medical Research Council, *Australian Dietary Guidelines* (2013); US Department of Agriculture and US Department of Health and Human Services, *Dietary Guidelines for Americans, 2010* (7th ed, US Government Printing Office, 2010). These guidelines are based on best available scientific evidence, and aim to provide information on the types and amounts of foods, food groups and dietary patterns that promote health and wellbeing, reduce the risk of diet-related conditions and reduce the risk of chronic disease.

34 See, for example, Felice Jacka, Arnstein Mykletun and Michael Berk, 'Moving Towards a Population Health Approach to the Primary Prevention of Common Mental Disorders' (2012) 10 *BMC Medicine* 149.

35 UK Department of Health, *Public Health Responsibility Deal* <https://responsibilitydeal.dh.gov.uk/about/>.

36 Ronald C Kessler et al, 'Age of Onset of Mental Disorders: A Review of Recent Literature' (2007) 20(4) *Current Opinion in Psychiatry* 359.

37 Ronald C Kessler and Philip S Wang, 'The Descriptive Epidemiology of Commonly Occurring Mental Disorders in the United States' (2008) 29 *Annual Review Public Health* 115.

38 Helen M Stallman, Sarah Lipsen and Daniel Eisenberg, 'A Population Approach to Mental Health of University Students' in J Tanner (ed), *Developing Mental Health in Emerging Adulthood* (forthcoming).

39 Stallman, above n1; Eisenberg et al, above n1.

40 Twenge et al, above n1.

41 Ronald C Kessler et al, 'Lifetime Prevalence and Age-of-Onset Distributions of DSM-IV Disorders in the National Comorbidity Survey Replication' (2005) 62 *Archives of General Psychiatry* 593.

42 Stallman, above n18.

43 Rachael Field and James Duffy, 'Law Student Psychological Distress, ADR and Sweet-Minded, Sweet-Eyed Hope' (2012) 23(3) *Australasian Dispute Resolution Journal* 195, 200.

44 Mary Ellen O'Connell, Thomas Boat and Kenneth Warner (eds), *Preventing Mental, Emotional, and Behavioral Disorders among Young People: Progress and Possibilitiess* (National Academies Press, 2009).

45 World Health Organization, 'Prevention of Mental Disorders: Effective Interventions and Policy Options' (WHO, 2004).

46 Helen M Stallman, David Kavanagh and Alan Ralph, 'thedesk: Promoting Student Success and Wellbeing' (Brisbane No University of Queensland, 2012) <https://www.thedesk.org.au>.

47 Helen M Stallman, 'On Track for Success Scale' in Helen M Stallman, David Kavanagh and Alan Ralph (eds), *thedesk* (University of Queensland, 2013).
48 Abraham H Maslow, 'A Theory of Human Motivation' (1943) 50(4) *Psychological Review* 370.
49 Helen M Stallman, *Success and Wellbeing Seminar* (University of Queensland, 2010).
50 Helen M Stallman, 'Embedding Resilience within the Tertiary Curriculum: A Feasibility Study' (2011) 30(2) *Higher Education Research and Development* 121.
51 Helen M Stallman, 'The Learning Thermometer: Engage, Link, Learn', *Creating Excellence in Scholarship of Teaching and Learning (CESoTL) eZine* (Brisbane).

16 Dealing With Resistance to Change by Legal Academics

Nick James[*]

Abstract

Many law schools have in recent years responded to the mounting evidence of unusually high levels of psychological distress experienced by law students by attempting to introduce measures intended to ameliorate such distress and foster law student wellbeing. The responses by individual legal academics to these wellness initiatives are varied. Some academics embrace them with enthusiasm, some are ambivalent . . . and some appear determined to resist and oppose any efforts to make legal education less stressful and difficult for law students. This chapter examines the nature of academic resistance to wellness initiatives: identifying the various forms of resistance engaged in by academics; describing the various reasons and justifications for the resistance; and offering some possible strategies for addressing the resistance.

Introduction

The well-known survey of Australian law students and lawyers conducted by the University of Sydney Brain and Mind Research Institute (BMRI) in 2008 found that over 35 per cent of the law students studied suffered from high to very high levels of psychological distress, and that almost 40 per cent reported distress severe enough to warrant clinical or medical intervention.[1] The report suggested that the high levels of distress experienced by law students were at least partly attributable to the competitive and adversarial nature of legal education and legal culture. Since the publication of the BMRI report, further Australian research has been conducted to affirm the report's findings; to identify the factors that contribute to law student distress; and to identify measures that successfully promote student wellness.[2] Some of the measures are extracurricular, and some call for changes to teaching and assessment practices within the law school curriculum. Both types of measure are important: Larcombe et al. recommend that in order to effectively promote student wellness, a 'whole of school' approach that encompasses curriculum design, assessment and law school culture is required.[3]

In March 2013, the Council of Australian Law Deans (CALD) issued a set of 10 good practice guidelines for law schools, with the aim of promoting law student wellbeing.[4] Many of these guidelines require law schools to rethink traditional approaches to the teaching of law. At least three of the guidelines – 4, 5 and 6 – relate directly to the teaching practices of law academics. Guideline 4 refers explicitly to the integration of 'strategies for the promotion of law student well-being into . . . teaching and learning practices'. The notes accompanying the guideline cite literature suggesting that the use of grading curves,[5] 100 per cent examinations and 24-hour take-home examinations appear to contribute to student distress and should therefore be minimized or abolished; and that engaged and active learning,[6] greater student autonomy[7] and team-based learning[8] may contribute to student wellbeing.[9]

A 'whole of school' approach to student wellness requires individual academics within the law school to reflect upon and reconsider their traditional teaching and assessment practices. The traditional emphasis within legal education upon individual effort and competition between students rather than group work and collaboration;[10] upon the passive learning of abstract doctrine and theory rather than active engagement by students in the learning process;[11] and upon teaching law students how to 'think like lawyers' by privileging reason, logic and objectivity above compassion, empathy and caring[12] are now seen as contributing to the wellness problem. However, when those seeking to introduce wellness initiatives within the law school endeavour to persuade their colleagues to reflect upon and reconsider their teaching practices, the responses are not always positive. Some colleagues appear to understand and be sympathetic to the need to modify their teaching to promote student wellness, and welcome the opportunity to reform and refine their own teaching practices. Some are not quite as enthusiastic about modifying their teaching practices, but nevertheless accept that reflection upon and development of their teaching is an unavoidable element of contemporary academic life. And some colleagues explicitly object to any and all attempts to influence their teaching practices; insist that they know how best to teach their particular subjects; and seem to take it as a personal insult whenever another academic, an administrator or a university policy suggests that they might need to make changes to how they teach. These are the academics who, when encouraged to reconsider their teaching and assessment practices in order to better promote student wellbeing, respond with statements such as 'if they [students] can't stand the heat they should get out of the kitchen'; or with arguments to the effect that since the practice of law is so challenging, a law school would be doing its students a disservice were it to support them in law school and thereby fail to 'toughen them up'.[13]

This chapter examines the nature of academic resistance to wellness initiatives. The emphasis is upon curricular initiatives requiring the cooperation of individual academics (such as changes to the content, delivery and assessment of law subjects) rather than extracurricular initiatives that can be introduced regardless of the views of individual academics (such as mindfulness, lifestyle and resilience workshops for students, or the provision of counselling and support services). The chapter begins by locating curricular wellness initiatives alongside other efforts to regulate and reform academic teaching practices within the broader discourse of 'educationalism'. It then describes the various ways in which institutional efforts to regulate and reform teaching practices are resisted by legal academics, and analyses that resistance by identifying its various causes and justifications. Finally, the chapter presents some of the ways in which resistance to teaching reform generally and to wellness initiatives in particular can be addressed.

The ideas presented in this chapter are informed and supplemented by a series of interviews with Associate Deans Teaching and Learning (ADTLs) and Directors of Teaching and Learning from six Australian law schools. The interviews sought to identify the ADTLs' views on the various forms of and justifications for resistance by law school academics to efforts to regulate and reform the teaching of law within their school or faculty. The observations and experiences of the various ADTLs are referred to in the final three parts of the chapter to support and illustrate various points.[14]

Wellness and Educationalism

I have argued elsewhere that 'legal education' is appropriately conceptualized as a dynamic nexus of competing discourses rather than as a stable body of knowledge and practices.[15] One such discourse is 'educationalism', a discourse characterized by the insistence that all academics, regardless of their discipline, should teach in a manner consistent with principles from orthodox education scholarship.[16] These principles include, for example:

- the notion that a student-centred approach to teaching is more appropriate than a teacher-centred or content-centred approach;[17]
- that reflective, evidenced-based approaches to teaching are preferable to approaches based on tradition, common practice or the demands of employers;[18]
- that teaching should be defined as the facilitation of learning rather than the transmission of knowledge;[19]
- that student engagement,[20] formative feedback,[21] authentic assessment,[22] transparency in learning objectives[23] and the alignment of objectives, teaching and assessment[24] are of fundamental importance; and
- that student wellbeing is at least partly the responsibility of academics and institutions rather than solely the responsibility of students.

Educationalism can be contrasted with other legal education discourses such as *doctrinalism* (characterized by an emphasis upon the transmission to students of a correct and detailed understanding of legal doctrine in isolation from law's diverse contexts); *vocationalism* (characterized by an emphasis upon the acquisition by students of practical skills in preparation for post-university employment); and *liberalism* (characterized by an emphasis upon a broad and diverse education rather than a narrowly specialized one, and upon lifelong education rather than education for employment). These and other discourses coexist within the discursive field that is 'legal education', often competing and sometimes aligning, with no discourse ever completely and consistently dominant, whether in terms of an individual academic's teaching practice or a law school's approach to curriculum design.[25]

Educationalism is a relatively new discourse within a discipline traditionally dominated by an emphasis upon black-letter law (doctrinalism) and preparation for legal practice (vocationalism). The propagation of educationalism within law schools is at least partially the result of efforts by some legal academics to shift the focus away from legal rules and legal practice, and to think more deeply about the student learning experience. These legal academics choose to familiarize themselves with general education scholarship; to incorporate insights from this scholarship into their own teaching practices; to write about what they have learned in legal education journals; and to encourage their colleagues to themselves incorporate educationalist concepts and notions into their own teaching practices. The recent spate of articles, reports, conferences and workshops concerned with student wellness is a good example of the way in which the educationalist focus on the student (rather than content) is being propagated amongst legal academics.[26]

However, if the propagation of educationalist notions was solely dependent upon voluntary engagement by legal academics, it would not be anywhere near as successful as it has been in recent years. The recent propagative success of educationalism generally – and of educationalist notions such as institutional and academic responsibility for student wellbeing in particular – is largely the result of the adoption by governments, regulators and university managers and administrators of educationalist concepts. Many others have commented upon the recent turn by universities towards corporatism, managerialism and the massification of education.[27] Law schools are no longer purely sites for the creation and dissemination of knowledge; they are now units within corporatized institutions with an obligation to minimize cost and maximize customer satisfaction and worker efficiency. For those seeking to monitor and regulate the teaching practices of academic workers, educationalism offers a plethora of standards against which those practices can be measured and evaluated, all supported by a large body of academic literature. Educationalism is a way for a university to regulate, improve and market the 'product' sold to its customers, the students. Educationalist notions such as the identification and communication to students of explicit learning objectives are no longer simply a 'good idea' that academics are welcome to adopt or reject as they see fit. They are now embedded within regulatory frameworks and university and faculty policies. Academics are no longer encouraged to provide students with informative subject outlines; instead they are obliged to use faculty- or university-produced templates that compel them to provide certain specific information to students. Academics are told what types of assessment are acceptable; how many assessment tasks they should set; what standards they should use when assessing students; and how much feedback they should provide. They are told to maintain subject websites and to record and stream their lectures. They are told to gather and act upon student feedback about their teaching practices. They are told to justify their teaching practices by reference to educationalist concepts and standards.

Many wellness initiatives are voluntary in the sense that individual academics can choose for themselves whether or not to engage with them. Examples of voluntary initiatives include faculty guidelines on promoting student wellness; faculty workshops and seminars on the topic of wellness; wellness interest groups and networks; and of course the academic literature on law student wellness. But the wellness issue is increasingly informing regulatory reform, and in that sense is mandatory rather than voluntary. Teaching policies and regulations that call for multiple forms of assessment in a subject; maximum weightings for individual items of assessment; minimum weightings for group work; minimum disclosure in subject outlines; limits upon the quantity of pre-class readings and student workloads; and concessions for students recognized as experiencing depression or anxiety are all informed, at least in part, by concerns about student wellness, and are all increasingly likely to be mandatory for academics rather than voluntary.

Institutional initiatives that seek to promote student wellness by modifying traditional teaching practices are part of the broader propagation of educationalism within law schools. The identification of law student wellness as an important issue took place within the literature, as do many of the ongoing efforts to identify the factors contributing to law student anxiety, stress and depression. But the responses by institutions and administrators – whether driven by a shared concern for student wellbeing, a corporatist concern to avoid potential legal liability, or a combination of both – are now likely to take the form of policy and regulation. Wellness initiatives, whether voluntary or mandatory, are now seen by many individual academics as part of a suite of unwelcome educationalist regulations. And opposition to wellness initiatives is part of a wider practice of academic resistance to mandatory educationalism generally.

Academic Resistance

Academics are already less inclined than most other categories of employee to accept direction unquestioningly. Academics are encouraged to think critically when engaging in research and scholarship, and so it is not surprising that academics are likely to question and challenge regulations and decision-making within their own workplace.[28] *Legal* academics are even more likely to resist regulation of their activities, a view espoused by a majority of the ADTLs interviewed by the author. For example, according to one ADTL:

> To some extent law training is directed towards autonomous kinds of thinking and a sort of a fierce independence in the way that one carries out one's work. [ADTL5]

Of course, not all legal academics engage in resistant practices; and those that do, do so in different ways and at different times. An individual academic might willingly accept regulation of some aspects of their work life but be passionately opposed to regulation of other aspects. Some academics will welcome regulation of their teaching practices, perhaps because that regulation is compelling all academics to do what that academic believes to be the right thing to do. Some will accept regulation as an unavoidable aspect of contemporary academic life. And some academics will criticize and oppose all efforts to influence their teaching, including those driven by a desire to promote student wellness. As one ADTL observed:

> There are members of staff in my experience who believe quite passionately that once they are employed as a law teacher, even if it's at level A, but

> certainly if they are employed at level C, D or E, that nobody should be questioning anything that they do or don't do within their own courses. That it's like a private domain and 'How dare you tell me what I should teach or how I should teach or how I should assess. And by the way don't ask me to teach all those skills because there's so much other stuff going on in this curriculum or in this course, and they're all so terribly important that I can't possibly do anything else.' [ADTL5]

Academic resistance takes a variety of forms.[29] Sometimes the resistance is explicit and deliberate. Academics complain loudly about the increasing level of regulation of their teaching in staff meetings and in corridor conversations. Academics write emails to Deans and Associate Deans challenging a proposed new teaching reform initiative. Academics respond to emailed announcements about new teaching and learning policies with sarcastic comments or detailed critiques (often clicking 'reply all' and sharing their views with everyone). Academics explicitly refuse to post content to their subject websites, provide written feedback to students or submit draft examination papers on time.

> People are not afraid to express their opinions in staff meetings or in the corridors. They will say if they think it is a waste of time or serves no obvious purpose. [ADTL1]

Many academics, however, appear to be uncomfortable with or unwilling to engage in such explicit acts of resistance. A tenured professor may be willing to publicly object to a new university teaching policy; but a more junior academic may be unwilling to risk censure from their supervisors and employers, regardless of their views. Thornton goes so far as to argue that dissent is stifled in the neoliberal university:

> Marginalisation, reprimands, disciplinary proceedings or even dismissal is the likely fate of any academic who is critical of his or her institution's captivation by market magic, regardless of the academic expertise they might possess.[30]

Resistance is never, however, entirely absent,[31] and where explicit dissent is discouraged, quiet, less obvious acts of resistance can still thrive. Examples of these passive forms of resistance include missing administrative deadlines and failing to comply with administrative requests without explicitly refusing to do so; 'forgetting' to comply with teaching policies; and complying with teaching initiatives minimally, grudgingly or in a manner consistent with the letter but not the spirit of the rule.

> Sometimes people don't comply with deadlines or they complain that something isn't necessary. For example, some academics question the need to provide descriptions of the work required for particular grades, they say that everyone knows what needs to be done for a certain grade. [ADTL1]

> We've been through a very long process of embedding graduate attributes in particular subjects and making sure certain subjects target certain graduate attributes and that the assessment in the subject outline shows the link between that graduate attribute. And lots of people would say that 'yes, we have done that' but when you actually drill down through their subject outline you find it's not quite as explicit as you would have liked. [ADTL2]
>
> There are some academics in the school who every semester miss deadlines for completing electronic course profiles or setting up course websites, or who claim not to understand how to do it, or who don't respond to email requests for weeks at a time, or who ignore email requests completely. [ADTL6]

Acts of workplace resistance are certainly not unique to law schools, or even academia. There are, however, reasons and justifications for this resistance that are distinctive to the academic workplace.

Reasons and Justifications

Krieger describes how many legal academics find it 'uncomfortable' to confront the issue of law student wellness, and prefer to participate in collective denial of the issue.[32] Hall attributes academic resistance to recognizing and accepting the existence of a wellness issue amongst law students to cognitive dissonance and rationalization.[33] According to Hall, many people respond to the discomfort associated with cognitive dissonance between what they expect or believe and what they perceive by engaging in unconscious strategies, including reinterpreting the situation that caused the dissonance and avoiding or denying the negative information.[34]

This chapter contends that academic resistance to wellness initiatives can also be attributed to the association of such initiatives with institutional efforts to regulate their teaching generally. This resistance to regulation generally is justified or at least accompanied by certain narratives.

One such narrative of resistance is 'academic freedom'.[35] Some academics justify their opposition to wellness initiatives and the regulation of their teaching generally by citing the traditional freedom by academics to teach and conduct research in the manner of their choosing. Efforts to transform the way law is taught are seen as unwelcome infringements upon academic freedom. Sometimes the resistance is explicitly justified by reference to academic freedom, and sometimes the justification takes the form of complaints that the academic's standing and autonomy as a 'professional' are being questioned:

> I think there is a sense that there is no reason for the university to regulate teaching that closely, that 'I'm a professional and I should be free to teach in the way that I see fit'. [ADTL1]
>
> I think . . . lots of academics don't like being told what to do. They'd much prefer just to be able to do what they want to do. They believe and they probably do have the students' best interests at heart. I don't have any worries

> [that] any of the academics aren't concerned about students' wellbeing and making sure they get a good subject delivered. But I just think they'd prefer to do it on their own terms, how and when they want to do it. [ADTL2]

Other academics justify their resistance to teaching reform initiatives by referring to their obligation to conduct research. They insist that teaching and research are mutually exclusive activities; that they are primarily researchers rather than teachers; and that when pressed for time they have an obligation to direct their efforts towards research rather than teaching. They point to the increasing pressure upon academics to do more with less, and to produce acceptable research outcomes in order to be promoted:

> People are very conscious that there is this division of their time between teaching and learning and research, and then community contribution. So there is this tension, 'If I have to spend more time on my subject and in my teaching preparation and preparing new exams every semester, then that's less time that I have to be finishing an article or doing some further research.' [ADTL2]

If an initiative intended to promote law student wellbeing is perceived as obliging academics to spend more time on their teaching and less time on their research it is more likely to be opposed and resisted.

There is also within some law schools a culture of explicit anti-educationalism. Some academics challenge the relevance of general education scholarship and principles to the teaching of law. Occasionally this anti-educationalism is the result of academic engagement with the education literature – including wellness scholarship – and informed disagreement with what that literature has to say. More often, however, the anti-educationalism appears to be the result of ignorance of this literature, and in some cases an explicit refusal to engage with it.

> Very often in legal academia we have colleagues who really have no idea about quality practice in learning and teaching and yet they believe that they know it all . . . 'What can an educationalist tell me for heaven's sake? I'm a lawyer. I know my work. I know how to teach students. I'll stand in the class and give them stories and anecdotes and that's good teaching.' They just seem to be trapped into a mindset which precludes them from recognizing that their own teaching practice is often severely limited. [ADTL5]

Feinman and Feldman claim that many legal academics are 'anti-intellectual' about the process of legal education, and explain that this anti-intellectualism:

> is characterized by an unwillingness to reflect on the goals of legal education, the content of the curriculum, the methods of teaching, and the ability of law school graduates to practice law competently. At most law schools, the purposes and methods of teaching are regarded as unfruitful, if not unfit, topics for conversation.[36]

Many initiatives introduced within the law school to promote law student wellbeing or to reform teaching generally confront academics with the possibility that their teaching practice may be in some sense inadequate, and that they perhaps do not know as much about education as they believed, despite years or even decades of teaching law. Some welcome this confrontation. Many do not.

Addressing Academic Resistance

Teaching and learning initiatives and policies designed to promote student wellness are often introduced with the best of intentions. It would be a mistake, however, for wellness advocates to assume moral superiority over those opposed to teaching reform. Resistance to wellness initiatives is not likely to be the result of heartlessness or a lack of compassion on the part of the resistant academics, but of the association of these wellness initiatives with educationalist regulation generally – regulation to which these resistant academics are ideologically opposed.

Resistance to regulation and reform is a pervasive and unavoidable phenomenon within all organizations, including the legal academy.[37] A useful analogy is that of the machine: all movement within the organizational machine is the result of power, and friction or resistance is an unavoidable aspect of that process. However, just as friction can be minimized, steps can be taken to reduce the level of conflict between reform and resistance. All of the ADTLs interviewed by the author offered suggestions about addressing academic resistance and minimizing the conflict between those advocating for the reform of law teaching and those resisting such reform.

One suggestion is a response to resistance based upon the ideal of academic freedom: where appropriate, teaching reform initiatives should be disengaged from compulsion, and academics should be encouraged rather than compelled to cooperate. This is not always possible, because more senior administrators and decision-makers may impose particular initiatives in the form of regulation. But where there is a choice between making compliance compulsory and making it optional, the latter is less likely to provoke resistance by academics.

One ADTL insisted that 'the last thing I want to do is regulate how people teach'. Another talked about getting a few academics to cooperate and then allowing others to slowly adopt the desired practices at their own pace:

> I also think if you've got some new idea that you wanted to implement, then if you've got the people who are with you and you work with these people then it can sort of trickle down to the other people later on. And if you have got somebody who really doesn't want to be a part of it, I think to a certain extent, at least in the beginning, you're best to sort of try and not get involved with that. Let them be and eventually when everyone else is moving down one track then I think often they'll get caught up along the way. [ADTL2]

Most ADTLs emphasized the importance of not rushing reform or pushing academics too hard to embrace change, recognizing that the more forceful the regulation the more likely it is that resistance will be provoked. Encouraging academics to voluntarily recognize the seriousness of the wellness problem and the importance of taking steps to address it is preferable to introducing a policy that compels all academics to change their teaching practices. Of course, making a reform initiative optional may, at least in the short term, reduce its chances of propagative success. In the longer term, however, a change embraced willingly is more likely to be sustained than one imposed quickly and forcefully.

Another suggestion by the ADTLs was a response to resistance based upon the self-identification by many academics as researchers rather than teachers: the assumption that teaching and research are two separate fields of endeavour, and that individual academics must choose between one or the other, can be challenged by highlighting the potential connections between the two. There is a substantial body of scholarship about what is often called either the 'teaching-research nexus' or 'research-led teaching' that can be drawn upon in this endeavour. Alternatively, if a particular wellness initiative is perceived by some academics as too time-consuming and a distraction from their research efforts, the wellness advocate can emphasize the potential for the initiative to produce time savings in the longer term by reducing the time spent by the academics dealing with distressed students.

This leads to the third suggestion by the ADTLs: advocates for reform should take the time to clearly explain to other academics the potential benefits of the reform initiatives. Some ADTLs advocated educating academics about the reasons for the initiatives in which they are being asked to participate and the possible benefits for students. Other ADTLs advocated encouraging compliance by emphasizing the importance of cooperation and collaboration within the law school, and by pointing to the practical benefits of compliance for individual academics (e.g. better student feedback, fewer student complaints or a lighter workload) or for the law school (e.g. better results in performance measures, better support or funding from the university or being 'left alone' by university administrators). According to one ADTL:

> Over the last couple of years I have tried to introduce new requirements and regulations by explaining to my colleagues the importance of complying for the good of the school as a whole. Instead of making regulations a negative thing, a burden, I try to portray it as an opportunity to promote the school, to make it look good. [ADTL1]

The final suggestion by the ADTLs is a response to resistance to reform based upon anti-educationalism: advocates for teaching reform should strive to create a culture that values *informed* debate about teaching. This is not the same as saying that reform advocates must convince all of their colleagues to accept the relevant scholarship without question. Rather, it is about creating the conditions where discussions about the most appropriate approaches to the teaching of law, including the importance of student wellness, are informed by evidence and scholarship rather than assumptions and ignorance. Claims by resistant academics that, for example, wellness initiatives make students less resilient and therefore less able to cope with the realities of legal practice, or that traditional approaches to the teaching of law have worked well enough in the past and continue to work well enough in other jurisdictions, can be rebutted by evidence to the contrary in the literature. Those academics opposed to wellness initiatives are entitled to their views, but they should still be expected to have engaged with the wellness scholarship, even if they do not agree with its claims.

This is only possible within a culture that values informed, scholarly debate about teaching. Most of the ADTLs talked about minimizing the conflict around teaching reform by effecting a gradual change of culture:

> I think you can over time build up a sufficient critical mass to tip the balance in favour of a culture that cares about [teaching and learning]. . . . You need a champion that really drives that, or a couple of champions, and then some institutional support. Then an early taste of success and then people get on the bandwagon because they like the idea, they see it working. [ADTL4]

All of the ADTLs acknowledged that resistance to teaching reform initiatives is much more likely if there is (within the school) a culture that does not recognize the importance of engagement with the relevant academic literature and informed, scholarly debate about the teaching of law.

Conclusion

Academic resistance to wellness initiatives and other efforts to transform teaching practices can never be abolished within a law school; nor should it. It is appropriate, if not unavoidable, that any discourse within the academy – even one informed by legitimate concern about a serious problem – be questioned, challenged and even opposed by alternative discourses and points of view. Advocates for reform can, however, take steps to better understand the reasons and justifications for resistant practices by academics. They can endeavour to introduce changes in ways that recognize the importance of academic freedom and the professional status of legal educators. They can take the time to explain the reasons for the reforms and emphasize the potential benefits of the reforms for students, for individual academics and for the institution. And they can strive to ensure that any debate about teaching reform is a debate informed by research and scholarship rather than a mere argument driven by ignorance of the available evidence, insecurity about teaching quality, or an unjustified bias in favour of the status quo.

Notes

* Nick James, BCom LLB LLM PhD, is a Professor, Faculty of Law, Bond University, Australia.

1 Norm Kelk et al, *Courting the Blues: Attitudes towards Depression in Australian Law Students and Legal Practitioners* (Brain and Mind Research Institute, 2009).

2 See e.g. Massimiliano Tani and Prue Vines, 'Law Students' Attitudes to Education: Pointers to Depression in the Legal Academy and Profession?' (2009) 19(1) *Legal Education Review* 3; Kath Hall, 'Do We Really Want to Know?: Recognizing the Importance of Student Psychological Well-Being in Australian Law Schools' (2009) 9(1) *QUT Law and Justice Journal* 122; Kath Hall, Molly Townes O'Brien and Stephen Tang,

'Developing a Professional Identity in Law School: A View from Australia' (2010) 4(19) *Phoenix Law Review* 19; Rachael Field and Sally Kift, 'Addressing the High Levels of Psychological Distress in Law Students through Intentional Assessment and Feedback Design in the First Year Law Curriculum' (2010) 1(1) *International Journal of the First Year in Higher Education* 65; James Duffy, Rachael Field and Melinda Shirley, 'Engaging Law Students to Promote Psychological Health' (2011) 36(4) *Alternative Law Journal* 250; Kate Galloway et al, 'Approaches to Student Support in the First Year of Law School' (2011) 21(2) *Legal Education Review* 235; Anna Huggins, Sally Kift and Rachael Field, 'Implementing the Self-Management Threshold Learning Outcome for Law: Some Intentional Design Strategies from the Current Curriculum Toolbox'(2011) 21(2) *Legal Education Review* 183; Anthony Lester, Lloyd England and Natalia Antolak-Saper, 'Health and Wellbeing in the First Year: The Law School Experience' (2011) 36(1) *Alternative Law Journal* 47; Molly Townes O'Brien, Stephen Tang and Kath Hall, 'Changing our Thinking: Empirical Research on Law Student Wellbeing, Thinking Styles and the Law Curriculum' (2011) 21 *Legal Education Review* 149; Penelope Watson and Rachael Field, 'Promoting Student Wellbeing and Resilience at Law School' in Sally Kift et al (eds), *Excellence and Innovation in Legal Education* (LexisNexis Butterworths, 2011) 389; Rachael Field and James Duffy, 'Better to Light a Single Candle Than to Curse the Darkness: Promoting Law Student Well-Being through a First Year Law Subject' (2012) 12(1) *QUT Law and Justice Journal* 133.

3 Wendy Larcombe et al, 'Does an Improved Experience of Law School Protect Students against Depression, Anxiety and Stress? An Empirical Study of Wellbeing and the Law School Experience of LLB and JD Students' (2013) 35(2) *Sydney Law Review* 407. See also Wendy Larcombe and Katherine Fethers, 'Schooling the Blues? An Investigation of Factors Associated with Psychological Distress among Law Students' (2013) 36(2) *UNSW Law Journal* 390.

4 Council of Australian Law Deans, *Promoting Law Student Well-Being: Good Practice Guidelines for Law Schools* (2013). The guidelines were developed by a Working Party established under the auspices of the CALD Standing Committee for Legal Education. The members of the Working Party were Professor Paula Baron (Chair), Dr Wendy Bonython, Dr Julie Clarke, Dr Rachael Field, Ms Kate Galloway, Dr Wendy Larcombe, Professor Maree Sainsbury, Professor Michael Stuckey, Ms Carmel Velleley and Mr David Wishart.

5 Citing Lawrence S Krieger, 'Institutional Denial about the Dark Side of Law School, and Fresh Empirical Guidance for Constructively Breaking the Silence' (2002) 52 *Journal of Legal Education* 112, 125.

6 Citing Duffy, Field and Shirley, 'Engaging Law Students to Promote Psychological Health', above n3, 251; Field and Duffy, above n3, 145.

7 Citing KM Sheldon and LS Krieger, 'Understanding the Negative Effects of Legal Education on Law Students: A Longitudinal Test of Self-Determination Theory' (2007) 33(6) *Personality and Social Psychology* 883, 894.

8 Citing Ann Iijima, 'The Collaborative Legal Studies Program: A Work in Progress' (2002–2003) 12 *Kansas Journal of Law and Public Policy* 143.

9 Council of Australian Law Deans, above n6, 5.

10 Lawrence S Krieger, 'Human Nature as a New Guiding Philosophy for Legal Education and the Profession' (2008) 47 *Washburn Law Journal* 24.

11 Field and Duffy, above n3,133.

12 Ian Gallacher, 'Thinking Like Non-Lawyers: Why Empathy Is a Core Lawyering Skill and Why Legal Education Should Change to Reflect Its Importance' (2010) 8 *Legal Communication and Rhetoric* 109; O'Brien, Tang and Hall, above n3.

13 The author encountered both of these responses in his efforts to have former colleagues consider the impact of their teaching upon law student wellbeing.

14 For a more detailed description of the interviews and the research project of which they formed a part, see Nickolas James, '"How Dare You Tell Me How to Teach!": Resistance to Educationalism within Australian Law Schools' (2013) 36(3) *UNSW*

Law Journal 779. The research project was approved by the University of Queensland Behavioural and Social Sciences Ethical Review Committee on 21 September 2010 (Project Number 2010001112).

15 Nickolas James, 'Australian Legal Education and the Instability of Critique' (2004) 28 *Melbourne University Law Review* 1.

16 James, above n15, 779.

17 See, e.g., Donna Brandes and Paul Ginnis, *A Guide to Student Centred Learning* (Blackwell, 1986). In the context of legal education, see, e.g., Jos C Moust and Herman J Nuy, 'Preparing Teachers for a Problem-Based, Student-Centred Law Course' (1987) 5 *Journal of Professional Legal Education* 16.

18 See, e.g., Stephen D Brookfield, *Becoming a Critically Reflective Teacher* (Jossey-Bass, 1995).

19 See, e.g., Anne Brockbank and Ian McGill, *Facilitating Reflective Learning in Higher Education* (Open University Press, 2nd ed, 2007); Stephen D Brookfield, *Understanding and Facilitating Adult Learning: A Comprehensive Analysis of Principles and Effective Practices* (Jossey-Bass, 1986).

20 See, e.g., Kerri-Lee Krause and Hamish Coates, 'Students' Engagement in First-Year University' (2008) 33 *Assessment and Evaluation in Higher Education* 493.

21 See, e.g., Neil J Cooper, 'Facilitating Learning from Formative Feedback in Level 3 Assessment' (2000) 25 *Assessment and Evaluation in Higher Education* 279.

22 See, e.g., Grant P Wiggins, *Assessing Student Performance: Exploring the Purpose and Limits of Testing* (Jossey-Bass, 1999).

23 See, e.g., D Royce Sadler, 'Specifying and Promulgating Achievement Standards' (1987) 13 *Oxford Review of Education* 191.

24 See, e.g., John Biggs and Catherine Tang, *Teaching for Quality Learning at University: What the Student Does* (Open University Press, 4th ed, 2011).

25 Above n15.

26 See above n2.

27 See, e.g., Margaret Thornton, 'Governing the Corporatised Academy' (2004) 1 *Journal for the Public University* 1; Mark Olssen and Michael A Peters, 'Neoliberalism, Higher Education and the Knowledge Economy: From the Free Market to Knowledge Capitalism' (2005) 20(3) *Journal of Education Policy* 313; Margaret Thornton, 'The Law School, the Market and the New Knowledge Economy' (2007) 17 *Legal Education Review* 1; Joyce E Canaan and Wesley Shumar, 'Higher Education in the Era of Globalization and Neoliberalism' in Joyce E Canaan and Wesley Shumar (eds), *Structure and Agency in the Neoliberal University* (Routledge, 2008); Margaret Thornton, *Privatising the Public University: The Case of Law* (Routledge, 2012).

28 Gina Anderson, 'Mapping Academic Resistance in the Managerial University' (2008) 15(2) *Organization* 251, 252.

29 In this section the various forms of academic resistance identified by the ADTLs are categorized according to the work of Anderson, above n29.

30 Above n28 (2012) 33.

31 Foucault insists that whenever power is exercised, resistance is formed: 'Where there is power there is resistance, and yet, or rather consequently, this resistance is never in a position of exteriority in relation to power . . . These points of resistance are present everywhere in the power network.' Michel Foucault, *The Will to Knowledge: The History of Sexuality 1* (Penguin, 1998), 96.

32 Krieger, above n6, 116.

33 Hall, above n3, 122.

34 Ibid., 126.

35 The ideal of academic freedom is one that has been associated with academic life for a long time: see Conrad Russell, *Academic Freedom* (Routledge, 1993) and, more recently, Robert R Kuehn and Peter A Joy, 'Lawyering in the Academy: The Intersection of Academic Freedom and Professional Responsibility' (2009–2010) 59 *Journal of Legal Education* 97.

36 Jay Feinman and Marc Feldman, 'Pedagogy and Politics' (1985) 73 *Georgetown Law Journal* 875, 875. Feinman and Feldman were writing about US legal education, but their comments are of direct relevance to legal academics elsewhere, including Australia.

37 According to Prasad and Prasad, there is 'a multitude of less visible and often unplanned oppositional practices in the everyday world of organisations': Anshuman Prasad and Pushkala Prasad, 'Everyday Struggles at the Workplace: The Nature and Implications of Routine Resistance in Contemporary Organizations' in Peter A Bamberger and William J Sonnenstuhl (eds), *Research in the Sociology of Organizations: Deviance in and of Organizations* (JAI, 1998) 227. According to Thomas and Davies, there are 'routinized, informal and often inconspicuous forms of resistance in everyday practice': Robyn Thomas and Annette Davies, 'Theorizing the Micro-Politics of Resistance: New Public Management and Managerial Identities in the UK Public Services' (2005) 26(5) *Organization Studies* 683, 686. And according to Scott, the 'quiet evasion' associated with everyday forms of resistance is more widespread, and often more effective, than direct, confrontational forms of resistance: James Scott, 'Everyday Forms of Peasant Resistance' in James C Scott and Benedict JT Kerkvliet (eds), *Everyday Forms of Peasant Resistance in South-East Asia* (Frank Cass, 1986) 5, 8.

Index

www.ingramcontent.com/pod-product-compliance
Ingram Content Group UK Ltd.
Pitfield, Milton Keynes, MK11 3LW, UK
UKHW011005180926
475701UK00004B/571
9780367596743